W9-DCC-542

WIN-WIN ADMINISTRATION
How To Manage An Organization So Everybody Wins

Stephen K. Blumberg

WITHDRAWN
by Unity Library

UNITY SCHOOL LIBRARY
UNITY VILLAGE, MISSOURI 64065

9/95

(Copyright 1983 Thomas Horton and Daughters)

26662 S. Newton
Sun Lakes, Az 85224
No part of this manuscript may be used or reproduced unless prior permission of
the author has been obtained.

Gift
e.f.

HD
31
.B525
1983
c.1

To my "Win-Win" family:
Andy, Dina, Ron, Dan, Wendy

CONTENTS

PREFACE

This book is the result of my perception that many of our organizations—public and private—are being run in ways which seem to demonstrate little real concern for the people who work in them. The prevailing attitude too often is one fostering a mechanistic culture of depersonalization. I knew, though, that exceptions exist, and that there are enlightened organizations operating under a new concept of humanistic people-oriented organizational values.

My goal was to put together a book of previously published articles revolving around the central theme of organizational teamwork. With such a book available to them, I hoped that more managers might be encouraged to try to run their organizations in such a fashion. In these days of citizen and customer frustration, tighter budgets, and diminishing profits this teamwork spirit may very well be the requisite response.

Knowing that some organizations were achieving positive results from the adoption of a more humane system of management, I sought to research the periodical literature in an attempt to find articles which would support and encourage this "win-win" philosophy. We searched for articles dealing with cooperation, participation, organizational democracy, humanism. In determining which of these articles to include in the book, I tried to select ones which were clearly written and which seemed to be most inspirational. Some three hundred articles were reviewed, and the twenty-two appearing here impressed me as the ones which most effectively made the point I'm trying to make with this book. The twenty-two selected all serve to advance the notion that our organizations, and the people served by them, can benefit from the adoption of a "win-win" spirit.

I am grateful to Professor Harold C. White of Arizona State University, Tempe for providing a detailed critique of the book when it was in manuscript form. His thoughtful suggestions improved the format and readability of the book.

The process of putting this book together has been substantially aided by the help of a number of research assistants. They performed various responsibilities, and each of them knows the extent to which they have played a role in bringing this book to life. I am very grateful and extend warm thanks to Dan Blumberg, Jack Campbell, Janet Carroll, Bill Dober, Maria Dzida, Patti Grace, Elbert Griffin, Fred Guerra, Lois O'Sullivan, Jennifer Reeves, and Rich Sletten.

My years of affiliation with the Center for Public Policy and Administration at California State University, Long Beach have been stimulating and rewarding. I appreciate the opportunities I've had to exchange ideas with many bright students; I've learned from them all. I thank the University and the Center for having given me these opportunities and for their support.

Finally, I thank Wendy Blumberg. As my wife for over twenty-six years, she knows what "win-win" is all about.

Stephen K. Blumberg
Manhattan Beach, California
August 1982

SECTION I

AN ARGUMENT FOR "WIN-WIN" ADMINISTRATION

PRELUDE

Everybody likes to win. For most it is a truism that we would rather win than lose. The problem with winning, however, is that most often when someone wins others lose. I win the election—you lose. He wins the contest—the other contestants lose. She wins the race—the other runners lose. Concerning individuals, these are obvious examples. More subtle is the winners versus losers syndrome found too frequently in many organizations.

Perhaps because of this win-lose mentality, organizational life typically tends to foster a destructive pattern. The boss wins—employees lose. The union wins—management loses. The store wins—customers lose. Unlike the more obvious situations where, for example, we simply count ballots to determine the winner, there are situations in organizations where winners prevail and losers despair. These winners emerge by virtue of having their will imposed on others. The despair is indeed real for those who must yield and become powerless. It certainly is not pleasant to frequently feel like a loser in one's workplace. Furthermore, if people throughout an organization feel like losers, levels of productivity will be adversely affected. Obviously, this is not healthy for the organization.

THE ORGANIZATIONAL PATH OF PROGRESS

Do we really want a society where many people daily put themselves into a work setting where they experience feelings of defeat? Do we really need to have organizational winners and organizational losers? The answer, most emphatically, is NO. It is entirely possible to foster an organizational climate of "Win-Win." This concept implies that instead of winners and losers there will be only winners. Such an organizational climate (or tone, value system, managerial style, atmosphere) will be one recognizing that a spirit of cooperative teamwork produces the best overall results. These results involve efficient and effective productivity, a motivated and satisfied workforce, productive management, and a satisfied community served by our organizations.

There can be little debate regarding the desirability of achieving this "win-win" atmosphere of results. My experience as a practitioner working with many organizations, and as an academician studying and teaching organizational behavior, has led me to develop a concept which I call *the organizational path of progress.* An awareness and understanding of this path of progress will help any organization to operate in a "win-win" manner. This concept recognizes that in any organizational system there is an intense interrelationship among the various elements, and these elements can be woven together to achieve a "win-win" spirit of cooperative teamwork.

The critical element beginning the path of progress is the *leadership* of the organization. The manager, chairman, president, or other leaders establish the climate which is pervasive throughout the organization. To achieve the most productive climate, the leaders must possess *self-confidence.* A self-confident manager is secure about his or her own ability and knowledge. Feeling secure will prevent leaders from feeling threatened by bright people in their organization. These managers will then be more likely to have *confidence in the people they are managing.*

Managerial confidence in the people throughout the organization leads to the next step along the path of progress: *open communication* back and forth, up and down, between all levels of the organization. There will be a sharing of information enabling everyone to feel that they know what's going on . This can lead to people sharing problems and feeling that they have a *common stake* in the organization.

People feeling that they have a common stake in the organization, fostered by open communication, leads to *participation.* Management encourages and promotes the participation of non-management in the organization's policies, and non-management welcomes the opportunites to participate. This partici-. pation leads to constructive *involvement;* such involvement stimulates enduring *commitment* to these policies.

As people within the organization experience this involvement and commitment they begin to feel as though they are a genuine member of the team, thus promoting a *sense of purpose* within the organization. This sense of purpose allows people to feel that they are personally contributing to the operation of the organization and gives them a gratifying reason for coming to work.

Having an organization full of people who want to come to work, who feel a sense of purpose, must certainly maximize *organizational effectiveness.* Such an atmosphere of *healthy productivity* originates from people who want to achieve results and accomplish tasks in their work setting. The healthy productivity allows people to feel a genuine sense of *job satisfaction* through their success and achievement. Self-confident management will, of course, recognize and acknowledge non-management's results.

The achievement of results leads to *contentment.* That wonderful glow of satisfaction following the completion of specific tasks and responsibilities is a feeling enjoyed and appreciated by anyone who experiences it. This contentment allows for feelings of *self-actualization:* a sense that "I am working toward my potential." Feeling that one is given the chance to use his or her talents and abilities allows those abilities to flourish.

The spirit of *cooperative teamwork* fostered by the various steps in this organizational path of progress leads to *organizational humanism.* It matters not whether we use the term organizational democracy, participatory management, quality of worklife, or any other term; following the path of progress will create a *humane organization.* The ultimate recipient of this organizational humanism is the society.

The result of completing the organizational path of progress is *societal benefit.* These societal benefits accrue from productive, creative members of the society who come out of these humane organizations. After all, these people who spend so much of their lives in organizations are also a part of the broader society. Their lives are greatly shaped and influenced by what goes on in their organization at work, and that influence has a profound impact on how they in turn relate to the society. Persons who are fortunate to work in "win-win" organizations where organizational humanism exists will have a more positive impact on society. It seems only natural that if people leave their workplaces with feelings of achievement, contentment and satisfaction, they will in turn be more apt to transmit these same positive feelings to those with whom they transact outside their organizations. In other words, the development of a more fulfilled workforce leads directly to a more productive and fulfilled society.

In summary, we find that the organizational path of progress starts with self-confident managers which leads them to have confidence in non-managers leading to open communication (sharing of information and sharing problems) causing a common stake in the organization, participation and involvement, leading to commitment and a sense of purpose which leads to organizational effectiveness and healthy productivity leading to job satisfaction, contentment and self-actualization all of which results in a spirit of "win-win" cooperative teamwork creating a humane organization which finally benefits the total society.

BENEFITS ACCRUING FROM "WIN-WIN"

It is, furthermore, a certainty that organizations where the prevailing atmosphere is "win-win" will do a better job for the people they serve than organizations without such an atmosphere: "win-win" governmental agencies will be more trusted by the citizenry and will provide services to the community in the most effective and efficient manner; "win-win" educational institutions will demonstrate more respect for, and responsiveness toward, their students, and the students will feel more positive toward their schools; private sector businesses and industries which promote "win-win" policies and practices will have more satisfied customers while operating more productively and profitably. Idealistic sounding? Perhaps. The evidence supporting this position, however, is abundant, and the articles appearing in the following sections of this volume represent just a small fraction of that evidence.

In recent years there has been substantial input indicating that organizations are in transition. The central reason for this seems to be the way people are changing within organizations. We hear of their increasing level of education, their different value systems, and their new life styles. The changing nature of the people who work in organizations is forcing organizational re-evaluation. The very survival of the organization as a viable entity will mandate various changes.

The essential change taking place in many organizations, change which should be taking place in many more organizations, is the change from a bureaucratic structure to a humane organization. Near the beginning of the twentieth century the German scholar Max Weber enunciated the components which comprise the bureaucracy. About the same time, working in the United States, Frederick Taylor gave birth to the concept of scientific management. While it is clear that some of Weber's principles of bureaucratic efficiency and Taylor's scientific management can assist organizations in accomplishing their mission, it is even more clear that this is not enough. The people want more. The people are asking for more. The society demands more. The humane organization called for requires a climate of humanistic management. This simply means that management will truly recognize the human element in the organization. Management in the humane organization will recognize that in addition to job skills people also have attitudes, beliefs, feelings, personal needs and values. This climate of humanistic management will provide an environment where people throughout the organization will have an opportunity for increasing their level of participation in decision making. It will provide more opportunity to obtain greater personal satisfaction on the job through more challenging and rewarding work. Humanistic management means that managers will more effectively develop their interpersonal skills and thus enable them to achieve greater cooperation between management and non-management as they all work toward accomplishing the goals of the organization. Ultimately of course, as has been previously stated, the people served by the organization will win as a result of this humanistic management. The victory by these people will be the most important factor in ensuring the organization's survival.

All managers must recognize, however, that their managerial responsibilities go far beyond the goal of organizational survival. They already know that they have services to provide, things to produce, or products to sell. Beyond all this, though, they must be aware that their organizations and the people in them are also a part of the community, a part of the broader society.

Contemporary organizations contain great numbers of people who are different in many respects from the organizational members of the past. These men and women, far less willing to passively accept oppressive organizational structures and autocratic managerial behavior, are concerned about the quality of their working lives. These people want to spend their work lives involved with tasks which have some meaning to them, tasks that satisfy their individual needs. They want to be part of an organization which acknowledges their worth as human beings. People are demanding, in various ways, that the organizations in which they spend their working lives adopt new ways of dealing with them.

Many people today expect to be able to grow and develop personally through their work organization. They want their organizations to help nurture their development, and they will resist those organizational policies and procedures which inhibit this growth. Organizations which facilitate the process of helping people become whole human beings will most assuredly be more productive, and simultaneously will provide better service to their consumers. This results in a "win-win" situation for everybody involved.

CONCLUSION

Enlightened organizations, recognizing the benefits of fostering a "win-win" spirit, are changing. They are questioning the wisdom of having so many organizational decisions emanate from the top. They are moving away from Weber's bureaucratic model with its emphasis on a rigid hierarchical structure and the impersonality of human relationships. They are recognizing that there are human beings in their organizations and that these human beings cannot productively function on a sustaining basis if treated like machines. These enlightened organizations are creating an environment in which the people in the organization have an opportunity to use their talents and abilities, to achieve healthy productivity, and to grow as human beings.

Emerging within these enlightened organizations is a new value system. It is a value system focusing on the human dimension, a value system recognizing that there are individual human beings in the organization. These enlightened organizations realize that the dignity of people, inside and outside the organization, must be respected.

The appeals/demands for organizational change are real. The challenge for organizations and for those who manage them is to respond to these burgeoning forces with sensitivity, with understanding and patient wisdom, and to respond responsively. The articles which follow represent an essential sample of the vast emerging literature documenting the beginnings of the response to these demands for organizational change.

SECTION II

INTRODUCING THE "WIN-WIN" CONCEPT

INTRODUCTION

The concept of "Win-Win" differs from the traditional ways in which too many organizations are managed. Some organizations seem to operate in a manner which tends to produce what appears to be a "lose-lose" situation for everyone involved. No-one "wins" in these organizations. More abundant is the experiential evidence of organizations where the "win-lose" approach is dominant.

The win-lose mentality dominating many organizations is one in which, as the term implies, some people win at the expense of others. The concept of "Win-Win," quite simply, promotes the notion that organizations can be managed in such a way that everybody "wins."

In 1966 Warren Bennis set the stage for many of the changes which some organizations have made in attempting to establish a "win-win" climate. His article is a literate discussion of various possibilities which need to be implemented if organizations expect to meet contemporary demands. The article provides a solid foundation for the validity of the points made by many of the authors of later articles appearing in subsequent sections of this book.

While the 1969 article by Robert Tannenbaum and Sheldon Davis is rather lengthy, and may be considered a bit dated by some readers, the message of these scholars is essential. In suggesting that an organizational environment must be created in which people can grow as human beings, they make a timeless point. Their article says that as organizations move away from the bureaucratic model a way must be found to help the organizations meet their own needs along with meeting the needs of individual organization members. They argue that changing values are required in order to meet this dual need, and that these newer values are basically humanistic ones.

In congruence with Tannenbaum and Davis' suggestion that organizations must adopt humanistic values, Stephen Blumberg presents a set of humanistic guidelines in his "Notes on the Art of Administration." While this article relates especially to *public* administration, the concepts presented are applicable for *all* organizations. Students of administration have been exposed, ever since they were presented in 1937, to a set of technical guidelines for administrative behavior contained in the acronym POSDCORB. This article proposes an additional set of administrative guidelines: the humanistic guidelines contained in the EVPOSDCORB acronym.

An awareness of the three articles in this section will serve as a background foundation for the articles in the remaining sections of this book.

CHANGING ORGANIZATIONS
WARREN G. BENNIS

THE IDEA OF CHANGE

Not far from where the new Government Center is going up, in downtown Boston, a foreign visitor walked up to an American sailor and asked why the ships of his country were built to last for only a short time. According to the foreign tourist, "The sailor answered without hesitation that the art of navigation is making such rapid progress that the finest ship would become obsolete if it lasted beyond a few years. In these words, which fell accidentally from an uneducated man, I began to recognize the general and systematic idea upon which your great people direct all their concerns."

The foreign visitor was that shrewd observer of American morals and manners, Alexis de Tocqueville, and the year was 1835. He would not recognize Scollay Square today. But he caught the central theme of our country—its preoccupation, its *obsession* with change. One thing, however, *is* new since de Tocqueville's time: the prevalence of newness, the changing scale and scope of change itself, so that, as Oppenheimer said, ". . . the world alters as we walk in it, so that the years of man's life measure not some small growth or rearrangement or moderation of what was learned in childhood, but a great upheaval."

Numbers have a magic all their own, and it is instructive to review some of the most relevant ones. In 1789, when George Washington was inaugurated, American society comprised fewer than 4 million persons, of whom 750,000 were Negroes. Few persons lived in cities; New York, then the capital, had a population of 33,000. In all, 200,000 individuals lived in what were then defined as "urban areas"—places with more than 2,500 inhabitants. In the past

Reprinted by permission of the author from *Journal of Applied Behavioral Science,* Volume 2, number 3 (July-September 1966).

ten years, Los Angeles has grown by 2,375,000, almost enough to people present-day Boston. In July, 1964, the population of the U.S. was about 192 million. The U.S. Census Bureau estimates that the population in 1975 will be between 226 and 235 million and that in 1980 it will be between 246 and 260 million. World population was over 3 billion in 1964. If fertility remains at present levels until 1975 and then begins to decline, the population of the world will reach 4 billion in 1977, 5 billion by about 1990.

In 1960, when President Kennedy was elected, more than half of all Americans alive were over 33 years of age and had received their formative experiences during the Great Depression, or earlier. By 1970, only ten years later, more than half of all Americans alive will be under 25 and will have been born after World War II. In one short decade the mid-age of the United States will have dropped by a full eight years—the sharpest such age drop recorded in history.

Observe the changes taking place in education. Thirty years ago only one out of every eight Americans at work had been to high school. Today four out of five attend high school. Thirty years ago 4 per cent or less of the population attended college. Now the figure is around 35 per cent, in cities about 50 per cent.

Consider one more example of social change. We are all aware of the momentum of the Scientific Revolution, whose magnitude and accelerating rate—to say nothing of its consequences—are truly staggering. By 1980 science will cut even a wider path, for in that year the government alone will spend close to $35 billion on research and development: $10 billion on arms and arms control, $7 billion on basic research, and $18 billion on vast civilian welfare programs and new technology.

"Everything nailed down is coming loose," an historian said recently, and it does seem that no exaggeration, no hyperbole, no outrage can realistically appraise the extent and pace of modernization. Exaggerations come true in only a year or two. Nothing will remain in the next ten years—or there will be twice as much of it.

And it is to our credit that the pseudo-horror stories and futuristic fantasies about *accelerations* of the rate of change (the rate of obsolescence, scientific and technological unemployment) and the number of "vanishing" stories (the vanishing salesman, the vanishing host, the vanishing adolescent, the vanishing village)—it is to our credit that these phenomenal changes have failed to deter our compulsive desire to invent, to overthrow, to upset inherited patterns and comfort in the security of the future.

No more facts and numbers are needed to make the point. We can *feel* it on the job, in the school, in the neighborhood, in our professions, in our everyday lives. Lyndon Johnson said recently, "We want change. We want progress. We want it both at home and abroad—and we aim to get it!" I think he's got it.

CHANGING ORGANIZATIONS

How will these accelerating changes in our society influence human organizations?

Let me begin by describing the dominant form of human organization employed throughout the industrial world. It is a unique and extremely durable social arrangement called "bureaucracy," a social invention perfected during the Industrial Revolution to organize and direct the activities of the business firm. It is today the prevailing and supreme type of organization wherever people direct concerted effort toward the achievement of some goal. This holds for university systems, for hospitals, for large voluntary organizations, for governmental organizations.

Corsica, according to Gibbon, is much easier to deplore than to describe. The same holds true for bureaucracy. Basically, bureaucracy is a social invention which relies exclusively on the power to influence through rules, reason, and the law. Max Weber, the German sociologist who developed the theory of bureaucracy around the turn of the century, once described bureaucracy as a social machine: "Bureaucracy," he wrote, "is like a modern judge who is a vending machine into which the pleadings are inserted together with the fee and which then disgorges the judgment together with its reasons mechanically derived from the code."

The bureaucratic "machine model" Weber outlined was developed as a reaction against the personal subjugation, nepotism, cruelty, and capricious and subjective judgments which passed for managerial practices in the early days of the Industrial Revolution. The true hope for man, it was thought, lay in his ability to rationalize, to calculate, to use his head as well as his hands and heart. Bureaucracy emerged out of the need for more predictability, order, and precision. It was an organization ideally suited to the values of Victorian Empire.

Most students of organizations would say that the anatomy of bureaucracy consists of the following "organs": a division of labor based on functional specialization, a well-defined hierarchy of authority, a system of procedures and rules for dealing with all contingencies relating to work activities, impersonality of interpersonal relations, and promotion and selection based on technical competence. It is the pyramidal arrangement we see on most organizational charts.

Allow me to leap-frog to the conclusion of my paper now. It is my premise that the bureaucratic form of organization is out of joint with contemporary realities; that new shapes, patterns, and models are emerging which promise drastic changes in the conduct of the corporation and of managerial practices in general. In the next 25 to 50 years we should witness, and participate in, the end of bureaucracy as we know it and the rise of new social systems better suited to twentieth-century demands of industrialization.

REASONS FOR ORGANIZATIONAL CHANGE

I see two main reasons for these changes in organizational life. One has been implied earlier in terms of changes taking place in society, most commonly referred to as the population and knowledge explosions. The other is more subtle and muted—perhaps less significant, but for me profoundly exciting. I have no easy name for it, nor is it easy to define. It has to do with man's historical quest for self-awareness, for using reason to achieve and stretch his potentialities and possibilities. I think that this deliberate self-analysis has spread to large and more complex social systems, to organizations. I think there has been a dramatic upsurge of this spirit of inquiry over the past two decades. A new depths and over a wider range of affairs, organizations are opening their operations up to self-inquiry and analysis. This really involves two parallel shifts in values and outlooks, between the men who make history and the men who make knowledge. One change is the scientist's realization of his affinity with men of affairs, and the other is the latter's receptivity and newfound respect for men of knowledge. I am calling this new development *organizational revitalization.* It is a complex social process which involves a deliberate and self-conscious examination of organizational behavior and a collaborative relationship between managers and scientists to improve performance.

This new form of collaboration may be taken for granted by many members of the Sloan School of Management. For myself, I have basked under the light of Professor Douglas McGregor's foresight and have simply come to regard reciprocity between the academician and the manager as inevitable and natural. But I can assure you that this development is unprecedented, that never before in history, in any society, has man, in his organizational context, so willingly searched, scrutinized, examined, inspected, or contemplated—for meaning, for purpose, for improvement.

I think this shift in outlook has taken a good deal of courage from both partners in this encounter. The manager has had to shake off old prejudices about "eggheads" and longhair intellectuals. More important, he has had to make himself and his organization vulnerable and receptive to external sources and to new, unexpected, even unwanted information—which all of you know is not such an easy thing to do. The academician has had to shed some of his natural hesitancies. Scholarly conservatism is admirable, I think, except to hide behind, and for a long time caution has been a defense against reality.

It might be useful to dwell on the role of academic man and his growing involvement with social action, using the field of management education as a case in point. Until recently, the field of business was disregarded by large portions of the American public, and it was unknown to or snubbed by the academic establishment. Management education and research were at best regarded there with dark suspicion, as if contact with the world of reality—particularly monetary reality—was equivalent to a dreadful form of pollution.

In fact, academic man has historically taken one of two stances toward The Establishment, *any* Establishment—that of rebellious critic or of withdrawn snob. The former (the rebel) can be "bought," but only in paperback books under such titles as: *The Power Elite, The Lonely Crowd, The Organization Man, The Hidden Persuaders, The Tyranny of Testing, Mass Leisure, The Exurbanites, The Death and Life of Great American Cities, The American Way of Death, Compulsory Mis-Education, The Status Seekers, Growing Up Absurd, The Paper Economy, Silent Spring, The Child Worshippers, The Affluent Society, The Depleted Society.* On the basis of these titles and reports of their brisk sales, I am thinking of writing one called *Masochism in Modern America,* practically a guaranteed success.

The withdrawn stance can be observed in some of our American universities, but less so these days. It is still the prevailing attitude in many European universities. There, the university seems intent to preserve the monastic ethos of its medieval origins, offering a false but lulling security to its inmates and sapping the curriculum of virility and relevance. Max Beerbohm's whimsical and idyllic fantasy of Oxford, *Zuleika Dobson,* dramatizes this: "It is this mild, miasmal air, not less than the grey beauty and the gravity of the buildings that has helped Oxford to produce, and foster, eternally, her peculiar race of artist-scholars, scholar-artists. . . . The buildings and their traditions keep astir in his mind whatsoever is gracious; the climate enfolding and enfeebling him, lulling him, keeps him careless of the sharp, harsh exigent realities of the outer world. These realities may be seen by him. . . . But they cannot fire him. Oxford is too damp for that."

"Adorable dreamer," said Matthew Arnold, in his valedictory to Oxford, "whose heart has been so romantic! who has given thyself so prodigally, given thyself to sides and to heroes not mine, only never to the Philistine! . . . what teacher could ever so save us from that bondage to which we are all prone . . . the bondage of what binds us all, the narrow, the mundane, the merely practical."

The intellectual and the manager have only recently come out of hiding and recognized the enormous possibilities of joint ventures. Remember that the idea of the professional school is new; this is true even in the case of the venerable threesome—law, medicine, and engineering—to say nothing of such recent upstarts as business and public administration. It is as new as the institutionalization of science, and even today, this change is not greeted with unmixed joy. Colin Clark, the economist, writing in a recent *Encounter,* referred to the "dreadful suggestion that Oxford ought to have a business school."

It is probably true that we in the United States have had a more pragmatic attitude toward knowledge than anyone else. Many observers have been impressed with the disdain European intellectuals seem to show for practical matters. Even in Russia, where one would least expect it, there is little interest in the "merely useful." Harrison Salisbury, the *New York Time's* Soviet expert, was struck during his recent travels by the almost total absence of liaison between research and practical application. He saw only one great agricultural experimental station on the American model. In that case, professors were working in the fields. They told Salisbury, "People call us Americans."

There may not be many American professors working in the fields, but they can be found, when not waiting in airports, almost everywhere else: in factories, in government, in less advanced countries, more recently in backward areas of our own country, in mental hospitals, in the State Department, in educational systems, and in practically all the institutional crevices Ph.D. recipients can worm their way into. They are advising, counseling, researching, recruiting, interpreting, developing, consulting, training, and working for the widest variety of client imaginable. This is not to say that the deep ambivalence which some Americans hold toward the intellectual has disappeared, but it does indicate that academic man has become more committed to action, in greater numbers, with more diligence, and with higher aspirations than at any other time in history.

Indeed, Fritz Machlup, the economist, has coined a new economic category called the "knowledge industry," which, he claims, accounts for 29 per cent of the gross national product. And Clark Kerr, the President of the University of California, said not too long ago, "What the railroads did for the second half of the last century and the automobile did for the first half of this century may be done for the second half of this century by the knowledge industry: that is, to serve as the focal point of national growth. And the university is at the center of the knowledge process."

CHANGES IN MANAGERIAL PHILOSOPHY

Now let us turn to the main theme and put the foregoing remarks about the reciprocity between action and knowledge into the perspective of changing organizations. Consider some of the relatively recent research and theory concerning the human side of enterprise which have made such a solid impact on management thinking and particularly upon the moral imperatives which guide managerial action. I shall be deliberately sweeping in summarizing these changes as much to hide my surprise as to cover a lot of ground quickly. (I can be personal about this. I remember observing Professor McGregor's class some seven years ago, when he first presented his new theories, and I remember the sharp antagonism his Theory X and Theory Y analysis then provoked. Today, I believe most of you would take these ideas as generally self-evident.)

It seems to me that we have seen over the past decade a fundamental change in the basic philosophy which underlies managerial behavior, reflected most of all in the following three areas:

1. A new concept of *man,* based on increased knowledge of his complex and shifting needs, which replaces the oversimplified, innocent push-button idea of man.

2. A new concept of *power,* based on collaboration and reason, which replaces a model of power based on coercion and fear.

3. A new concept of *organizational values,* based on humanistic-democratic ideals, which replaces the depersonalized mechanistic value system of bureaucracy.

Please do not misunderstand. The last thing I want to do is overstate the case. I do not mean that these transformations of man, power, and organizational values are fully accepted or even understood, to say nothing of implemented, in day-to-day affairs. These changes may be light-years away from actual adoption. I do mean that they have gained wide intellectual acceptance in enlightened management quarters, that they have caused a tremendous amount of rethinking and search behavior on the part of many organizations, and that they have been used as a basis for policy formulation by many large-scale organizations.

I have tried to summarize all the changes affecting organizations, resulting both from the behavioral sciences and from trends in our society, in the chart of human problems confronting contemporary organizations on the following page. These problems (or predicaments) emerge basically from twentieth-century changes, primarily the growth of science and education, the separation of power from property and the correlated emergence of the professional manager, and other kinds of changes which I will get to in a minute. The bureaucratic mechanism, so capable of coordinating men and power in a stable society of routine tasks, cannot cope with contemporary realities. The chart shows five major categories, which I visualize as the core tasks confronting the manager in coordinating the human side of enterprise:

1. The problem of integration grows out of our "consensual society," where personal attachments play a great part, where the individual is appreciated, in which there is concern for his well-being—not just in a veterinary-hygiene sense but as a moral, integrated personality.

2. The problem of social influence is essentially the problem of power, and leadership studies and practices reveal not only an ethical component but an *effectiveness* component: people tend to work more efficiently and with more commitment when they have a part in determining their own fates and have a stake in problem solving.

3. The problem of collaboration grows out of the same social processes of conflict, stereotyping, and centrifugal forces which inhere in and divide nations and communities. They also employ the same furtive, often fruitless, always crippling mechanisms of conflict resolution: avoidance or suppression, annihilation of the weaker party by the stronger, sterile compromises, and unstable collusions and coalitions. Particularly as organizations become more complex they fragment and divide, building tribal patterns and symbolic codes which often work to exclude others (secrets and noxious jargon, for example) and on occasion to exploit differences for inward (and always, fragile) harmony. Some large organizations, in fact, can be understood only through an

Figure 1. Human Problems Confronting Contemporary Organizations

Problem		Bureaucratic Solutions	New Twentieth-Century Conditions
Integration	The problem of how to integrate individual needs and management goals	No solution because of no problem. Individual vastly oversimplified, regarded as passive instrument or disregarded.	Emergence of human sciences and understanding of man's complexity. Rising aspirations. Humanistic-democratic ethos.
Social Influence	The problem of the distribution of power and sources of power and authority	An explicit reliance on legal-rational power but an implicit usage of coercive power. In any case, a confused, ambiguous, shifting complex of competence, coercion, and legal code.	Separation of management from ownership. Rise of trade unions and general education. Negative and unintended effects of authoritarian rule.
Collaboration	The problem of managing and resolving conflicts	The "rule of hierarchy" to resolve conflicts between ranks and the "rule of coordination" to resolve conflict between horizontal groups. "Loyalty."	Specialization and professionalization and increased need for interdependence. Leadership too complex for one-man rule or omniscience.
Adaptation	The problem of responding appropriately to changes induced by the environment of the firm	Environment stable, simple, and predictable; tasks routine. Adapting to change occurs in haphazard and adventitious ways. Unanticipated consequences abound.	External environment of firm more "turbulent," less predictable. Unprecedented rate of technological change.
"Revitalization"	The problem of growth and decay	?	Rapid changes in technologies, tasks, manpower, norms and values of society, and goals of enterprise and society all make constant attention to the processes of the firm and revision imperative.

analysis of their cabals, cliques, and satellites, their tactics resembling a sophisticated form of guerrilla warfare; and a venture into adjacent spheres of interest is taken under cover of darkness and fear of ambush.

(The university is a wondrous place for these highly advanced battle techniques, far overshadowing their business counterparts in subterfuge and sabotage. Quite often a university becomes a loose collection of competing departments, schools, and institutes, largely noncommunicating because of the multiplicity of specialist jargons and interests and held together, as Robert Hutchins once said, chiefly by a central heating system, or as Clark Kerr amended, by questions of what to do about the parking problem.)[2]

[2]For this quote, as well as for other major influences, I want to thank Professor Kenneth D. Benne.

4. The real *coup de grâce* to bureaucracy has come as much from our turbulent environment as from its incorrect assumptions about human behavior. The pyramidal structure of bureaucracy, where power was concentrated at the top—perhaps by one person or a group who had the knowledge and resources to control the entire enterprise—seemed perfect to "run a railroad." And undoubtedly, for tasks like building railroads, for the routinized tasks of the nineteenth and early twentieth centuries, bureaucracy was and is an eminently suitable social arrangement.

Nowadays, due primarily to the growth of science, technology, and research and development activities, the organizational environment of the firm is rapidly changing. Today it is a turbulent environment, not a placid and predictable one, and there is a deepening interdependence among the economic and other facets of society. This means that economic organizations are increasingly enmeshed in legislation and public policy. Put more simply, it means that the government will be in about everything, more of the time. It may also mean, and this is radical, *that maximizing cooperation,* rather than competition between firms—particularly if their fates are correlated—may become a strong possibility.

5. Finally, there is the problem of revitalization. Alfred North Whitehead sets it neatly before us: "The art of free society consists first in the maintenance of the symbolic code, and secondly, in the fearlessness of revision. . . . Those societies which cannot combine reverence to their symbols with freedom of revision must ultimately decay." Organizations, as well as societies, must be concerned with those social conditions that engender buoyancy, resilience, and fearlessness of revision. Growth and decay emerge as the penultimate problem where the environment of contemporary society is turbulent and uncertain.

FORECAST OF ORGANIZATIONS OF THE FUTURE

A forecast falls somewhere between a prediction and a prophecy. It lacks the divine guidance of the latter and the empirical foundation of the former. On thin empirical ice, I want to set forth some of the conditions that will dictate organization life in the next 25 to 50 years.

The Environment

Those factors already mentioned will continue in force and increase. Rapid technological change and diversification will lead to interpenetration of the government—its legal and economic policies—with business. Partnerships between business and government will be typical. And because of the immensity and expense of the projects, there will be fewer identical units competing for the same buyers and sellers. The three main features of the environment will be interdependence rather than competition, turbulence rather than steadiness, and large-scale rather than small-scale enterprises.

Population Characteristics

The most distinctive characteristic of our society is, and will become even more so, its education . Peter Drucker calls us the "educated society," and for good reason: within 15 years, two-thirds of our population living in metropolitan areas will have attended college. Adult education is growing even faster. It is now almost routine for the experienced physician, engineer, and executive to go back to school for advanced training every two or three years. Some 50 universities, in addition to a dozen large corporations, offer advanced management courses to successful men in the middle and upper ranks of business. Before World War II, only two such programs existed, both new and struggling to get students.

All of this education is not just "nice" but necessary. For as W. Willard Wirtz, the Secretary of Labor, recently pointed out, computers can do the work of most high school graduates—and they can do it cheaper and more effectively. Fifty years ago education used to be regarded as "nonwork," and intellectuals on the payroll (and many staff workers) were considered "overhead." Today, the survival of the firm depends, more than ever before, on the proper exploitation of brain power.

One other characteristic of the population which will aid our understanding of organizations of the future is increasing job mobility. The lowered cost and growing ease of transportation, coupled with the real needs of a dynamic environment, will change drastically the idea of "owning" a job—or "having roots," for that matter. Participants will be shifted from job to job and even employer to employer with little concern for roots and homestead.

Work Values

The increased level of education and mobility will change the values we hold about work. People will be more intellectually committed to their jobs and will probably require more involvement, participation, and autonomy in their work.

Also, people will tend to be more "other-directed," taking cues for their norms and values more from their immediate environment than from tradition. We will tend to rely more heavily on temporary social arrangements, on our immediate and constantly changing colleagues. We will tend to be more concerned and involved with relationships than with relatives.

Tasks and Goals

The tasks of the firm will be more technical, complicated, and unprogrammed. They will rely more on intellect than muscle. And they will be too complicated for one person to comprehend, to say nothing of control. Essentially, they will call for the collaboration of specialists in a project or team form of organization.

There will be a complication of goals. Business will increasingly concern itself with its adaptive or innovative-creative capacity. In addition, meta-goals —that is, supragoals which shape and provide the foundation for the goal structure—will have to be articulated and developed. For example, one meta-goal might be a system for detecting new and changing goals; another could be a system for deciding priorities among goals.

Finally, there will be more conflict and contradiction among diverse standards of organizational effectiveness, just as in hospitals and universities today there is conflict between teaching and research. The reason for this is the increased number of professionals involved, who tend to identify more with the goals of their profession than with those of their immediate employer. University professors can be used as a case in point. More and more of their income comes from outside sources, such as foundations which grant them money and industries for whom they consult. They tend not to be good "company men" because they divide their loyalty between their professional values and organizational goals.

Structure

The social structure of organizations of the future will have some unique characteristics. The key word will be "temporary"; there will be adaptive, rapidly changing *temporary systems*. These will be problem-oriented "task forces" composed of groups of relative strangers who represent a diverse set of professional skills. The groups will be arranged on an organic rather than a mechanical model; they will evolve in response to a problem rather than to programmed role expectations. The "executive" thus will become a coordinator or "linking pin" among various task forces. He must be a man who can speak the diverse languages of research, with skills to relay information and to mediate between groups. People will be differentiated not vertically according to rank and status but flexibly and functionally, according to skill and professional training.

Adaptive, problem-solving, temporary systems of diverse specialists, linked together by coordinating and task-evaluating specialists in an organic flux—this is the organizational form that will gradually replace bureaucracy as we know it. As no catchy phrase comes to mind, I call this an organic-adaptive structure.

Motivation

The organic-adaptive structure should increase motivation, and thereby effectiveness, since it will enhance satisfactions intrinsic to the task. There is a harmony between the educated individual's need for meaningful, satisfactory, and creative tasks and a flexible organizational structure.

There will, however, also be reduced commitment to work groups, for these groups, as I have already mentioned, will be transient and changing.

While skills in human interaction will become more important, due to the growing needs for collaboration in complex tasks, there will be a concomitant reduction in group cohesiveness. My prediction is that in the organic-adaptive system people will have to learn to develop quick and intense relationships on the job and learn to bear the loss of more enduring work relationships. Because of the added ambiguity of roles, more time will have to be spent on the continual search for the appropriate organizational mix.

In general, I do not agree with those who emphasize a new utopianism in which leisure, not work, will become the emotional-creative sphere of life. Jobs should become more rather than less involving; man is a problem-solving animal, and the tasks of the future guarantee a full agenda of problems. In addition, the adaptive process itself may become captivating to many.

At the same time, I think that the future I describe is not necessarily a "happy" one. Coping with rapid change, living in temporary work systems, developing meaningful relations and then breaking them—all augur social strains and psychological tensions. Teaching how to live with ambiguity, to identify with the adaptive process, to make a virtue out of contingency, and to be self-directing will be the task of education, the goal of maturity, and the achievement of the successful manager. To be a wife in this era will be to undertake the profession of providing stability and continuity.

In these new organizations, participants will be called on to use their minds more than at any other time in history. Fantasy, imagination, and creativity will be legitimate in ways that today seem strange. Social structures will no longer be instruments of psychic repression but will increasingly promote play and freedom on behalf of curiosity and thought.

Bureaucracy was a monumental discovery for harnessing the muscle power of the Industrial Revolution. In today's world, it is a lifeless crutch that is no longer useful. For we now require structures of freedom to permit the expression of play and imagination and to exploit the new pleasure of work.

One final word: While I forecast the structure and value coordinates for organizations of the future and contend that they are inevitable, this should not bar any of us from giving the inevitable a little push here and there. And while the French moralist may be right that there are no delightful marriages, just good ones, it is possible that if managers and scientists continue to get their heads together in organizational revitalization, they *might* develop delightful organizations—just possibly.

I started with a quote from de Tocqueville and I think it would be fitting to end with one: "I am tempted to believe that what we call necessary institutions are often no more than institutions to which we have grown accustomed. In matters of social constitution, the field of possiblities is much more extensive than men living in their various societies are ready to imagine."

VALUES, MAN, AND
ORGANIZATIONS

Robert Tannenbaum and Sheldon A. Davis

INTRODUCTION

". . . we are today in a period when the development of theory within the social sciences will permit innovations which are at present inconceivable. Among these will be dramatic changes in the organization and management of economic enterprise. The capacities of the average human being for creativity, for growth, for collaberation, for productivity (in the full sense of the term) are far greater than we have recognized . . . it is possible that the next half century will bring the most dramatic social changes in human history."[1]

For those concerned with organization theory and with organizational development work, this is an exciting and challenging time. Probably never before have the issues at the interface between changing organizations and maturing man been so apparent, so compelling, and of such potentially critical relevance to both. And to a considerable extent the sparks at the interface reflect differences in values both within organizations and within man—human values which are coming loose from their moorings, whose functional relevance is being re-examined and tested, and which are without question in transition.

Many organizations today, particularly those at the leading edge of technology, are faced with ferment and flux. In increasing instances, the bureaucratic model—with its emphasis on relatively rigid structure, well-defined functional specialization, direction and control exercised through a formal

Reprinted from "Values, Man, and Organizations" by Robert Tannenbaum and Sheldon A. Davis, INDUSTRIAL MANAGEMENT REVIEW, Vol. 10, (Winter 1969), pp. 67–86, by permission of the publisher. Copyright © 1969 by the Sloan Management Review Association. All rights reserved.

[1]McGregor[5], p. 244.

hierarchy of authority, fixed systems of rights, duties, and procedures, and relative impersonality of human relationships—is responding inadequately to the demands placed upon it from the outside and from within the organization. There is increasing need for experimentation, for learning from experience, for flexibility and adaptability, and for growth. There is a need for greater inventiveness and creativity, and a need for collaboration among individuals and groups. Greater job mobility and the effective use of temporary systems seem essential. An environment must be created in which people will be more fully utilized and challenged and in which people can grow as human beings.

In his recent book. *Changing Organizations,* Warren Bennis has pointed out that the bureaucratic form of organization "is becoming less and less effective, that it is hopelessly out of joint with contemporary realities, and that new shapes, patterns, and models . . . are emerging which promise drastic changes in the conduct of the corporation and in managerial practices in general."[2] At least one of the newer models, the one with which our recent experience is most closely connected, is organic and systems-oriented. We feel that, for the present at least, this model is one which.can suggest highly useful responses to the newer demands facing organizations.

At this historical juncture, it is not just organizations which are in flux. Man, perhaps to an extent greater than ever before, is coming alive; he is ceasing to be an object to be used, and is increasingly asserting himself, his complexity, and his importance. Not quite understanding why or how, he is moving slowly but ever closer to the center of the universe.

The factors underlying man's emergence are complex and interrelated. They include higher levels of educational attainment, an increased availability of technology which both frees man from the burdens of physical and routine labor and makes him more dependent on society, an increasing rate of change affecting his environment which both threatens and challenges him, and higher levels of affluence which open up opportunities for a variety and depth of experiences never before so generally available.

The evidences of this trend are many. They are to be found, for example, in the gropings within many religions for more viable modes and values. They are to be found in the potent thrusts for independence of minorities everywhere, and in the challenges of our youths who find our values phony and often materialistically centered. They are to be found in the involvement of so many people in psychotherapy, in sensitivity training, and in self-expression activities in the arts and elsewhere. They are also to be found in the continuing and growing interest in writings and ideas in the general direction of the humanistic-existential orientation to man.

Organizations are questioning and moving away from the bureaucratic model, in part because man is asserting his individuality and his centrality, in

---

[2]See Bennis [1].

part because of growing dissatisfaction with the personally constraining impact of bureaucracies. In this flux, organizations and man must find a way with each other. In our view, this way will be found through changing values—values which can hopefully serve the needs for effectiveness and survival of organizations and the needs for individuality and growth of emergent man. Those concerned with organization theory and with organizational development have, in our judgment, a most important role to play in this quest.

VALUES IN TRANSITION

Deeply impressed with the managerial and organizational implications of the increasing accumulation of knowledge about human behavior, Professor Douglas McGregor formulated his assumptions of Theory Y.[3] According to him, these assumptions were essentially his interpretations, based upon the newer knowledge and on his extensive experience, of the nature of man and of man's motivation. In our view, McGregor was overly cautious and tentative in calling the Theory Y tenets "assumptions" and in limiting them to being his "interpretations." In trying to be "scientific," he seemed reluctant in his writing to assert explicity as *values* those elements (including the Theory Y assumptions) which so much affected his organizational theory and practice. He was not alone in his reluctance. Perhaps the most pervasive common characteristic among people in laboratory training and in organizational development work is their values, and yet, while organizational development academicians and practitioners are generally aware of their shared values and while these values implicitly guide much of what they do, they too have usually been reluctant to make them explicit.

We want here not only to own our values but also to state them openly. These values are consistent with McGregor's assumptions and in some instances go beyond this. They are not scientifically derived nor are they new, but they are compatible with relevant "findings" emerging in the behavioral sciences. They are deeply rooted in the nature of man and are therefore basically humanistic. As previously suggested, many of the values underlying the bureaucratic model and its typical implementation have been inconsistent with the nature of man, with the result that he has not been fully utilized, his motivator, has been reduced, his growth as a person stunted, and his spirit deadened. These outcomes sorely trouble us, for we believe organizations can in the fullest sense serve man as well as themselves.

Growing evidence strongly suggests that humanistic values not only resonate with an increasing number of people in today's world, but also are highly consistent with the effective functioning of organizations built on the

---

[3]See McGregor[5].

newer organic model.[4] As we discuss a number of these values below, we will provide some face validity for their viability by illustrating them with cases or experiences taken from our involvements with or knowledge of a number of organizations which recently have been experimenting with the interface between the organizational and humanistic frontiers described above. The illustrations come primarily from TRW Systems, with which we have had a continuing collaboration for more than four years. Other organizations with which one or both of us have been involved include Aluminum Company of Canada, Ltd., U.S. Department of State, and the Organizational Behavior Group of Case Institute of Technology.

We clearly recognize that the values to which we hold are not absolutes, that they represent directions rather than final goals. We also recognize that the degree of their shortrun application often depends upon the people and other variables involved. We feel that we are now in a period of transition, sometimes slow and sometimes rapid, involving a movement away from older, less personally meaningful and organizationally relevant values toward these newer values.[5]

Away from a View of Man as Essentially Bad Toward a View of Him as Basically Good. At his core, man is not inherently evil, lazy, destructive, hurtful, irresponsible, narrowly self-centered, and the like. The life experiences which he has, including his relationships with other people and the impact on him of the organizations with which he associates, can and often do move him in these directions. On the other hand, his more central inclination toward the good is reflected in his behavior as an infant, in his centuries-long evolution of ethical and religious precepts, and in the directions of his strivings and growth as a result of experiences such as those in psychotherapy and sensitivity training. Essentially man is internally motivated toward positive personal and social ends; the extent to which he is not motivated results from a process of demotivation generated by his relationships and/or environment.

We have been impressed with the degree to which the fairly pervasive cultural assumption of man's badness has led to organizational forms and practices designed to control, omit, push, check upon, inhibit, and punish. We are also increasingly challenged by the changes in behavior resulting from a growing number of experiments with organizational forms and practices rooted in the view of man as basically good.

-----

[4]This contention is supported by the further discussion of Theory Y by McGregor [6] by the discussion of System 5 by Likert [4]; and by the discussion of 9, 9 management by Blake and Mouton [2].

[5]On reading an earlier draft to this paper, a corporation executive commented; "I think the perspective is wrong when the impression is created that these values are widespread. They are probably spreading from an infinitesimal fraction to a tiny fraction of the world's population, but at an accelerating rate"

Within an organization it is readily apparent to both members and perceptive visitors whether or not there is, in general, an atmosphere of respect for the individual as a person. Are people treated arbitrarily? Are there sinister coups taking place? How much of the time and energy of the members of the organization is devoted to constructive problem solving rather than to playing games with each other, back-biting, politicking, destructive competition, and other dysfunctional behavior? How does management handle problems such as the keeping of time records? (Some organizations do not have time clocks and yet report that employees generally do not abuse this kind of a system). One of the authors can remember a chain of retail stores which fired a stock clerk because he had shifty eyes, although he was one of the best stock boys in that chain. There are all kinds of negative assumptions about man behind such an incredible action.

For a long period of time, two senior engineers, Taylor and Durant, had real difficulty in working together. Each had a negative view of the other; mutual respect was lacking. Such attitudes resulted in their avoiding each other even though their technical disciplines were closely related. A point in time was reached when Taylor sorely needed help from Durant. Caught up in his own negative feelings, however, he clearly was not about to ask Durant for help. Fortunately, two of Taylor's colleagues who did not share his feelings prodded him into asking Durant to work with him on the problem. Durant responded most positively, and brought along two of his colleagues the next day to study the problem in detail. He then continued to remain involved with Taylor until the latter's problem was solved. Only a stereotype had kept these men apart; Taylor's eventual willingness to approach Durant opened the door to constructive problem solving.

Away from Avoidance or Negative Evaluation of Individuals Toward Confirming Them as Human Beings. One desire frequently expressed by people with whom we consult is "I wish I knew where I stand with my boss [with this organization] [with my colleagues] [with my subordinates]. I'd really like to know what they think of me personally." We are not referring to the excessively neurotic needs of some persons for attention and response, but rather to the much more pervasive and basic need to know that one's existence makes a difference to others.

Feedback that is given is generally negative in character and often destructive of the individual instead of being focused on the perceived shortcomings of a given performance. It seems to be exceedingly difficult for most of us to give positive feedback to others—and, more specifically, to express genuine feelings of affection and caring.

When people are seen as bad, they need to be disciplined and corrected on the issue only; when they are seen as good, they need to be confirmed. Avoidance and negative evaluation can lead individuals to be cautious, guarded, defensive. Confirmation can lead to personal release, confidence, and enhancement.

A senior executive reported to one of us that he did not get nearly as much feedback as he wanted about how people thought about him as a person and whether or not they cared for him. He reported that one of the most meaningful things that had happened to him in this regard occurred when the person he reported to put his arm around him briefly at the end of a working session, patted him on the shoulder, and said, "Keep up the good work," communicating a great deal of warmth and positive feelings towards the person through this behavior. This event had taken place two years ago and lasted about five seconds, yet it was still fresh in the senior executive's memory and obviously has had a great deal of personal meaning for him. In our culture, most of us are grossly undernourished and have strong need for the personal caring of others.

Away from a View of Individuals as Fixed Toward Seeing Them as Being in Process. The traditional view of individuals is that they can be defined in terms of given interests, knowledge, skills, and personality characteristics: they can gain new knowledge, acquire additional skills, and even at times change their interests, but it is rare that people really change. This view, when buttressed by related organizational attitudes and modes, insures a relative fixity of individuals, with crippling effects. The value to which we hold is that people can constantly be in flux, groping, questing, testing, experimenting, and growing. We are struck by the tremendous untapped potential in most individuals yearning for discovery and release. Individuals may rarely change in core attributes, but the range of alternatives for choice can be widened, and the ability to learn how to learn more about self can be enhanced.

Organizations at times question whether it is their responsibility to foster individual growth. Whether or not it is, we believe that for most organizations, especially those desiring long-term survival through adaptability, innovation, and change, it is an increasing necessity. Further, evidence suggests that to have people in process requires a growth-enhancing environment. Personal growth requires healthy organizations. This value, then, carries with it great implications for work in organizational development. In organizations, people continuously experience interpersonal difficulties in relating to the other people with whom they must work. Some reasons for the difficulties are that people listen very badly to each other, attribute things of a negative nature to another person, and make all kinds of paranoid assumptions, with the result that communication breaks down rather severely.

There have been many instances within TRW Systems of people, who, in the eyes of others around them, produce some fairly significant changes in their own behavior. Most of these changes have been reported quite positively. In some cases there have been rather dramatic changes with respect to how a person faces certain kinds of problems: how he handles conflicts, how he conducts staff meetings, etc. In those cases, an individual who is perceived as having changed quite often reports that these changes are personally rewarding, that he feels better about himself and more optimistic and expansive about life.

TRW Systems is committed to a continuation and improvement of its Career Development program, which places considerable emphasis on the personal and professional growth of its members. Although the original commitment was perhaps largely based on faith, experience gained in recent years strongly suggests that one of the most productive investments the organization can make is in the continuing growth of its members and in the health of the environment in which they work.

Away From Resisting and Fearing Individual Differences Toward Accepting and Utilizing Them. The pervasive and long-standing view of man as bad takes on even more serious implications when individual differences among men appear—differences in race, religion, personality (including personal style), specialties, and personal perceptions (definitions of truth or reality). A bad man poses sufficient problems but a strange bad man often becomes impossible.

Organizations and individuals are frequently threatened by what they consider questioning of or challenge to their existing values and modes, represented by the presence of alternative possibilities. And they choose to avoid the challenge and the related and expected conflicts, discomforts, and the like which might follow. As a result, they achieve drabness, a lack of creativity, and a false sense of peace and security. We firmly believe that the existence of differences can be highly functional. There is no single truth, no one right way, no chosen people. It is at the interface of differences that ferment occurs and that the potential for creativity exists. Furthermore, for an organization to deny to itself (in the name of harmony or some similar shibboleth) the availability of productive resources simply because they do not conform to an irrelevant criterion is nothing short of madness. To utilize differences creatively is rarely easy, but our experience tells us that the gains typically far outweigh the costs.

In the play "Right You Are," Pirandello makes the point that truth in a particular human situation is a collection of what each individual in the situation sees. Each person will see different facets of the same event. In a positive sense, this would lead us to value seeing all the various facets of an issue or problem as they unfold in the eyes of all the beholders and to place a positive value on our interdependence with others, particularly in situations where each of us can have only part of the answer or see part of the reality.

An organization recently faced the problem of filling a key position. The man whose responsibility it was to fill the position sat down with five or six people who, due to their various functional roles, would have a great deal of interaction with the person in that position and with his organization. The man asked them to help him identify logical candidates. The group very quickly identified a number of people who ought to be considered and the two or three who were the most logical candidates. Then the group went beyond the stated agenda and came up with a rather creative new organizational notion, which was subsequently implemented and proved to be very desirable. After this took

place, the executive, who had called the meeting in order to get the help for
the decision he had to make, reported that it was very clear to him that doing
the job became much easier by getting everyone together to share their varying
perceptions. This meant that he had more relevant data available to him in
making his decision. Furthermore, the creative organizational concept only
came about as a result of the meeting's having taken place.

In most organizations persons and groups with markedly different training, experience, points of view, and modes of operating frequently bump into
each other. Project managers face functional performers, mechanical engineers
face electrical engineers, designers face hardware specialists, basic researchers
face action-oriented engineers, financial specialists face starry-eyed innovators.
Each needs to understand and respect the world of the other, and organizations should place a high value upon and do much to facilitate the working
through of the differences which come into sharp focus at interfaces such as
these.

**Away from Utilizing an Individual Primarily with Reference to his Job
Description Toward Viewing Him as a Whole Person.**   People get pigeon-
holed very easily, with job description (or expectations of job performance)
typically becoming the pigeon hole. A cost accountant is hired, and from then
on he is seen and dealt with as a cost accountant. Our view is that people
generally have much more to contribute and to develop than just what is
expected of them in their specific positions. Whole persons, not parts of persons, are hired and available for contribution. The organizational challenge is
to recognize this fact and discover ways to provide outlets for the rich, varied,
and often untapped resources available to them.

One of many personal examples that could be cited within TRW System
is that of a person trained as a theoretical physicist. Having pursued this
profession for many years, he is now effectively serving also as a part-time
behavioral science consultant (a third-party process facilitator) to the personnel organization within the company. This is an activity for which he had no
previous formal training until a new-found interest began asserting itself. The
organization has supported him in this interest, has made a relevant learning
opportunity available to him, and has opened the door to his performing an
additional function within the organization.

An organizational example involves the question of charters that are
defined for particular sub-elements of the organization: divisions, staffs, labs,
etc. What are their functions? What are they supposed to do? To state the
extreme, an organizational unit can have very sharply defined charters so that
each person in it knows exactly what he is supposed to do and not do. This
can lead to very clean functional relationships. Another approach, however,
is to say that the *core* of the charter will be very clear with discrete responsibilities identified, but the outer edges (where one charter interacts with others) will
not be sharply defined and will deliberately overlap and interweave with other
charters. The latter approach assumes that there is a potential synergy within

an organization which people can move toward fully actualizing if they can be constructive and creative in their interpersonal and intergroup relations. Very different charters are produced in this case, with very different outcomes. Such charters must, by definition, not be clean and sharply described, or the innovative and coordinated outcomes that might come about by having people working across charter boundaries will not occur.

Away from Walling-Off the Expression of Feelings Toward Making Possible Both Appropriate Expression and Effective Use. In our culture, there is a pervasive fear of feelings. From early childhood, children are taught to hide, repress, or deny the existence of their feelings, and their learnings are reinforced as they grow older. People are concerned about "losing control," and organizations seek rational, proper, task-oriented behavior, which emphasizes head-level as opposed to gut-level behavior. But organizations also seek high motivation, high morale, loyalty, team work, commitment, and creativity, all of which, if they are more than words, stem from personal feelings. Further, an individual cannot be a whole person if he is prevented from using or divorced from his feelings. And the energy dissipated in repression of feelings is lost to more productive endeavors.

We appreciate and are not afraid of feelings, and strongly believe that organizations will increasingly discover that they have a reservoir of untapped resources available to them in the feelings of their members, that the repression of feelings in the past has been more costly, both to them and to their members, than they ever thought possible.

One of the relevant questions to ask within an organization is how well problems stay solved once they are apparently solved. If the feelings involved in such problems are not directly dealt with and worked through, the problem usually does not remain solved for very long. For example, if two subordinates are fighting about something, their supervisor can either intervene and make the decision for them or arbitrate. Both methods can solve the immediate difficulty, but the fundamental problem will most likely again occur in some other situation or at some other time. The supervisor has dealt only with the symptoms of the real problem.

The direct expression of feelings, no matter what they are, does typically take place somewhere along the line, but usually not in the relevant face-to-face relationship. A person will attend a staff meeting and experience a great deal of frustration with the meeting as a whole or with the behavior of one or more persons in it. He will then talk about his feelings with another colleague outside the meeting or bring them home and discuss them with or displace them on his wife or children, rather than talking about them in the meeting where such behavior might make an important difference. To aid communication of feelings, participants at a given staff meeting could decide that one of the agenda items will be: "How do we feel about this meeting; how is it going; how can it be improved?" They could then talk face-to-face with each other while the feeling is immediately relevant to the effective functioning of the staff group.

The outcomes of the face-to-face confrontation can be far more constructive than the "dealing-with symptoms" approach.

Away from Maskmanship and Game-Playing Toward Authentic Behavior. Deeply rooted in existing organizational lore is a belief in the necessity or efficacy of being what one is not, both as an individual and as a group. Strategy and out-maneuvering are valued. Using diplomacy, wearing masks, not saying what one thinks or expressing what one feels creating an image— these and other deceptive modes are widely utilized. As a result, in many interpersonal and intergroup relations, mask faces mask, image faces image, and much energy is employed in dealing with the other person's game. That which is much more basically relevant to the given relationship is often completely avoided in the transaction.

To be that which one (individual or group) truly is—to be authentic—is a central value to us. Honesty, directness, and congruence, if widely practiced, create an organizational atmosphere in which energies get focused on the real problems rather than on game-playing and in which individuals and groups can genuinely and meaningfully encounter each other.

Recently, two supervisors of separate units within an organization got together to resolve a problem that affected both of them. At one point in their discussion, which had gone on for some time and was proving not to be very fruitful, one of them happened to mention that he had recently attended a sensitivity training laboratory conducted by the company. At that point, the other one mentioned that sometime back he had also attended a laboratory. They both quickly decided "to cut out the crap," stop the game they were playing, and really try to solve the problem they had come to face. Within a very short period of time, they dramatically went from a very typical organizational mode of being very closed, wearing masks, and trying to outmaneuver each other, to a mode of being open and direct. They found that the second mode took less energy and that they solved the problem in much less time and were able to keep it solved. But, somehow, at least one of them had not felt safe in taking off his mask until he learned that the other one had also gone through a T-Group.

When people experience difficulty with others in organizations, they quite often attribute the difficulty to the fact that the other person or group is not trustworthy. This attitude, of course, justifies their behavior in dealing with the other. On numerous occasions within TRW Systems, groups or individuals who are experiencing distrust are brought together and helped to articulate how they feel about each other. When the fact that "I do not trust you" is out on the table, and only then, can it be dealt with. Interestingly, it turns out that when the feeling is exposed and worked through, there are not really very many fundamentally untrustworthy people. There certainly are all kinds of people continuously doing things that create feelings of mistrust in others. But these feelings and the behavior that triggers them are rarely explored in an effort to work them through. Instead, the mistrust escalates, continues to

influence the behavior of both parties, and becomes self-fulfilling. Once the
locked-in situation is broken through and the people involved really start
talking to each other authentically, however, trust issues, about which people
can be very pessimistic, become quite workable. This has happened many,
many times in organizational development efforts at TRW Systems.

**Away from Use of Status for Maintaining Power and Personal Prestige
Toward Use of Status for Organizationally Relevant Purposes.** In organizations, particularly large ones, status and symbols of status can play an important role. In too many instances, however, they are used for narrowly personal
ends, both to hide behind and to maintain the aura of power and prestige.
One result is that dysfunctional walls are built and communication flow
suffers.

We believe that status must always be organizationally (functionally)
relevant. Some people know more than others, some can do things others
cannot do, some carry more responsibility than others. It is often useful for
status to be attached to these differences, but such status must be used by its
holder to further rather than to wall off the performance of the function out
of which the status arises. An organization must be constantly alert to the role
that status plays in its functioning.

It is relatively easy to perceive how status symbols are used within an
organization, how relatively functional or dysfunctional they are. In some
organizations, name dropping is one of the primary weapons for accomplishing
something. A person can go to a colleague with whom he is having a quarrel
about what should be done and mention that he had a chat with the president
of the organization yesterday. He then gets agreement. He may or may not
have talked with the president, he may or may not have quoted him correctly;
but he is begging the question by using a power figure in order to convince the
other person to do it his way. In other organizations we have observed that
people very rarely work a problem by invoking the name of a senior executive,
and that, in fact, those who do name-drop are quickly and openly called to
task.

At TRW Systems, with only minor exceptions, middle- and top-level
executives, as well as key scientists and engineers, are typically available for
consultation with anyone in the organization on matters of functional relevance to the organization. There is no need to use titles, to "follow the organization chart," to obtain permission for the consultation from one's boss or
to report the results to him afterwards. As a result, those who can really help
are sought out, and problems tend to get worked at the point of interface
between need on the one hand and knowledge, experience, and expertise on
the other.

Away from Distrusting People Toward Trusting Them. A corollary of
the view that man is basically bad is the view that he cannot be trusted. And
if he cannot be trusted, he must be carefully watched. In our judgment, many
traditional organizational forms exist, at least in part, because of distrust.

Close supervision, managerial controls, guarding, security, sign-outs, etc., carry with them to some extent the implication of distrust.

The increasing evidence available to us strongly suggests that distrusting people often becomes a self-confirming hypothesis—distrusting another leads to behavior consciously or unconsciously designed by the person or group not trusted to "prove" the validity of the distrust. Distrust begets distrust. On the other hand, the evidence also suggests that trust begets trust; when people are trusted, they often respond in ways to merit or justify that trust.

Where distrust exists, people are usually seen as having to be motivated "from the outside in," as being responsive only to outside pressure. But when trust exists, people are seen as being motivated "from the inside out," as being at least potentially self-directing entities. One motivational device often used in the outside-in approach involves the inculcation of guilt. Rooted in the Protestant ethic, this device confronts the individual with "shoulds," "oughts," or "musts" as reasons for behaving in a given way. Failure to comply means some external standard has not been met. The individual has thus done wrong and he is made to feel guilty. The more trustful, inside-out approach makes it possible for the individual to do things because they make sense to him, because they have functional relevance. If the behavior does not succeed, the experience is viewed in positive terms as an opportunity to learn rather than negatively as a reason for punishment and guilt.

Organizations which trust go far to provide individuals and groups with considerable freedom for self-directed action backed up by the experience-based belief that this managerial value will generate the assumption of responsibility for the exercise of that freedom. In California, going back about 27 years, a forward-looking director of one of our state prisons got the idea of a "prison without walls." He developed and received support for an experiment that involved bringing prisoners to the institution where correctional officers, at that time called guards, carried no guns or billy clubs. There were no guards in the towers or on the walls. The incoming prisoners were shown that the gate was not locked. Under this newer organizational behavior, escape rates decreased, and the experiment has become a model for many prisons in this country and abroad.

An organizational family embarked upon a two-day team-development lab shortly after the conclusion was reached from assessment data that the partial failure of a space vehicle had resulted from the non-functioning of a subsystem developed by his team. At the outset of the lab, an aura of depression was present but there was no evidence that the team had been chastised by higher management for the failure. Further, in strong contrast with what most likely would have been the case if they had faced a load of guilt generated from the outside, there was no evidence of mutual destructive criticism and recriminations. Instead, the team was able in time to turn its attention to a diagnosis of possible reasons for the failure and to action steps which might be taken to avoid a similar outcome in the future.

During a discussion which took place between the head of an organization and one of his subordinates (relating to goals and objectives for that subordinate for the coming year) the supervisor said that one of the things he felt very positive about with respect to that particular subordinate was the way he seemed to be defining his own set of responsibilities. This comment demonstrated the large degree of trust that was placed in the subordinates of this particular supervisor. While the supervisor certainly made it clear to this individual that there were some specific things expected of him, he consciously created a large degree of freedom within which the subordinate would be able to determine for himself how he should spend his time, what priorities he ought to have, what his function should be. This is in great contrast to other organizations which define very clearly and elaborately what they expect from people. Two very different sets of assumptions about people underlie these two approaches.

Away from Avoiding Facing Others with Relevant Data Toward Making Appropriate Confrontation. This value trend is closely related to the one of "from maskmanship toward authenticity," and its implementation is often tied to moving "from distrust toward trust."

In many organizations today there is an unwillingness to "level" with people, particularly with respect to matters which have personal implications. In merit reviews, the "touchy" matters are avoided. Often incompetent or unneeded employees are retained much longer than is justified either from the organization's or their own point of view. Feelings toward another accumulate and at times fester, but they remain unexpressed. "Even one's best friends won't tell him."

Confrontation fails to take place because "I don't want to hurt Joe," although in fact the non-confronter may be concerned about being hurt himself. We feel that a real absurdity is involved here. While it is widely believed that to level is to hurt and, at times, destroy the other, the opposite may often be the case. Being left to live in a "fool's paradise" or being permitted to continue with false illusions about self is often highly hurtful and even destructive. Being honestly confronted in a context of mutual trust and caring is an essential requirement for personal growth. In an organizational setting, it is also an important aspect of "working the problem."

A quite dramatic example of confrontation and its impact occurred in a sensitivity training laboratory when one executive giving feedback to a colleague said to him that he and others within the organization perceived him as being ruthless. This came as a tremendous jolt to the person receiving the feedback. He had absolutely no perception of himself as ruthless and no idea that he was doing things which would cause others to feel that way about him. The confrontation was an upending experience for him. As a result, he later began to explore with many people in the organization what their relationship with him was like and made some quite marked changes in his behavior after getting additional data which tended to confirm what he had recently heard.

In the absence of these data (previously withheld because people might not want to hurt him), he was indeed living in a fool's paradise. A great deal of energy was expended by other people in dealing with his "ruthlessness," and a considerable amount of avoidance took place, greatly influencing the productivity of everyone. Once this problem was exposed and worked through, this energy became available for more productive purposes.

Away from Avoidance of Risk-Taking Toward Willingness to Risk. A widely discernable attribute of large numbers of individuals and groups in organizations today is the unwillingness to risk, to put one's self or the group on the line. Much of this reluctance stems from not being trusted, with the resulting fear of the consequences expected to follow close upon the making of an error. It often seems that only a reasonable guarantee of success will free an individual or group to take a chance. Such a stance leads to conformity, to a repetition of the past, to excessive caution and defensiveness. We feel that risk-taking is an essential quality in adaptable, growthful organizations; taking a chance is necessary for creativity and change. Also, individuals and groups do learn by making mistakes. Risk-taking involves being willing "to take the monkey on my back," and it takes courage to do so. It also takes courage and ingenuity on the part of the organization to foster such behavior.

At TRW Systems, the president and many of the senior executives were until recently located on the fifth floor of one of the organization's buildings, and part of the language of the organization was "the fifth floor," meaning that place where many of the power figures resided. This phrase was used quite often in discussion: "the fifth floor feels that we should . . ." In working with groups one or two levels below the top executives to explore what they might do about some of the frustrations they were experiencing in getting their jobs done, one of the things that dominated the early discussions was the wish that somehow "the fifth floor" would straighten things out. For example, a group of engineers of one division was having problems with a group of engineers of another division, and they stated that "the fifth floor" (or at least one of its executives) ought to go over to the people in the other division and somehow "give them the word." After a while, however, they began to realize that it really was not very fruitful or productive to talk about what they wished someone else would do, and they began to face the problem of what they could do about the situation directly. The discussion then became quite constructive and creative, and a number of new action items were developed and later successfully implemented—even though there was no assurance of successful outcomes at the time the action items were decided upon.

Away from a View of Process Work as Being Unproductive Effort Toward Seeing it as Essential to Effective Task Accomplishment. In the past and often in the present, productive effort has been seen as that which focused directly on the production of goods and services. Little attention has been paid to the processes by which such effort takes place; to do so has often been viewed as a waste of time. Increasingly, however, the relevance to task accomplishment of such activities as team maintenance and development diagnosis and working through of interpersonal and intergroup communication barriers, confrontation efforts for resolution of organizationally dysfunctional personal and interpersonal hangups, and assessment and improvement of existing modes of decision-making is being recognized. And, in fact, we harbor growing doubts with respect to the continued usefulness of the notion of a task-process dichotomy. It seems to us that there are many activities which can make contributions to task accomplishment and that the choice from among these is essentially an economic one.

Within TRW Systems, proposals are constantly being written in the hope of obtaining new projects from the Department of Defense, NASA, and others. These proposals are done under very tight time constraints. What quite often happens is that the request for the proposal is received from the customer and read very quickly by the principals involved. Everybody then charges off and starts working on the proposal because of the keenly felt time pressure. Recently, on a very major proposal, the proposal manager decided that the first thing he should do was spend a couple of days (out of a three month period of available time) meeting with the principals involved. In this meeting, they would not do any writing of the proposal but would talk about how they were going to proceed, make sure they were all making the same assumptions about who would be working on which subsystem, how they would handle critical interfaces, how they would handle critical choice points during the proposal period, and so on. Many of the principals went to the meeting with a great deal of skepticism, if not impatience. They wanted to "get on with the job," which to them meant writing the proposal. Spending a couple of days talking about "how we're going to do things" was not defined by them as productive work. After the meting, and after the proposal had been written and delivered to the customer, a critique was held on the process used. Those involved in general reported very favorably on the effects of the meeting which took place at the beginning of the proposal-writing cycle. They reported things such as: "The effect of having spent a couple of days as we did meant that at that point when we then charged off and started actually writing the proposal, we were able to function as if we had already been working together for perhaps two months. We were much more effective with each other and much more efficient, so that in the final analysis, it was time well spent." By giving attention to their ways of getting work done, they clearly had facilitated their ability to function as well as a team.

Away from a Primary Emphasis on Competition Toward a Much Greater Emphasis on Collaboration.   A pervasive value in the organizational milieu is competition. Competition is based on the assumption that desirable resources are limted in quantity and that individuals or groups can be effectively motivated through competing against one another for the possession of these resources. But competition can often set man against man and group against group in dysfunctional behavior, including a shift of objectives from obtaining the limited resource to blocking or destroying the competitor. Competition inevitably results in winners and losers, and at least some of the hidden costs of losing can be rather high in systemic terms.

Collaboration, on the other hand, is based on the assumption that the desirable limited resources can be shared among the participants in a mutually satisfactory manner and, even more important, that it is possible to increase the quantity of the resources themselves.

As organizational work becomes more highly specialized and complex, with its accomplishment depending more and more on the effective interaction of individuals and groups, and as the organic or systems views of organizational functioning become more widely understood, the viability of collaboration as an organizational mode becomes ever clearer. Individuals and groups are often highly interdependent, and such interdependency needs to be facilitated through collaborative behavior rather than walled off through competition. At the same time, collaborative behavior must come to be viewed as reflecting strength rather than weakness.

In organizations which have a high degree of interdependency, one of the problems people run into regarding the handling of this interdependency is that they look for simple solutions to complex problems. Simple solutions do not produce very good results because they deal with the symptoms rather than with the real problems. A major reorganization recently took place within TRW Systems. The president of the organization sketched out the broad, general directions of the reorganization, specifying details only in one or two instances. He assigned to a large number of working committees the development of the details of the new organization. The initial reaction of some people was that these were things that the president himself should be deciding. The president, however, did not feel he had enough detailed understanding and knowledge to come up with many of the appropriate answers. He felt strongly that those who had the knowledge should develop the answers. This was an explicit, conscious recognition on his part of the fact that he did indeed need very important inputs from other people in order to effect the changes he was interested in making. These working committees turned out to be very effective. As a result of the president's approach, the reorganization proceeded with far less disruption and resistance than is typically the case in major reorganizations.

Another example involved a major staff function which was experiencing a great deal of difficulty with other parts of the organization. The unit having the trouble made the initial decision to conduct briefings throughout the organization to explain what they were really trying to accomplish, how they were organized, what requirements they had to meet for outside customers, and so on. They felt that their job would be easier if they could solicit better understanding. What actually took place was quite different. Instead of conducting briefings to convince the "heathen," the people in this unit revised their plan and met with some key people from other parts of the company who had to deal with them to ask what the unit was doing that was creating problems at the interface. After receiving a great deal of fairly specific data, the unit and the people with whom they consulted developed joint collaborative action items for dealing with the problems. This way of approaching the problem quickly turned interfaces that had been very negative and very hostile into ones that were relatively cooperative. The change in attitude on both sides of the interface provided a positive base for working toward satisfactory solutions to the problems.

SOME IMPLICATIONS OF THESE VALUES IN TRANSITION

Many people would agree with the value trends stated in this paper and indeed claim that they use these guidelines in running their own organizations. However, there is often quite a gap between saying that you believe in these values and actually practicing them in meaningful, important ways. In many organizations, for example, there is a management-by-objectives process which has been installed and used for several years—an approach which can involve the implementation of some of the values stated earlier in this paper. If, however, one closely examines how this process takes place in many organizations, it is in fact a very mechanical one, one which is used very defensively in some cases. What emerges is a statement of objectives which has obtained for the boss what he really wants, and, at the end of the year, protects the subordinate if he does not do everything that his boss thought he might do. It becomes a "Pearl Harbor file." The point that needs emphasis is that the payoff in implementing these values by techniques is not in the techniques themselves but in how they are applied and in what meaning their use has for the people involved.

To us, the implementation of these values clearly involves a bias regarding organizational development efforts. Believing that people have vast amounts of untapped potential and the capability and desire to grow, to engage in meaningful collaborative relationships, to be creative in organizational contexts, and to be more authentic, we feel that the most effective change interventions are therapeutic in nature. Such interventions focus directly on the hangups, both personal and organizational, that block a person from realizing his potential. We are referring to interventions which assist a person in breaking through the neurotic barriers in himself, in others around him, and in the ongoing culture.

We place a strong emphasis on increasing the sanity of the individuals in the organization and of the organization itself. By this we mean putting the individuals and the organization more in touch with the realities existing within themselves and around them. With respect to the individual, this involves his understanding the consequences of his behavior. How do people feel about him? How do they react to him? Do they trust him? With respect to the organization, it involves a critical examination of its culture and what that culture produces: the norms, the values, the decision-making processes, the general environment that it has created and maintained over a period of time.

There are obviously other biases and alternatives available to someone approaching organizational development work. One could concentrate on structural interventions. How should we organize? What kind of charters should people in various functional units have? The bias we are stating does not mean that structure, function, and charters are irrelevant, but that they are less important and have considerably less leverage in the early stages of organizational development efforts than working with the individuals and groups in a therapeutic manner. Furthermore, as an individual becomes more authentic and interpersonally competent, he becomes far more capable of creative problem-solving. He and his associates have within them more resources for dealing with questions of structure charters, and operating procedures, in more relevant and creative ways, than does someone from outside their system. Such therapeutic devices include the full range of laboratory methods usually identified with the National Training Laboratories: sensivitity training, team building, intergroup relationship building, etc. They also include individual and group counseling within the organization, and the voluntary involvement of individuals in various forms of psychotherapy outside the organization.

In order to achieve a movement towards authenticity, focus must be placed on developing the whole person and in doing this in an organic way. The program cannot be something you crank people through; it must be tailored in a variety of ways to individual needs as they are expressed and identified. In time, therapy and individual growth (becoming more in touch with your own realities) become values in and of themselves. And as people become less demotivated and move toward authenticity, they clearly demonstrate that they have the ability to be creative about organization matters, and this too becomes a value shared within the organization. Once these values are introduced and people move towards them, the movement in and of itself will contain many forces that make for change and open up new possibilities in an organization. For example, as relationships become more trustworthy, as people are given more responsibility, as competition gives way to collaboration, people experience a freeing up. They are more apt to challenge all the given surroundings, to test the limits, to try new solutions, and to rock the boat. This can be an exciting and productive change, but it can also be troublesome, and a variety of responses to it must be expected.

Therapeutic efforts are long-term efforts. Movement towards greater authenticity, which leads to an organization's culture becoming more positive, creative, and growthful, is something that takes a great deal of time and a great deal of energy. In this kind of approach to organizational development, there is more ambiguity and less stability than in other approaches that might be taken. Patience, persistence, and confidence are essential through time if significant change is to occur and be maintained.

For the organizational development effort to have some kind of permanency, it is very important that it becomes an integral part of the line organization and its model of operating. Many of the people involved in introducing change in organizations are in staff positions, typically in personnel. If, over time, the effort continues to be mainly one carried out by staff people, it is that much more tenuous. Somehow the total organization must be involved, particularly those people with line responsibility for the organization's success and for its future. They must assimilate the effort and make it a part of their own behavior within the organization. In other words, those people who have the greatest direct impact on and responsibility for creating, maintaining, and changing the culture of an organization must assume direct ownership of the change effort.

In the transition and beyond it, these changes can produce problems for the organization in confronting the outside world with its traditional values. For example, do you tell the truth to your customers when you are experiencing problems building a product for them, or do you continue to tell them that everything is going along fine? For the individual, there can be problems in other relationships around him, such as within his family at home. We do not as yet have good methods developed for dealing with these conflicts, but we can certainly say that they will take place and will have to be worked out.

As previously stated, the Career Development program at TRW Systems, now in its fifth year of operation, is an effort in which both authors have been deeply involved. We feel it is one of the more promising examples of large-scale, long-term, systematic efforts to help people move toward the values we have outlined.[6]

One question that is constantly raised about efforts such as the Career Development program at TRW Systems relates to assessing their impact. How does one know there has been a real payoff for the organization and its members? Some behavioral scientists have devised rather elaborate, mechanical tools in order to answer this question. We feel that the values themselves suggest the most relevant kind of measurement. The people involved have the capacity to determine the relevance and significance to them and to their organizational units of what they are doing. Within TRW Systems, a very pragmatic approach is taken. Questions are asked such as: Do we feel this has been useful? Are these kinds of problems easier to resolve? Are there less hidden agenda now? Do we deal more quickly and effectively with troublesome intergroup problems? The payoff is primarily discussed in qualitative terms, and we feel this is appropriate. It does not mean that quantitative judgments are not possible, but to insist on reducing the human condition to numbers, or to believe that it can be done, is madness.

---

[6]This program is described in detail in Davis [3].

The role of the person introducing change (whether he is staff or in the line) is a very tough, difficult, and, at times, lonely one.[7] He personally must be as congruent as he can with the values we have discussed. If people perceive him to be outside the system of change, they should and will reject him. He must be willing and able to become involved as a person, not merely as the expert who will fix everybody else up. He, too, must be in process. This is rewarding, but also very difficult.

Introducing change into a social system almost always involves some level of resistance to that change. Accepting the values we have described means that one will not be fully satisfied with the here and now because the limits of man's potential have certainly not been reached. All we know for sure is that the potential is vast. Never accepting the status quo is a rather lonely position to take. In effect, as one of our colleagues has put it, you are constantly saying to yourself, "Fifty million Frenchmen are wrong!" From our own experience we know that this attitude can produce moments when one doubts one's sanity: "How come nobody else seems to feel the way I do, or to care about making things better or to believe that it is possible to seek improvements?" Somehow, these moments must be worked through, courage must be drawn upon, and new actions must follow.

We are struck with and saddened by the large amounts of frustration, feelings of inadequacy, insecurity, and fear that seem to permeate groups of behavioral science practitioners when they meet for seminars or workshops. Belief in these values must lead to a bias towards optimism about the human condition. "Man does have the potential to create a better world, and I have the potential to contribute to that effort." But in addition to this bias towards optimism, there has to be a recognition of the fundamental fact that we will continuously have to deal with resistance to change, including resistances within ourselves. People are not standing in line outside our doors asking to be freed up, liberated, and upended. Cultures are not saying: "Change us, we can no longer cope, we are unstable." Commitment to trying to implement these values as well as we can is not commitment to an easy, safe existence. At times, we can be bone weary of confrontation questioning, probing, and devil's-advocating. We can have delightful fantasies of copping out on the whole mess and living on some island. We can be fed up with and frightened by facing someone's anger when we are confronting him with what is going on around him. We can be worn out from the continuous effort to stretch ourselves as we try to move towards living these values to the fullest.

On the other hand, the rewards we experience can be precious, real, and profound. They can have important meaning for us individually, for those with whom we work, and for our organizations. Ultimately, what we stand for can make for a better world—and we deeply know that this is what keeps us going.

---

[7]Each Winter Quarter, UCLA's Graduate School of Business Administration offers a residential program in Organizational Development for individuals instrumental in the change activities of the organizations

REFERENCES

1. Bennis, W. G. *Changing Organizations.* New York, McGraw-Hill, 1966.
2. Blake, R. R., and Mouton, J. S. *The Managerial Grid.* Houston, Gulf, 1964.
3. Davis, S. A. "An Organic Problem-Solving Method of Organizational Change." *Journal of Applied Behavioral Science,* Vol. 3, no. 1 (1967), pp. 3–21.
4. Likert, R. *The Human Organization.* New York, McGraw-Hill, 1967.
5. McGregor, D. M. *The Human Side of Enterprise.* New York, McGraw-Hill, 1960.
6. McGregor, D. M. *The Professional Manager.* New York, McGraw-Hill, 1967.

NOTES ON THE ART OF
ADMINISTRATION

Stephen K. Blumberg

In 1936, as a member of President Roosevelt's Committee on Administrative Management, Luther Gulick prepared a memorandum titled "Notes on the Theory of Organization - with Special Reference to Government in the United States."[1] In addition to being a member of this presidential committee, Gulick was also Eaton Professor of Municipal Science and Administration at Columbia University and Director of the Institute of Public Administration in New York. Today, at the age of eighty-nine, he is Chairman of the Board of Trustees of this same Institute of Public Administration.

In this classic memorandum, building on the theories of Henri Fayol,[2] Gulick made up a word to identify an executive's activities and duties. The word is POSDCORB, an acronym made up of the initials of these major management actitivies: Planning, Organizing, Staffing, Directing, Coordinating, Reporting, and Budgeting.

Ever since, students of administration have been exposed to POSDCORB. We have been taught that in order to be an effective executive we need to know and understand these functions. These functions can be called the "technical guidelines" of administration. To be sure, they are important guidelines, and

Reprinted by permission of *Midwest Review of Public Administration* from volume 14, number 3(September 1980).

The author wishes to express deep thanks to Daniel M. Blumberg whose talented efforts were instrumental in making this essay more literate than earlier drafts.

[1]Luther Gulick, "Notes on the Theory of Organization," in *Papers on the Science of Administration,* ed. by Luther Gulick and L. Urwick (New York: Institute of Public Administration, Columbia University, 1937).

[2]Henri Fayol, *Industrial and General Administration,* trans. by J. A. Coubrough (Geneva: International Management Association, 1930).

any competent administrator will need to follow them in order to effectively manage an organization. However, a critically needed dimension was inadvertently left out of the POSDCORB prescription. This dimension, in the broadest sense, is the human element. Professor Gulick, some forty years after establishing POSDCORB, has written:

> How interesting it is historically that we all assumed in the 1930's that all management, especially public management, flowed in a broad, strong stream of value-filled ethical performance. Were we blind or only naive until Nixon came along? Or were we so eager to "take politics out of administration" that we threw the baby out with the bath water?[3]

It was never Gulick's intention to encourage administrators to ignore the human element. Unfortunately, this has too often been the case. Morris Janowitz, University of Chicago Professor of Sociology, recently said that "our universities have been too oriented to technical education instead of emphasizing humanistic education."[4] In our current contemporary society this lack of humanistic emphasis has become a serious problem. There is the problem of distrust and cynicism many citizens have toward government. There is the problem of alienation and frustration felt by many public employees. The problem is one which is both internal and external to public organizations.

Within the organization managers are facing a more hostile internal environment. The work force is more highly educated and less tolerant of many previous management approaches; these are people who frequently want to satisfy more than just economic needs through their jobs. Many people are determined to participate more in helping to shape the activities of the organization in which they spend most of their waking hours. Mills says that our organizations must help in the fulfillment of positive human aspirations.[5] Bennis argues some missing key ingredients are needed in organizations in order to respond to the new kinds of people coming into organizations.[6] Marrow makes the point clearly:

> The feelings of restlessness, anger and hatred that creep out of . . . office buildings, and into the streets and homes of Americans, come from jobs that provide no challenge or variety, and from *bosses who are inconsiderate and autocratic.* The on-coming generation . . . is unwilling to pay the

---

[3]Letter from Luther Gulick to the author, January 24, 1978.

[4]Morris Janowitz, "Outlook for Middle Class: 'I am Mildly Optimistic'," *U. S. News and World Report* (May 2, 1977), p. 57.

[5]Ted Mills, "Human Resources-Why the New Concern?" *53 Harvard Business Review* (March-April, 1975), pp. 120–134.

[6]Warren Bennis, *The Unconscious Conspiracy* (New York: AMACOM, 1976).

crushing price of loss of pride, mind-killing monotony, dehumanization and stress diseases in return for the highest wages in history. Their idea of success revolves around a form of self-fulfillment, toward *more humanistic ways of living*. Material rewards alone turn them off.[7] (Emphasis added.)

Insofar as the enviroment *outside* the organization is concerned, it is argued by Pfiffner that following POSDCORB is not enough, and that management "must adopt a scheme of social values." He persuasively advocates that the more important responsibility of administration "is to make this world a better one in which humans are to live."[8]

It is clear that new public administration is vitally concerned with the impact public agencies have on their surrounding communities. An essential message of this "new" attitude, so articulately compiled by Marini, is expressed by Frederickson's hope that we have moved "light years away from the POSDCORB image."[9]

The image conjured up by POSDCORB is one of our problems. We need a new image of public administrative behavior. We must expand the limiting constraints of technical dictates to include a set of humanistic guidelines upon which administrators can focus their attention. It is not that the technical dictates of POSDCORB will be dismissed, it is simply that they must be complemented with an additional set of guidelines. One might argue that humanistic guidelines would come naturally for public administrators, but perhaps because the public bureaucracy lends itself to being impersonal, a set of humanistic guidelines must be identified and brought more sharply to our attention. These guidelines will coexist, and in fact the humanistic guidelines can help to make the execution of the technical dictates more effective.

The balance of this paper will identify the humanistic guidelines—what Bennis indicated as the missing administrative ingredients. Incorporating these guidelines into the administrative management process will help to reduce the number of what Marrow called "inconsiderate bosses" and begin to create more "humanistic ways of living." Following this proposed set of humanistic guidelines will assist in restoring some of government's lost trust and credibility.

---

[7]A. J. Marrow, "Management by Participation," in *Man and Work in Society,* ed. by Cass and F. G. Zimmer (New York: Van Nostrand Reinhold Co., 1975), pp. 35–36.

[8]John M. Pfiffner, "Why Not Make Social Science Operational?" *22 Public Administration Review* (September, 1962), p. 112.

[9]H. George Frederickson, "Toward a New Public Administration," in *Toward a New Public Administration: The Minnowbrook Perspective,* ed. by Frank Marini (Scranton: Chandler Publishing Co., 1971), p. 331.

HUMANISTIC GUIDELINES

The humanistic guidelines are found in a new acronym: EVPOSDCORB. Gulick's word has been used deliberately as the foundation of this new acronym to emphasize that any effective administrator must have a combination of technical and humanistic skills. Henceforth it will be clear that POSD-CORB represents the needed technical dictates of administrative behavior while EVPOSDCORB symbolizes the equally needed humanistic guidelines.

Ethics

It is too often true that public employees and officials are viewed by the citizenry as little more than crooks. One vividly remembers former President Nixon saying on national television, "I am not a crook." Especially after Watergate, ethical standards must be expressed in action. Ethics includes honesty, integrity, decency, and regard for others. Talking about ethics is nice; practicing ethics is what is called for.

Each individual is a member of society; the level at which we practice honesty, integrity, decency, and regard for others affects our society. We need these standards of moral and intellectual sincerity on which to base our individual conduct.[10]

Administrators, indeed all public employees, realize that ethics has always concerned itself with questions of good and bad, right and wrong. The public administrator's first priority will be to do that which he feels honestly is right.

Values

Each individual does of course possess his own set of values. Recognizing these values is a challenge eloquently presented in *Hamlet* when Shakespeare writes, "This above all: to thine own self be true. And it must follow, as the night the day, thou canst not then be false to any man."[11] Nierenberg echoes this theme by arguing that the process of human interaction must begin with "an intimate examination of one's sense of values,"[12] while Bennis urges us to find things to believe in with passionate conviction and integrity.[13] Possessing these convictions helps to establish our personal values.

Public employees especially need to constantly remind themselves that their fundamental responsibility—their predominant value—is to provide ser-

[10]Bennis, *The Unconscious Conspiracy.*

[11]Shakespeare, *Hamlet* I. iii.

[12]Gerad I. Nierenberg, *The Art of Negotiating* (New York: Hawthorn Books, Inc., 1977), p. 48.

[13]Bennis, *The Unconscious Conspiracy.*

vice to the community. They too must begin with an intimate examination of their own value system; an effective way to achieve this is to follow the Golden Rule of treating others as we wish to be treated. The remaining humanistic guidelines help establish and clarify these personal values and simultaneously shape the organizational values.

Patience

Today's organizations are confronted with stress and tension; public organizations are also confronted with angry citizens. Dealing with this situation requires people who possess an abundance of patience. Calling again on Shakespeare, we are told to "take each man's censure, but reserve thy judgement."[14]

Public employees are required to be patient with citizens who sometimes perceive only how they might personally be affected by a given issue without seeing the total picture. Patience is also needed to be receptive, with genuine interest and understanding, to the diverse views and opinions of others.

Dealing appropriately with the problems of contemporary society requires a certain degree of organizational innovativeness. Public administrators, therefore, need patient tolerance to hear input, try new ideas, and accept the fact that not everything will work out positively. This necessitates some patience for the "mistakes" which will sometimes be made within organizations.

There are times when it is appropriate for administrators to give more time and thought to a particular situation before making a decision. This patient delay may help to prevent an unwise decision, and lead to a more productive humanistic response to the situation.

Openness

Just as patience is required to hear new ideas, there must be an open willingness to listen to new suggestions.[15] This openness will help to generate more confidence toward public administrators and their organizations. A genuinely open public organization will demonstrate the way it is serving the community and encourage more trust in itself.

Beyond this kind of openness, an administrator must be willing and able to withstand an additional test of openness when making decisions. This test has been classically provided by Cleveland who tells us to ask this question before making a decision: "If this action were held up to public scrutiny, would I still feel that it is what I should have done and how I should have done it?"[16]

---

[14]Shakespeare, *Hamlet* I. iii.

[15]Bennis, *The Unconscious Conspiracy.*

[16]Harlan Cleveland, *The Future Executive* (New York: Harper and Row Publishers, Inc., 1972), p. 104.

Asking this question will eliminate secrecy and "smoke-filled backroom" decisions and ensure that decision-makers can be honestly comfortable with their actions.

Sensitivity

Administrators' sensitivity is important when relating to people inside and outside their organizations. This involves constant awareness of the effect decisions might have on others. Making decisions requires genuine feelings of empathy and a recognition of how these decisions and subsequent actions might be perceived by the people who are affected by them.

Public administrators especially must recognize that they do not function in a vacuum; as part of a very open system, their decisions create vast ramifications for the public. We can erect sensitive antennae toward the people with whom we work—and the people we serve—to help make the organization more productive and satisfying for all.

Dignity

A true sensitive concern for the dignity of humankind is a major consideration for public administrators. Dvorin and Simmons persuasively argue that decision-makers must leave behind the constraints of neutral decision-making and replace it with a humane bureaucracy which focuses on human dignity.[17] This will enable staff and constituents to be dealt with as human beings—not as automatons.

There is a need to eliminate the too-prevalent attitude of treating others as inferiors or subordinates; the clerk typist deserves the same respect as the assistant manager. Even the term "subordinate" has a demeaning, dependency-laden connotation. Instead, according to Tannenbaum and Schmidt, use of the term "non-manager" will make the terminological difference between managers and non-managers functional rather than hierarchical.[18]

Creating humanizing work is an objective of a productive society, and Rosow says that this translates to increasing human dignity at the workplace.[19] This requires organizations to provide more personnel development. Rosow further argues that in order to advance human dignity in the public sector it is important to turn attention to greater employee participation.

---

[17]Eugene P. Dvorin and Robert H. Simmons, *From Amoral to Humane Bureaucracy* (San Francisco: Canfield Press, 1972).

[18]Robert Tannenbaum and Warren H. Schmidt, "How to Choose a Leadership Pattern and a Retrospective Comment," *51 Harvard Business Review* (May-June, 1973).

[19]Jerome M. Rosow, "Human Dignity in the Public-Sector Workplace," *8 Public Personnel Management* (January-February, 1979).

Co-operation

Contemporary organizations are complex; an individual cannot make an effective decision in isolation. Managers do not have all the answers; if they did, they would still have to recognize that the rest of the people in the organization want to feel a sense of participation. To cooperate means to work together, to unite in producing a common goal. Organizations must allow their members to develop in a cooperative and supportive environment.

In establishing a cooperative spirit of participatory management and teamwork, administrators will be perceived as having evolved from "taskmasters" to "task-sharers." This spirit can pervade the organization and positively affect the people within it. Likewise, this cooperative atmosphere will be sensed by the community, thus creating a better relationship between the organization and the public.

One of the major benefits which can accrue as a result of this spirit of co-operation throughout the organization is an overall philosophy of "winwin." In this "no-lose" situation all parties feel they have benefited. Nierenberg posits that human transactions involve a process of negotiation; he suggests that we "think of negotiation as a cooperative enterprise. If both parties enter the situation on a cooperative basis, there is a strong likelihood that they will be persuaded to strive for goals that can be shared equally."[20] With a feeling of equality and cooperation the "win-win" philosophy will be achieved.

Responsiveness

The atmosphere found too frequently in many organizations is one which is symbolized by people saying, "nobody listens to me." The development of a responsive attitude in the organization will go a long way toward improving this negative atmosphere. A widely accepted technique to reduce "nobody listens" feelings has been developed by Carl Rogers. He advocates active listening as a means of hearing what people are feeling in addition to what they are saying.[21] An effective, responsive listener enhances the degree of credibility, trust, and respect which others feel toward him.

Being responsive also involves a positive attitude toward requests, suggestions, and complaints. However, this does not necessitate the mandatory consent to every request; rather it implies a willingness to acknowledge and listen to the concerns which people express.

Finally, responsiveness means readily going out of our way to attempt to be helpful to others. This may require spending a bit more time, but will inevitably help people feel better about our organization.

---

[20]Nierenberg, *The Art of Negotiating,* pp. 24–25.

[21]Carl Rogers and R. E. Farson, "Active Listening," in *Readings on Behavior in Organizations,* ed. by E. F. Huse, J. L. Bowditch, and D. Fisher (Reading, Mass.: Addison-Wesley Publishing Company, 1975).

Beneficence

This final guideline is one which serves to unify all the humanistic guidelines. Public administrators are in a unique position to provide beneficence: the quality of being kind or of doing good. The preceding humanistic guidelines help to define what is good and kind.

There may be times when providing beneficence appears to the administrator to involve a certain amount of personal risk while following humanistic guidelines. In order to avoid this perceived risk or harm, many people seem to practice only benign beneficence. Benign beneficence is being kind or doing good only when the actor senses a minimal risk to himself.[22]

The effective administrator, following humanistic guidelines without the constraints of only benign beneficence, will take risks when necessary. The foundation for this type of behavior was well established when Darwin said that

> it is the most noble of all the attributes of man, leading him without a moment's hesitation to risk his life for that of a fellow creature; or after due deliberation, impelled simply by the deep feeling of right or duty, to sacrifice it in some great cause.[23]

While public administrators may not literally need to risk their lives, the point is that they must be innovative and willing to exert themselves in establishing a spirit of beneficence throughout their organizations.

CONCLUSION

There is an intentional unifying thread of commonality weaving throughout these humanistic guidelines tying them together. This common bond is a *sincere concern for people*. As basic or simplistic as this concept may appear, it must be acknowledged that there are too many administrators, as well as others charged with the responsibility for serving the public, for whom this concern does not appear to be paramount.

It must again be stressed that no argument is being made for the elimination of POSDCORB. The technical guidelines are critical and the effective administrator will routinely use them. The argument being made is that Gulick's POSDCORB does not go far enough in delineating the administrator's functions. An awareness of what is represented by EVPOSDCORB will expand the administrator's focus of attention in managing his organization, and

---

[22]Stephen K. Blumberg, "Benign Beneficence: The Theory of Doing 'Good' If It Won't Hurt You" (unpublished article developed from unpublished Ph.D. dissertation, University of Southern California, 1975).

[23]Charles Darwin, *The Descent of Man* (New York: A. L. Burt Company, 1874), p. 110.

also make the execution of the technical aspects of his work more productive. Blake and Mouton have found that attention to humanistic guidelines, in terms of concern for people, will serve to increase the level of organizational productivity.[24]

It is important to recognize that following EVPOSDCORB is called for in private organizations as well as in public administration. In part this is necessary because these guidelines affect the people with whom administrators work—the internal personnel of the organization—as well as the people served—the organizational external community.

We must further be aware that the behavior of individuals throughout an organization influences the overall organizational culture. If there is a spirit of EVPOSDCORB pervading the organization, the total organization is more likely to achieve maximum effectiveness.

Administrators exposed to what is symbolized by EVPOSDCORB will bring to their technical responsibilities a new dimension of executive leadership. This new dimension will foster a humanistic atmosphere in organizations; an atmosphere of trust and respect needed in contemporary society. This atmosphere will help to decrease the growing sense of alienation that is prevalent today.

Practicing the humanistic guidelines of EVPOSDCORB is not the total answer to society's problems. It may very well represent, though, an effective starting point. We can only hope that it will help to advance the broad goals of contemporary public administration and make the world a better one in which to live.

---

[24]Robert R. Blake and Jane S. Mouton, "Grid Organization Development," *30 Personnel Administration* (January-February, 1967).

SECTION III

THE "WIN-WIN" ORGANIZATION

INTRODUCTION

Anyone who has experienced organizational life—whether from the inside or as a recipient of the organization's services—knows that the organization's basic "climate" is an important determinant of how people are treated. An organization, not unlike an individual, tends to have its own personality. This personality is established in part by the dominant value system or culture of the organization, and based upon this organizational personality one can categorize the organization. Is it bureaucratic? Humanistic? Friendly? Aloof? Is the organization one with which people feel comfortable or one which people would rather avoid dealing with? It is fair to accept as a truism that the organization's basic typology influences the way in which the organization deals with its employees and also the way the organization treats the people it serves.

If one wishes to manage an organization so that everybody "wins," then certainly one must be concerned with the way with which people are dealt. The organization's structure plays a role in this regard. Every organization has a structure, and of course that structure is one of the factors in determining the organization's personality. James Gibson is vitally concerned with organizational structure. His article is an excellent over-view of the influences which various eras have had on the development of the field of organization theory. He argues that value premises and consideration of human nature must influence the way an organization is structured and run. Considering human nature is an essential step toward achieving a "win-win" organization.

There are other elements, in addition to its structure, which comprise an organization. An organization has a technological system, formal and informal activities geared toward accomplishing its goals and objectives, a value system, and a whole network of interpersonal relationships. All of these elements combine to shape the organization's total environment. Ronald Webb, citing several research studies, finds that a supportive environment is needed to achieve a "win-win" spirit. This supportive environment is one where open communication and shared decision-making are part of the organization's value system, and Webb has found that this type of climate is an essential ingredient of an effective organization. A new definition for an effective organization may very well be one in which "win-win" is the organization's primary focus.

Having a focus within an organization is important, but translating that focus into results is critical. A "win-win" organization achieves good results, reaches high levels of productivity. Dennis Briscoe says that organizations which expect to accomplish their tasks must recognize the importance of the people in their organization. The organization must realize that it is dealing with human beings rather than some mechanical resource, and it must learn to deal with its employees as whole people. The organization must be aware of people as total human beings.

The articles in this section are all concerned with the organizational setting. The points made by the three authors, discussing the issue from slightly different perspectives, all lead to the establishment of a "win-win" organization.

ORGANIZATION THEORY AND THE NATURE OF MAN

James L. Gibson

A recent contribution to the literature of organization theory raises serious questions about the nature of men who participate in organizations.[1]

If Anthony Downs' hypotheses are correct, William H. Whyte's quietly-conservative, status-conscious and security-seeking organization man has been replaced by a new variety whose characteristics are even less admirable than those of his predecessor. If Downs is correct, the organization man of today is suspicious, distrustful, jealous, deceitful, self-centered, apathetic, and immature. He is intolerant of differences, unable to communicate in depth with his fellows, and short-sighted. In short, here is a man whose integrity and moral fiber should be seriously questioned.[2]

Downs, however, is not the only writer to introduce some interesting organizational characters. Robert Presthus developed three personality types to be found in organizations which he called the upward-mobiles, the indifferents, and the ambivalents.[3] Victor A. Thompson and others suggest similarly evocative concepts to describe some of the more irrational behavior of organizations (bureaupathology) and to portray the behavior of some individuals in organizations (bureausis).[4]

If the views of these writers are correct, there is need for a great deal of research and study directed at finding ways of making life in modern organizations more meaningful. I share the value system of those who believe "that work which permits autonomy, responsibility, social connection, and self-actualization furthers the dignity of the human individual, whereas work without these characteristics limits the development of personal potential and is therefore to be negatively valued."[5] And I value negatively the behavior of

Reprinted by permission of the author and The Academy of Management from *Academy of Management Journal,* Volume 9 (September 1966).

organization members who "inevitably distort information which they relay upwards to their superiors or downward to their subordinates,"[6] or who "distort the orders they receive from their superiors, interpreting them to their own benefit ... as they develop the implications of those orders for their subordinates."[7]

To say the least, the conclusion from the above statements is simply that some organization men are dishonest; to the extent that organizations create conditions which encourage and reward such behavior, to that extent, organization theorists should be concerned.

In the remainder of this article, I outline the development of organization theory in terms of its underlying assumptions regarding the nature of man. My purpose is to stimulate thought and action on two fronts:

1. To urge organization theorists and practitioners to express explicitly their assumptions about the nature of man; and,
2. To urge more analysis of ongoing organizations to determine the causes of behavior which Downs, Presthus, and Thompson describe.

This discussion seeks to add to the literature on the philosophy of organizations by emphasizing the value premises which underlie some of the major strands of thought.

The vehicle used to develop the literature is a classification system of three categories: the *mechanistic tradition;* the *humanistic challenge;* and, the *realistic synthesis.* An essential feature of the literature classified in the *mechanistic tradition* category is the view of man as a constant without peculiar features and malleable without incident into the organization structure; man is characterized as a machine—predictable, repairable, and replaceable. The literature of the *humanistic* challenge is characterized by an awareness of man as a unique element in the organization structure; man is viewed as having a need structure and individual differences are tolerated. The literature of the *realistic synthesis* is not easily characterized, but its essential feature is to treat man as one of a number of variables in the organization all of which are interdependent and interacting. Man is seen as being acted upon and as acting on the organization environment.

THE MECHANISTIC TRADITION

The writers of the mechanistic tradition focused on *two* aspects of organization theory.

At *one level,* Frederick W. Taylor and others analyzed the basic tasks of the individual members. The objective of Taylor and his followers was to reduce the contributions of each workman to the smallest, most specialized unit of work possible and to eliminate any uncertainty about the expected outcome. Elementary to such analysis were (and are) work simplification

studies which break down manual labor tasks into definite repetitive movements and motion and time studies which establish time standards for the
accomplishment of each movement. As Taylor himself said:

> Perhaps the most prominent single element in modern scientific manage-
> ment is the task idea. The work of every workman is fully planned out by
> the management at least one day in advance, and each man receives in
> most cases complete written instructions, describing in detail the task
> which he is to accomplish, as well as the means to be used in doing the
> work. And the work planned in advance in this way constitutes a task
> which is to be solved, as explained above, not by the workman alone, but
> in almost all cases by the joint effort of the workman and the management.
> This task specifies not only what is to be done but how it is to be done and
> the exact time allowed for doing it.[8]

To assure that each task is performed according to the plan, the worker
is paid on an incentive basis which rewards him for meeting the expectations
of the organization and punishes him if he does not. The application of scien-
tism tended to reduce the skills of craftsmen to routine, procedural predictable
sequences of movement; workers were to be as interchangeable as the cogs in
Eli Whitney's cotton gin.

Underlying the procedural prescriptions of scientific management were
definite assumptions about the nature of man. Taylor said:

> A reward, if it is to be effective in stimulating men to do their best work,
> must come soon after the work has been done. But few men are able to
> look forward for more than a week or perhaps at most a month, and work
> hard for a reward which they are to receive at the end of this time.[9]

Later, in discussing the reasons for the failure of profit sharing schemes, he
said: "Personal ambition always has been and will remain a more powerful
incentive to exertion than a desire for the general welfare."[10] The view that
man is motivated solely and predictably by economic considerations and is an
isolated factor of production independent of social and group pressures guided
the development of scientific management theories and practices.

The postulates of scientific management were quite appealing to those
who were concerned with administrative aspects of organizations—the *second
level* of analysis.

Wolin suggests that Saint-Simon[11] laid the foundations of organization
theory "with the conscious intent of establishing a defense against political
instability and social disorder" in the aftermath of the French Revolution.[12]
However, it was one hundred years later before a theory of organization
structuring was articulated.

The most prominent writers of what is often called "Classical Organization Theory" were Luther Gulick,[13] Henri Fayol,[14] James D. Mooney and A.

C. Reiley,[15] and L. Urwick[16] all of whom wrote from the perspective of business or military organizations. These writers owe an intellectual debt to Max Weber who provided the "ideal type" of administrative organization which he called a bureaucracy.[17] Even though Weber's model is based primarily on the European methods of organizing the civil servants (chiefly the Prussian experience), the characteristics of his "ideal type" are illustrative of the main features of classical organization theory.

According to Weber, the essential characteristics of the "ideal type" are as follows:[18]

1. All tasks necessary for the accomplishment of the goals are broken down into the smallest possible unit; the division of labor is carried out to the extent that specialized experts are responsible for the successful performance of specified duties.
2. Each task is performed according to a "consistent sytem of abstract rules"[19] to assure uniformity and coordination of different tasks. This uncertainty in the performance of tasks due to individual differences is theoretically eliminated.
3. Each member or office of an organization is accountable to a superior for his or its decisions as well as for his or its subordinates. The authority is based on expert knowledge and is sanctioned and made legitimate by the ultimate source of authority—the chief official at the top of the hierarchial pyramid.
4. Each official in the organization conducts the business of his office in an impersonal, rationalistic manner. He maintains a social distance between himself and his subordinates and between himself and the clients of the organization. The purpose of this impersonal detachment is to assure that personalities do not interfere with the efficient accomplishment of the mission.
5. "Employment in the bureaucratic organization is based on technical qualifications and is protected against arbitrary dismissal."[20] Promotions are based on seniority and achievement. Because employment is considered a career and the vagaries of making a living are eliminated, a high degree of loyalty for the organization is engendered in the members.

The inherent logic of the bureaucratic structure led Weber to believe that the bureaucratic form of administration is "superior to any other form in precision, in stability, in the stringency of its discipline, and in its reliability. It thus makes possible a particularly high degree of calculability of results for the heads of the organization and for those acting in relation to it."[21] Thus Weber presented the case for bureaucratic administration on precisely the same grounds that the Taylorites presented the case for Scientific Management. In fact Weber himself drew the analogy: "The fully developed bureaucratic mechanism compares with other organizations exactly as does the machine with nonmechanical modes of production."[22]

The bureaucratic form of organization was (and is) prominent in business practice. The proponents of its use in this context formulated "principles" which are obviously in the Weberian tradition. Haynes and Massie have codified these principles as follows:[23]

1. The Unity of Command principle: No member of an organization should report to more than one superior.
2. The Span of Control principle: No superior should have responsibility for the activities of more than five to eight subordinates.
3. The Exception principle: A superior should delegate responsibility for routine matters to subordinates.
4. The Scalar principle: Every organization should have a well defined hierarchial structure.

One is struck by the prescriptive nature of these principles, by their similarity to the characteristics of Weber's ideal type, and by their concern for order and certainty in carrying on the activities of the organization.

The evidence supplied in the foregoing discussion suggests the assumptions regarding the nature of man underlying scientific management and classical organization theory. March and Simon observe that two "views" of organization members are pervasive: "First, in general there is a tendency to view the employee as an inert instrument performing the tasks assigned to him. Second, there is a tendency to view personnel as a given rather than as a variable in the system."[24] Mason Haire has been less polite: "These are the implicit assumptions about man on which classical organization theory seems to me to be based: He is lazy, short-sighted, selfish, liable to make mistakes, has poor judgment, and may even be a little dishonest."[25]

From another perspective, William F. Whyte argues that there are three assumptions underlying the theory: First, it is assumed that "man is a rational animal concerned with maximizing his economic gains," second, "each individual responds to economic incentives as an isolated individual," and third, "men, like machines, can be treated in a standardized fashion."[26]

THE HUMANISTIC CHALLENGE

It was only in the 1930's that these assumptions and their implications for organization theory and practice were seriously challenged. The body of concepts that developed during the initial thrust of the industrial revolution and which I have characterized as mechanistic was soon confronted with evidence that seriously challenged its validity. This challenge (which I call the humanistic challenge) came from two sources:

1. There were those who questioned the basic assumptions of the scientific management approach regarding the motivation of men; and,

2. There were those who questioned the efficiency of the bureaucratic form of organization.

Although the two sources of challenge were seemingly unrelated, the emphasis of both was the same, namely: the participants of organizations are not constants and cannot be regarded as givens; and, a large mass of empirical evidence was soon available to show that participants adjust the environment to meet their individual and group needs. And part of this adjustment process is related to motivations, as some industrial engineers were to discover.

In 1924, engineers at the Hawthorne Works, a division of the Western Electric Company in Chicago, began a series of tests to determine the relationship between certain variables and the rate of production.[27] A number of frustrating experiments caused the scientists to reject their original hypothesis (that a high and positive correlation exists between working conditions and the rate of output) and they formulated alternative hypotheses. The major sources of data for testing the revised hypotheses were the voluminous recordings of interpersonal conversations that the experimenters had accumulated. These conversations between workers and the scientists revealed that the workers were members of closely knit work groups and that these work groups had established acceptable patterns of behavior for the members. These patterns of behavior, in turn, were based on the sentiments of the members of the group, but these sentiments were easily disguised and difficult to isolate. Nevertheless, the scientists discarded their statistical techniques and "denuded of their elaborate logical equipment"[28] they went into the shop to learn the things that were important to the workers.

The findings of the Hawthorne studies challenged the basic assumptions of earlier organization theory, namely the social isolation of the worker and the primacy of economic incentives. For these two assumptions, the human relations school substituted the view that man desires "first, a method living in social relationship with other people, and, second, as part of this an economic function for and value to the group."[29] Thus man (according to Mayo and his followers) "is a uniquely social animal who can achieve complete 'freedom' only by fully submerging himself in the group."[30] Based on the notion of man as a gregarious animal, the human relations school included in their ideology a view of a society in which man could best achieve his freedom. But the industrial society is not such a society and in fact the process of industrialization destroys the cultural traditions of former times which had enhanced social solidarity. The results of industrialization are social disorganization and unhappy individuals.

According to Mayo the responsibility for restoring the bases for social stability belongs to administrators of large industrial firms. With leadership that is human-oriented rather than production-oriented the prospects for social stability and its concomitant, a meaningful life for the individual, are enhanced. In fact Mayo has said: "If our social skills (that is, our ability to secure cooperation between people) had advanced step by step with our technical skill, there would not have been another European war."[31] Thus the ideology of the founders of the "human relations" approach consisted of three parts: (1) a view of man as a social animal, (2) a view of industrial society as incompatible with the basic nature of man, and (3) a view of the solution to man's dilemma as resting with industrial leaders.

The findings of the Hawthorne experiments were exceedingly important to those members of society primarily concerned with rational industrial supervision.[32] It had long been a mystery why workers would restrict output and produce far below standards established by exacting analyses. The Hawthorne studies provided both diagnosis and prescription. The practical application of human relations theory required careful consideration of the informal organization, work teams, and symbols that evoke worker response. Unions were viewed in a new dimension and were seen as making a contribution to effective organization rather than as the consequence of malfunctions in the organization.[33] Participative management, employee education, junior executive boards, group decisions and industrial counseling became important means for improving the performance of workers in the organization. Industrial leaders were spurred on by researchers whose findings indicated that "every human being earnestly seeks a secure, friendly, and supportive relationship and one that gives him a sense of personal worth in the face-to-face groups most important to him."[34] Thus, in practice, the "herd hypothesis" replaced the "rabble hypothesis."

The research methodology, the ideology, and the practice of human relations have been attacked on several points. The methodology of the supporting research is criticized for dealing with only immediate variables and for ignoring the external environment; the work is viewed as static and subject to little change over time. The findings of single case studies do not provide sufficient data for the construction of a rigorous theory of man and his organizations. But at a more fundamental level, the ideological view of man is attacked. "They (the human relations advocates) begin by saying that man dislikes isolation and end by consigning him to the care of the managerial elite for his own salvation."[35] Thus by losing his identity man becomes free or so assert the Mayo-ites.[36]

Critics of the practice of human relations have pointed to a number of defects. Most vehemently criticized has been the use of human relations techniques as means of manipulating workers to accept the superior's view of reality. Indeed, one has said: "I am totally unable to associate the *conscious practice of human relations skill* (in the sense of making people happy in spite of themselves or getting them to do something they don't think they want to do) with the *dignity of an individual person created in God's image.*"[37]

This tendency toward manipulation is, at least in part, due to a misunder-standing of the purpose of the social sciences, "to the belief that the function of the social sciences is the same as that of the physical sciences, namely, to gain control of something outside."[38]

A second misunderstanding, and one springing directly from the ideology of human relations, is the belief that the business firm is a total institution which provides for all the needs of its members and that such an institution has the "right" to demand total loyalty. The attempt to gain total loyalty underlies much of personnel and human relations work; administrators frequently use the tags "loyal service" and "loyal employee" to describe the record of a retiring organization member. On this point Peter Drucker has said: "It is not only not compatible with the dignity of man, but it is not permissible to believe that the dignity of man can or should be realized totally in a partial institution."[39] The present state of human relations theory might be expressed as follows: "Let's treat people like people, but let's not make a big production of it."[40]

The findings of post-Weber studies of bureaucratic behavior are similar to the findings of the Hawthorne studies—the reaction of individuals to organizational factors is not always predictable.[41] Merton,[42] Selznick,[43] and Gouldner[44] suggest that treating people as machines not only leads to unforeseen consequences but can actually reinforce the use of the "machine model." Each researcher studied some form of procedure designed to control the activities of the members of the organization.

Merton analyzed the organizational need for control and the consequent concern for reliability of members' behavior. In order to get the desired results, the organization implements standard rules and procedures. Control is achieved by assuring that the members are following the rules. Merton points out three consequences that result from concern for reliability of behavior: (1) officials react to individuals as representative of positions having certain specified rights and privileges; (2) rules assume a positive value as ends rather than as means to ends; and, (3) decision-making becomes routine application of tried and proven approaches and little attention is given to alternatives not previously experienced.[45] The organization becomes committed to activities that insure the status quo at the expense of greater success in achieving organization objectives.

Selznick studied the consequences of a second technique for achieving control and reliability—the delegation of authority. As intended, the specialized competence required to carry out the delegate tasks has the positive effect of achieving organization goals, but there are unintended consequences. Delegation of authority "results in departmentalization and an increase in the *bifurcation of interests* among the subunits in the organization."[46] Members of the organization become increasingly dependent upon the maintenance of subunits and there is a growing disparity between the goals of the subunit and the goals of the organization. The content of decisions is increasingly concerned with subunit objectives and decreasingly concerned with organization goals, except that there must not be too great a disparity between the two. Subunit officials seek to make legitimate their activities by squaring their decisions with precedent. Again there seems to be an inherent tendency in the bureaucratic structure toward conservatism and the maintenance of the status quo.[47]

Gouldner gives additional support to the thesis that organizational techniques designed to implement control often entail unanticipated results. In his study of industrial organization he found, among other things, that the improvisation of rules to assure control results in the knowledge of *minimum acceptable levels of behavior* and that members of organizations gear their activities to these minimum levels of behavior if there is a high level of bifurcation of interest. As officials perceive this low performance, they react by increasing the closeness of supervision and by enacting additional rules and procedures. Again, the unintended consequences are increasing tension among members, increasing nonacceptance of organization goals, and increasing the use of rules to correct matters.[48]

To summarize, the essence of the humanistic challenge is that man in organizations is socially oriented and directed. He has multiple needs which affect and are affected by the work environment; he reacts unpredictably, yet predictably, to stimuli encountered in the organization. The "unintended consequences" of bureaucratic methods imply that man may be incompatible with organization needs. The scene is set, then, for contemporary organization theorists to devise a synthesis of the two polar positions.

THE REALISTIC SYNTHESIS[49]

An important feature of modern organization theory[50] is the systems approach which treats organizations as complex sets of mutually dependent and interacting variables. In this framework the participants are one set of variables which act on all other variables. Because this paper is concerned only with the place of man in organization theory, I will outline the features of the systems approach (which I term the realistic synthesis) and then return to the discussion of man as a variable in the system.

The systems approach to organization theory presents the opportunity to view the organization as a totality. The emphasis is on the parts of the system, the nature of interaction among the parts, the processes which link the parts, and the goals of the system.[51] The key parts are the individual and his unique personality, the formal structure of jobs, the informal groups, the status and role patterns within the groups, and the physical environment. Relating these parts are complex patterns of interactions which modify the behavior and expectations of each. The basic parts are linked together by certain organizational processes including structured roles, channels of communication, and decision-making. These processes provide means for overcoming the centrifugal tendency of the parts[52] and for directing the parts toward the ultimate goals of the organization—growth, stability and social interaction.[53]

The systems approach is a realistic synthesis because it views the individual as only one of many parts, because it allows for modification of the parts, because it views conflict within the organization as a natural byproduct of group endeavor, and because it *anticipates dynamic* rather than static patterns of interaction.

The realistic view of man in the organization acknowledges the contributions of the Hawthorne experiments, but it has added certain ideas that go beyond "human relations." The basic premise seems to be that man's needs and the organization's needs are inconsistent.[54] Man's behavior is seen to be motivated by a hierarchy of needs and once the most basic needs are satisfied, the individual turns to the ultimate source of satisfaction—self-actualization. But to achieve self-actualization requires that the healthy individual be "independent, creative . . . exercise autonomy and discretion, and . . . develop and express . . . unique personality with freedom."[55] The organization, however, presents barriers to this development of self-actualization and requires that the individual be dependent upon others for goalsetting and direction and conform to norms far below the level of his ability or expectations. The results of this conflict are immature behavior and frustration-oriented activites, the overt expression being determined by the unique personality of the individual. Argyris' studies indicate that an organization member experiencing frustration and conflict may behave in any one of the following ways.[56]

a. He may leave the organization.
b. He may work hard and become president.
c. He may adapt through the use of defense mechanisms.
d. He may adapt by lowering his work standards and by becoming apathetic.

Other students of organizational behavior also perceive basic conflicts between the organization and the individual. Presthus argues that the reactions of members can be characterized by three bureaucratic types: the upwardmobiles; the indifferents; and, the ambivalents. The upwardmobiles are those who react positively to the organizational requirements and by adopting the sanctioned behavioral patterns succeed in it.[57] The indifferents are the great majority who view their jobs as means to secure off-work satisfactions and who neither seek nor expect on-job satisfaction.[58] The ambivalents are a small minority who are unable to play the organizationally defined role which would enable them to realize their ambitions.[59] The similarity between these three patterns of behavior and the adaptive responses which Argyris lists is evident.

Thus, the contemporary view of the nature of man in organizations recognizes the essential conflict that exists. Whereas: the mechanistic tradition considered conflict to be dysfunctional to organizational purposes and felt that it could be neutralized by monetary payments; and, the humanist challenge viewed conflict as dysfunctional but believed that human relations techniques could control it; the realistic synthesis assumes that conflict is a normal aspect of organization life.

The problem posed then is how to harness the energies of conflict such that *both organizational and individual needs are realized.* Given the problem, we can accept at the outset that neither will be met perfectly—this being the essence of the conflict.[60] And whether conflict or cooperation is the *essential* nature of man does not seem to be relevant,[61] since research indicates that many *organization members are in fact in conflict with the requirements of the organization.*

ASSUMPTIONS HAVE CONSEQUENCES

I offer no final conclusions as to where recent efforts in organization theory and organization structuring will lead us;[62] all the evidence is not in and final arguments have not been heard. However, it is not difficult to concur with Haire's statement:

> Whenever we try to plan what an organization should be like, it is necessarily based on an implicit concept of man. If we look ... at the outline of a "classical" organization theory and some more modern alternatives, we begin to see the change in the concept of man.[63]

Of course, to point out the importance of the assumptions which underlie organization theory is my major purpose. Anthony Downs would, perhaps, argue that these modern alternatives are not being tried since his findings indicate that much of classical organization theory is still with us. Perhaps again, the reason for its continued use is that those of us *who study organizations have not given sufficient attention to questions that are value-laden.*

Specifically, in what kinds of organizations do men behave in the very unattractive ways which Downs depicts? Or more basically, do we consider such behavior to be unattractive? What are the particular features of ongoing organizations that create the climate for such behavior? What variables are controlling and controllable? Or can we dismiss the problem by suggesting that the pressure-packed and anxiety-ridden culture of the times is the real culprit? But if it is concluded that such behavior is a necessary concomitant of organizations, I for one will count it a cost.

ENDNOTES

1. Anthony Downs, "A Theory of Bureaucracy," *American Economic Review, Papers and Proceedings* (May, 1965), pp. 439–446.

2. Downs does not make such harsh indictments of the nature of man; he states only that officials distort information and orders, fear investigations of their activities, champion the status quo, seek consensus of goals, and perform acts that would be embarrassing if publicly known. The adjectives that I use to describe the behavior are my own. The reader is invited to study Downs' paper and draw his own conclusions.

3. Robert Presthus, *The Organizational Society* (New York: Alfred A. Knopf, 1962).

4. Victor A. Thompson, *Modern Organization* (New York: Alfred A. Knopf, 1961) and Marshall E. Dimock, *Administrative Vitality* (New York: Harper and Brothers, 1959).

5. Robert Blauner, *Alienation and Freedom* (Chicago: The University of Chicago Press, 1964), p. 15. fn. 1.

6. Downs, *op. cit.*, p. 443.

7. *Ibid.*, pp. 443–444.

8. Frederick W. Taylor, *Scientific Management* (New York: Harper and Brothers 1911), p. 39.

9. *Ibid.*, p. 94.

10. *Ibid.*, p. 95.

11. See Henri de Saint-Simon, *Social Organization, The Science of Man, and other Writings*, edited and translated by Felix Markham (New York: Harper and Row, 1965).

12. Sheldon S. Wolin, *Politics and Vision* (Boston: Little, Brown and Co., 1960), p. 376.

13. HLuther Gulick and L. Urwick (eds.), *Papers on the Science of Administration* (New York: Institute of Public Administration, 1937).

14. HHenri Fayol, *General and Industrial Management* (London: Sir Isaac Pitman and Sons, 1949).

15. J. D. Mooney and A. C. Reiley, *Principles of Organization* (New York: Harper and Brothers, 1939).

16. L. Urwick, *The Elements of Administration* (New York: Harper and Brothers, 1943).

17. Max Weber, *The Theory of Social and Economic Organization*, translated by A. M. Henderson and Talcott Parsons (New York: Oxford University Press, 1947). Michel Crozier in *The Bureaucratic Phenomenon* (Chicago: University of Chicago Press, 1964), a study of the French experience in organization of the civil service, points out three usages of the term bureaucracy: (1) the "traditional usage" is the political science concept of government by bureaus but without participation by the governed; (2) The Weberian usage is the sociological concept of rationalization of collective activities; and, (3) the vulgar usage is the laymen's concept which implies the dysfunctional nature of "bureaucratic" organizations, i.e., red tape, procedural delays, frustrations of agents and clients, p. 3.

18. Weber, *ibid.*, pp. 329–340. For more reflective analyses of the "ideal type" see Peter M. Blau, *Bureaucracy in Modern Society* (Chicago: University of Chicago Press, 1956), pp. 27–56 and Victor A. Thompson, *op. cit.*, pp. 12–21.

19. Weber, *ibid.,* p. 330.
20. Blau, *op. cit.,* p. 30.
21. Weber, *op. cit.,* p. 334.
22. *From Max Weber: Essays in Sociology,* translated by H. H. Gerth and C. Wright Mills (New York: Oxford University Press, 1946), p. 214 and quoted in Blau, *op. cit.,* p. 31.
23. W. Warren Haynes and Joseph L. Massie, *Management* (Englewood Cliffs, N.J.: Prentice-Hall, Inc., 1961), pp. 39–43. Other writers, notably L. Urwick, *op. cit.,* pp. 119–129 have lengthened the list, but the four here seem to be primary. Herbert A. Simon refers to such principles as "proverbs" in *Administrative Behavior* (New York: The Macmillan Co., 1945), pp. 20–36 because they have neither empirical verification nor universality of application.
24. James G. March and Herbert A. Simon, *Organizations* (New York: John Wiley and Sons, 1958), p. 29.
25. George B. Strother (ed.), *Social Science Approaches to Business Behavior* (Homewood, Illinois: The Dorsey Press, Inc., 1962), p. 175. And lest one think that contemporary organizations are free of such assumptions, consider this statement by E. F. Scoutten, Vice-President, Personnel, Maytag Company: "Operating management has long since known what academic experts appear to reject. Many people, perhaps the majority, prefer to accept instruction, direction, and order without question, and in fact are uncomfortable and, therefore, resist being placed in situations where they are required to evaluate or otherwise exercise independent thought." Mason Haire, (ed.), *Organization Theory in Industrial Practice* (New York: John Wiley and Sons, 1962), p. 86.
26. William F. Whyte, *Money and Motivation* (New York: Harper and Brothers, 1955), pp. 2–3.
27. The Hawthorne Studies are reported in T. N. Whitehead, *The Industrial Worker,* 2 volumes (Cambridge, Massachusetts: Harvard University Press, 1938), Fritz J. Roethlisberger and William J. Dickson, *Management and the Worker* (Cambridge, Massachusetts: Harvard University Press, 1947), Fritz J. Roethlisberger, *Management and Marale* (Cambridge, Massachusetts: Harvard University Press, 1941), and Elton Mayo, *The Human Problems of an Industrial Civilization* (New York: The Macmillan Co., 1933).
28. F. J. Roethlisberger, *ibid.,* p. 16.
29. Mayo, *op. cit.,* p. 18.
30. Clark Kerr, *Labor and Management in Industrial Society* (Garden City, New York: Doubleday and Co., Inc., 1964), p. 54.
31. Elton Mayo, *The Social Problems of an Industrial Civilization* (Boston: Division of Research, Graduate School of Business Administration, Harvard University, 1947), p. 33.
32. Burleigh B. Gardner, *Human Relations in Industry* (Chicago: Richard D. Irwin, Inc., 1945) is a "classic" of this tradition.
33. See William F. Whyte, *Pattern for Industrial Peace* (New York: Harper and Brothers, 1951).
34. Rensis Likert, *Motivation: The Core of Management* (New York: American Management Association, 1953). Reprinted in Harry Knudson, *Human Elements of Administration* (New York: Holt, Rinehart, and Winston, 1963), p. 81.

35. Kerr, *op. cit.,* p. 57.
36. It is not quite fair to say that Mayo "asserts" in this connection. In *Human Problems of an Industrial Civilization, op. cit.,* he analyzes various traditional cultures and presents as evidence of the social nature of man the many practices designed to achieve social integration, e.g., ritual custom, codes, family and tribal instincts.
37. Malcolm P. McNair. "Thinking Ahead: What Price Human Relations?" *Harvard Business Review* (March-April, 1957), pp. 15–23. Reprinted in Harold Koontz and Cyril O'Donnell, *Readings in Management* (New York: McGraw-Hill Book Co., Inc., 1959), p. 279.
38. Peter Drucker, "Human Relations: Where Do We Stand Today?" in Knudson, *op. cit.,* p. 264. The purpose of the social sciences is to gain understanding of one's self as Drucker explains.
39. *Ibid.,* p. 364.
40. McNair, *op. cit.,* p. 285.
41. This discussion is based on March and Simon, *op. cit.,* pp. 36–47.
42. Robert K. Merton, "Bureaucratic Structure and Personality," *Social Forces,* Vol. 18 (1940), pp. 560–568.
43. Philip Selznick, *TVA and the Grass Roots* (Berkeley: The University of California Press, 1949).
44. Alvin W. Gouldner, *Patterns of Industrial Bureaucracy* (New York: The Free Press of Glencoe, 1954).
45. March and Simon, *op. cit.,* pp. 38–39.
46. *Ibid.,* p. 41.
47. Such is the thesis of Robert Michels, *Political Parties* (Glencoe, Illinois: The Free Press, 1949), whose concept of the "iron law of oligarchy" is a classic description of the tendency of organizations to become conservative as the demands for more specialized competence intensify.
48. March and Simon, *op. cit.,* p. 45. *Those studies are classics in the development of our knowledge of organizational behavior.* It is obvious that many of Downs' hypotheses are suggested by this literature, particularly the hypotheses that organizations value status quo solutions and consensus and that the content of decisions is limited to precedents.
49. Some third dimension as a basis for synthesis and the criteria for its selection are a concern to many students of organization theory. The work of Warren B. Bennis and many others could be cited. The focus of this paper, however, is on *values* more than the whole panorama.
50. Some presentations *of modern organization theory* are March and Simon, *op. cit.;* Mason Haire (ed.). *Modern Organization Theory* (New York: John Wiley and Sons, 1959); Albert II. Rubenstein and Chadwick J. Haberstroh, *Some Theories of Organization* (Homewood Illinois: The Dorsey Press, Inc., 1960); Jose A. Litterer, *The Analysis of Organizations* (New York: John Wiley and Sons, 1965); and Theodore Caplow, *Principles of Organizations* (New York: Harcourt, Brace and World, Inc., 1964).
51. William G. Scott, "Organization Theory: An Overview and an appraisal," *Academy of Management Journal* (April, 1961), pp. 7–26. Reprinted in Joseph A. Litterer (ed.), *Organizations: Structure and Behavior* (New York: John Wiley and Sons, 1963), p. 19.

52. John M. Pfiffner and Frank P. Sherwood, *Administrative Organization* (Englewood Cliffs, N.J.: Prentice-Hall, Inc, 1960), pp. 116–117.
53. Scott, *op. cit.,* p. 22.
54. This view is developed by Chris Argyris in *Personality and Organization* (New York: Harper and Brothers, 1957) and more recently in *Integrating the Individual and the Organization* (New York: John Wiley and Sons, 1964).
55. George Strauss, "Some Notes on Power-Equalization" in Harold J. Leavitt, editor, *The Social Science of Organization* (Englewood Cliffs, N.J.: Prentice-Hall, Inc., 1963), p. 46.
56. *Personality and Organization* . . . pp. 78–79.
57. Robert Presthus, *op. cit.,* pp. 164–204.
58. *Ibid.,* pp. 205–256.
59. *Ibid.,* pp. 257–285.
60. Conflict and struggle for power in organizations lead to patterns of behavior that are political in nature. Melville Dalton in *Men Who Manage* (New York: John Wiley and Sons, 1959) analyzes organizational politics.
61. Nor is there a final answer since some men (e.g. Thomas Hobbes) have viewed the essence of man to be conflict while others (e.g. John Locke) have viewed man as essentially cooperative. Realization of the individual through the group is not characteristic of Rousseau.
62. See William W. Cooper, Harold J. Leavitt, and Maynard W. Shelly, *New Perspectives in Organization Research* (New York: John Wiley and Sons, Inc., 1964) for some indications.
63. Strother, *op. cit.,* pp. 170–171.

SUPPORTIVENESS: A RECURRING THEME IN ORGANIZATIONAL EFFECTIVENESS

Ronald J. Webb

Those in responsible positions of leadership have always sought to do things in a more effective way. A classic example is Jethro's explanation of the concepts of span of control and delegation of authority to his son-in-law Moses. Jethro had perceived the tremendous responsibility of leadership given to Moses and was suggesting how this responsibility could be exercised in a more effective manner. Management history since then is replete with examples of interest in more effective organizational functioning. This inherent concern of managers for greater effectiveness has been the impetus for much of the development of the knowledge we now have about management.

However, a systematic study of "organizational effectiveness" has been quite neglected over the years and is only a relatively recent phenomena. Within the last ten years several theoretical formulations have been developed as well as a significant number of research studies. Both research and theory have dealt with various types of organizations and forms of analysis. As a result, the body of knowledge about "organizational effectiveness" is not really a "body" but an increasing wealth of information with no particular shape or form. The purpose of this article is to suggest what this author believes to be a recurring theme in much of the literature relating to organizational effectiveness. This theme may be what is needed to give meaningful shape to what we know about organizational effectiveness.

RESEARCH STUDIES

The common determinent of organizational effectiveness seems to be "supportiveness." A number of research studies as well as theoretical formulations seem

Reprinted by permission of *University of Michigan Business Review* from volume 28 (July 1976).

to be pointing to this one unifying factor. However, not all refer to this generalized characteristic in the same terminology.

In 1967 Mahoney reported on a model of organizational effectiveness that he had developed for general business organizations.[1] The respondents to Mahoney's research were managers from many different companies engaging in a variety of business activities. The managers were asked to describe a total of 283 subordinate organizational units in terms of 114 organizational characteristics. These managers also made independent judgments of the overall effectiveness of the organizational units. Factor analysis of the 283 descriptions yielded a structure of 24 factors accounting for 65 percent of the variance in the 114 organizational descriptions. All of the 114 organizational characteristics had been suggested as criteria of organizational effectiveness, therefore, the factors or dimensions identified were interpreted as independent dimensions of a general concept of effectiveness.

Using stepwise multiple regression, a combination of the dimensions was developed to predict judgments of overall effectiveness. A model consisting of four independent variables was generated. This final model accounted for 56 percent of the variance in managers' judgments of overall effectiveness and included the following characteristics: productivity-support-utilization, planning, reliability, and initiative.

Productivity-support-utilization was the independent variable having the most significant impact on the general business model. This dimension was actually composed of three separate concepts so closely interrelated in the original analysis that Mahoney chose to combine them and treat them as a single empirical dimension. Support means numerous things in Mahoney's analysis. It means that authority is respected in the organization and that people stand behind and uphold the leadership. There is also respect for individual competence. In addition, support is two-sided in the sense that organizational leaders should have a direct interest in, and concern for, the welfare of organizational members.

This research also recognized cohesion as being important, although that particular independent variable is not part of the final regression model. Mahoney says, "Supportive relationships within the organization . . . appear to be a function of the cohesion obtained within the workforce and the supervisory support provided the work force."[2] Cohesion, therefore, appears to be an integral part of developing supportiveness in this model.

Later, Mahoney and Weitzel reported on another model of organizational effectiveness which they developed for research and development organizations.[3] The research methodology was the same as used in the previous research, but this time a much more homogenous sample had been selected. The regression model developed in this study explained 50 percent of the variance in the independent judgments of organizational effectiveness and included three organizational characteristics: reliability, cooperation, and development.

Reliability (the accomplishment of objectives without constant contact and supervision) and development (the continuing refinement of one's skills) appear to be somewhat unique to this R & D study, but cooperation is related to the previous study in many ways. Achievement of cooperation in research and development units is accomplished through coordination of scheduling and flexibility in changing and adjusting assignments.

In another study of research scientists, Pelz and Andrews reached some related conclusions.[4] They found that coordination of activities was an essential ingredient in effective research and development units. They also found that the most effective researchers were those who undertook several specialties and changed assignments periodically. Cooperation as well as coordination are necessary to maintain effectiveness in such a free environment.

There is a degree of similarity between cooperation and the two characteristics (cohesion and support) discussed in the *general business* model. Cohesion refers to the working relationships among the members while support refers to the degree to which members stand behind and, in general, acknowledge the rights of others. Both of these characteristics are certainly part of the enlarged concept of cooperation.

A few years later, in 1971, Paine developed a government model of organizational effectiveness.[5] The methodological approach used was similar to that of Mahoney and Weitzel, however, the independent variables used by Paine were somewhat different. The sample for Paine's investigation consisted of 127 professionals involved in assessing of the management of human resources in over 130 organizational units in a large nationwide government organization. In addition to a judgment of the overall effectiveness of the unit being assessed, a descriptive judgment was made by these professionals using 51 organizational characteristics. These 51 items were combined into 16 dimensions and stepwise multiple regression analysis was used to fit the 16 dimensions and the judgments of overall effectiveness to the model. The final regression model accounted for 60 percent of the variance in the independent judgments of overall effectiveness and included the following characteristics: goal consensus and clarity, integration, supportiveness, planning adequacy, and cooperation. Again, supportiveness (with cooperation) appears as a dominant characteristic in explaining organizational effectiveness.

Most recently, a study by Webb investigated the determinents of organizational effectiveness for voluntary organizations.[6] In this study, the institutional church was used as the research base. Specifically, the group studied was a large protestant body with more than 100 churches. More than 500 qestionnaires were mailed to randomly-selected church members. The respondents were asked to provide an independent judgment of the effectiveness of their particular congregation based on a complex index that had been developed specificially for the study. The respondents were to provide descriptive judgement of their congregations similar to the previously mentioned studies of organizational effectiveness. Stepwise multiple regression analysis was performed with the data and the model that was generated explained 45 percent of the variance in the independent judgements of effectiveness as given by the church members. This model included four organizational characteristics: cohesion, efficiency, adaptability and support. Again, cohesiveness and support are significantly related to measured organizational effectiveness with cohesiveness being the dominant characteristic. Cohesiveness refers to a positive working relationship among the membership. A team spirit or esprit de corps is also indicative of a cohesive unit.

Communication also was an independent variable in this study, but it did not happen to be included in the final regession model. It is interesting to note, however, that the correlation matrix of the independent variables showed a strong degree of relationship between communication and support (correlation coefficient of .73). There appears to be a direct, positive relationship between the level and quality of communication in a church and its measure of support.

The four research studies reported here have uncovered numerous organizational characteristics having a significant impact on measured organizational effectiveness. In all of them, however, the idea of supportiveness is present in one form or another. There is great diversity in the kinds of organizations studied and yet the necessity for building a cohesive organization with sustaining power seems to be a recurring theme.

THEORY AND PRACTICE

Rensis Likert, in his "System 4" design, also stresses the importance of supportiveness in organizational effectiveness.[7] According to Likert, an effective organization is one which encourages supervisors to "focus their primary attention on endeavoring to build effective work groups with high performance goals."[8] Likert contends that organizations can be described in terms of eight dimensions, each of which is a continuum with classically designed organizations at one extreme and System 4 organizations at the opposite end. The eight dimensions are leadership, motivation, communication, interaction-influence, decision making, goal setting, control and performance goals. Those organizations operating at the System 4 end of the continuum for the eight dimensions are most likely to achieve a high degree of effectiveness.

In the System 4 design, managers are encouraged to decentralize decision-making, control, and goal-setting processes so that these are shared by all members at all levels of the organization. Communications also should flow throughout the organization. In addition to the traditional downward flow of communication, organizations should encourage upward communication. Conditions also should be such that there is a smooth flow of communication in a horizontal manner. These practices are intended to implement the basic assumption of System 4 which states that an organization will be optimally effective to the extent that its processes are "such as to ensure a maximum probability that in all interactions and in all relationships within the organization, each member, in the light of his background, values, desires, and expectations, will view the experience as supportive and one which builds and maintains his sense of personal worth and importance."[9]

Supportiveness is also deeply embedded in the theory of Management by Objectives. In a recent article, Reif and Bassford point out numerous organizational benefits that they believe accrue from an MBO program.[10] One of these they have described as "improved superior-subordinate relationships." They say that, "under MBO, the subordinate moves from a position of dependence to one of independence. He experiences greater freedom, is directly involved in decisions that affect him and his job, and receives more open communication about the organization and his role in it. The subordinate views his relationship with his boss as supportive and, for the help he receives in satisfying his needs, he is willing to commit his best efforts to meeting the requirements of the organization."[11] Another benefit they attribute to MBO is improved coordination. They suggest that effective coordination is really the "essence of organization" and that it cannot be achieved without a common purpose and a sense of direction. Well-defined objectives developed in an MBO program help integrate the range of activities of complex organizations and help elicit the voluntary cooperation of those whose contributions are essential to their achievement. An attitude of supportiveness is what builds this necessary coordination.

APPLICATIONS

One small manufacturing plant of Uniroyal, Inc, has been experiencing the benefits of a "supportiveness"-minded management and it appears more plants within the organization will adopt the same strategy.[12] Within three years of its start-up, this small hose manufacturing plant was producing high-quality hydraulic and automotive hose at 120 percent of its projected capacity; the scrap rate was half what it had been at an older plant; absenteeism was only 1.7 percent, and only four of the 140 employees had quit within the past year-none, apparently, for job-connected reasons.

This Kennett (Mo.) plant has adopted a participatory management strategy which includes the following:

(1) All employees earn salaries instead of hourly wages. (This makes the low absenteeism rate all the more significant.)
(2) Machine operators inspect their own output, draw up work rules, and participate in other management decisions.
(3) Managers work constantly on improving communication, both up and down.

Since many organizations around the world have begun experimenting with this concept, what makes the Kennett plant so unusual? It began in 1969 when John W. Gorman was selected by Howard Norris, production manager for the Industrial Products Division, to start up the new plant. Gorman had been managing a department in one of the division's older plants. Prior to assuming the leadership role, Gorman prepared himself by visiting a number of plants operating on a total salary basis and also by reading widely the theories of management psychologists.

This preparation led to a system that leans heavily on a worker's sense of responsibility. This has been referred to by Norris as "trust."[13] After the initial training period, a machine operator at Kennett is trusted to know what has to be done and to do it without direction. This idea makes sense to Kennett's machine operators and vastly reduces the amount of in-process quality inspection needed as well as the manpower and paperwork that goes with it. This trust did not come overnight, but as Gorman's successor Lloyd Spalter has said, "The biggest thing Gorman learned was that the more trust you put in people, the more they respond."[14]

Another big word that is practiced at Kennett is *"respect."* The philosophy that every job is important means that all employees should be treated respectfully. At Kennett that means no executive dining room, restrooms or parking slots. Cleanliness is stressed both in the plant and the workers' leisure areas. It means that a machine operator's request for time off is treated the same as if it had come from one of the management team. "There is no caste system here," says Spalter, the new plant manager.

Trust and respect lead naturally to the involvement of workers in making decisions, and this is true at Kennett. Output standards are set by operators, some of whom are even experimenting with rotation of jobs. Operators also are included in troubleshooting meetings when problems occur on the production line.

Communication also is treated as a necessity rather than a luxury at Kennett. The most regular form of communication is a daily notice emphasizing production information but also including general information about who may be visiting the plant that day. In addition, meetings with employees are held at least once a month at which staff changes may be announced along with other information employees need.

Many strategies for building a supportive environment are available to organizations. Let me suggest two organizational processes and elaborate on a few strategies whereby supportiveness may be easily developed. The two processes are common to all organizations, but the importance of building a supportive environment (as indicated by the analysis earlier in this paper) has not been given the emphasis it deserves.

The communication process. Communication permeates all important components of the management process and therefore is an obvious place to begin building a supportive environment. Most organizations preserve and perpetuate the theme that communications in general and initiation of communication in particular is a vertical, topdown activity. While this topdown approach to communication is important there are two other dimensions that receive relatively little managerial attention and are equally important in building the kind of cohesive organization we have been talking about. These two dimensions are the upward and lateral (or diagonal) flows of communications.

Media specialists have devised numerous techniques for transmitting information from the higher levels of an organization directly to individual members. Company magazines, newsletters, paycheck inserts and bulletin boards are just a few of the techniques used to create a sense of belonging. Some believe downward communications should pull the entire organization together and unite it behind particular task objectives.[15]

The degree to which this downward-oriented communication flow is successful in building supportiveness is a function of a number of things. Only two will be discussed here. *First,* the hierarchical structure (authority structure) must be one that minimizes role conflict. An organization cannot afford to have members taking conflicting orders from multiple sources. This situation destroys the validity of communication and discourages organizational members from complying with any formal, action-oriented communique. The identity of what to support is simply lost.

A *second* factor affecting success of downward communication is perception. Every attempt at communication represents a stimulus with a meaning that must be perceived. A common perception model illustrates the numerous difficulties facing managers. Before the stimulus ever reaches the receiver it will likely be altered and distorted. And because every member of the organization is a unique "personality," it is unlikely that everyone will perceive same stimulus in the same manner. The more aware management is of these non-qualifiable variables, the more successful will be the communication process. And the more successful the communication process, the greater the likelihood of developing employees' support.

Communication from bottom to top of the organization is also of great importance. This feedback process enables management to obtain information needed to evaluate and, when necessary, correct its downward communication. In addition, without some mechanisms through which employees can ask questions, express dissatisfactions, register complaints, or make suggestions, management may remain completely unaware of major problem areas and threats to organizational effectiveness.[16]

Unfortunately, most studies dealing with upward communication have found it particularly prone to distortion. Experimental research with small laboratory groups has shown that distortion and suppression of information tends to increase as status differentials between the lower-level sender and the higher-level receiver becomes greater.[17] It would seem appropriate, therefore, for organizations to reduce as much as possible those status differentials which restrain the upward flow of communication. The Uniroyal plant mentioned earlier has apparently recognized this form of inhibition and is trying to do something about it.

Other organizations also are recognizing the benefits of specific forms of upward communication. Industrial Motivation is now selling a radically different "suggestion-box" system called BAD—for "Buck-a-day," a catch-phrase suggesting that even small savings mount up over time.[18] This program is essentially a one-shot effort: a three-week blitz featuring posters, newsletters, bumper stickers, and small prizes. The publicity barrage that whips employees into a suggesting mood, (employee participation is never below 80 percent), is based on the use of the word "bad" in a variety of catchy phrases such as: "BAD news is good news," "A BAD idea makes sense." Although employees receive no monetary rewards for suggestions (only a token coffee cup), weekly newsletters highlight the best ideas, and those employees with worthy ideas are featured on mock "wanted" posters. The designer of this program says, "What we're really after is participation. It makes everybody feel that they're part of the company."[19] The program stresses the need to cut costs and, in so doing, emphasizes that any idea, no matter how unimportant it seems, will be welcomed and given recognition. Participation that is welcomed *and* recognized can only help to build a supportive environment.

The *decision-making* process. The information communicated throughout the organization provides the input for the decision-making process that occurs continually in all organizations. And as communication permeates all important components of the management process, so does decision making. Certainly attempts to build a supportive environment through the delegation process are not new. However, we are all aware that the assumption made by classical management theorists concerning the equality of delegated authority and responsibility is quite unrealistic. Although this inequality does not account for all the problems in the delegation process, it is an ever present characteristic of organizations that only inhibits the fostering of supportive attitudes. Only when mutual trust and respect are present can we expect those in supervisory positions to delegate the authority necessary to accomplish the delegated responsibilities. This ideal state can be developed only over time through a variety of organizational practices.

One obvious practice that will involve subordinates is input to the selection process. It would be presumptuous to say that this practice would be relevant for all organizations or at all levels within organizations; however, it does have merit in building support. A supportive environment is one in which organizational members stand behind and uphold each other. Can we realistically expect this kind of environment when subordinates are given no opportunity to provide input in deciding who will fill vacancies?

Another way to build cohesiveness and support is through consensus decision making. The most common approach to decision making in organizations is the vote. But the vote tends to divide not unite. The vote approach to decision making forces individuals to argue and attempt to convince, rather than help them work together to reach mutually agreeable solutions. Consensus decision making emphasizes group unity and may very well increase cooperation. It forces individuals to consider what is good for all, not just what is good for themselves. A consensus is a shared conviction that a particular decision is the right one and therefore merits support from all.

In day-to-day operations, many organizations encourage member output with the hope of gaining support for decisions that are made. This support will be gained only when there is genuine respect for organizational members and their contributions to ultimate decisions. It appears that support must begin first at the top and move downward throughout the organization.

CONCLUSIONS

In a cursory review of more than twenty-five management and organizational behavior texts, I have found the concept of "supportiveness" almost totally neglected. Related concepts were used in some texts but none had the same thrust as supportiveness. On the basis of research being conducted in the area of organizational effectiveness, this omission is deplorable.

A final word of caution, however. Any organization that believes supportiveness can be developed by installing the right "program" will be sadly disappointed. Programs do not build trust and respect, people do. Organizations must start with a close look at their human resources and the kind of people they are attracting and developing. People are the starting point in building an organization which really practices supportiveness.

NOTES

1. Thomas A. Mahoney, "Managerial Perceptions of Organizational Effectiveness," *Management Science* XIV (October, 1967): B76-B91.
2. Thomas A. Mahoney and William Weitzel, "Managerial Models of Organizational Effectiveness," *Administrative Science Quarterly* XIV (September, 1968): p. 360.
3. *Ibid.,* pp. 357-65.
4. Donald C. Pelz and Frank M. Andrews. *Scientists in Organizations* (New York: John Wiley and Sons, Inc., 1966).
5. Frank T. Paine, "Assessment Model of Government Organization Effectiveness" (unpublished manuscript, University of Maryland, 1971).
6. Ronald J. Webb, "Organizational Effectiveness in Voluntary Organizations," *The Academy of Management Journal* (in press).
7. Rensis Likert, *The Human Organization* (New York: McGraw-Hill Book Company, 1967).

8. Rensis Likert, *New Patterns of Management* (New York: McGraw-Hill Book Company, 1961). p. 7.

9. *Ibid,* p. 103.

10. William E. Reif and Gerald Bassfond, "What MBO Really Is," *Business Horizons* XVI (June, 1973).

11. *Ibid.,* p. 30.

12. "A Plant Where Workers Like Their Jobs," *Business Week,* September 8, 1973, pp. 64T-64W.

13. *Ibid.,* p. 64T.

14. *Ibid.*

15. L. R. Boulware, *The Truth About Boulwarison* (Washington, D. C.: Bureau of National Affairs Books, 1969).

16. John B. Miner and Mary Green Miner, *Personnel and Industrial Relations* (New York: The MacMillan Company, 1973).

17. D. C. Barnlund and C. Harland, "Propinquity and Prestige as Determinants of Communication Networks," *Sociometry* XXVI (1963): 467-479.

18. "When Employees Rush to Turn in 'BAD' Ideas," *Business Week,* January 12, 1974, pp. 52C-52F.

19. *Ibid.,* p. 52C.

ORGANIZATIONAL DESIGN: DEALING WITH THE HUMAN CONSTRAINT

Dennis R. Briscoe

Organizations exist to facilitate the doing of complex tasks in a complex environment with complex people. Organizational environments, including their people, are highly variable, unstable, and unpredictable. By limiting variability, instability, and unpredictability, organizations can accomplish much larger and more difficult objectives than would otherwise be the case.

Organizations are also social instruments. Traditionally, organizations have taken the position that there is one best way to reduce and limit the volatility of the human element: bureaucracy. The increasing complexity and volatility of the organizational environment has brought into question this approach.

This article tries to integrate diverse approaches to consideration of the human element in organizational design. It looks at why people are important, what about them is important, and discusses the impact of these things on organizational design. It then presents a model for viewing and understanding potential design options that respond to the human constraint.

INDIVIDUAL DIFFERENCES

In some respects all people are alike:

- They are motivated.
- Their behavior is purposeful.
- Their behavior is directed toward satisfaction of personal needs and goals.

© 1980 by the Regents of the University of California. Reprinted from CALIFORNIA MANAGEMENT REVIEW, volume XXIII, no. 1, pp. 71 to 80 by permission of the Regents.

And yet people come to organizations with widely varying backgrounds: their education and experience differ, as do their exposures to previous and current environments, psychological and biochemical makeups, behavioral repertoires, and perceptual styles. Organizations try to limit these natural variances as they are reflected in individual behavior; still, differences remain. The problem of designing organizations is a problem of integration. A variety of people must be integrated so they can collectively contribute to the accomplishment of singular organizational objectives.

Much has been written about the relationships between different characteristics of people and work organizations. The following list includes many of the variables researchers and practitioners have found important:

- biographical variables, such as age, sex, race and level of education;
- work-related attitudes, including sources of satisfaction and dissatisfaction, motivation, work ethics, and career values;
- life and career stages, including the stages of exploration, trial, establishment and advancement, maintenance, and decline;
- organizational commitment;
- psychological and personal variables, such as emotionality, activation, extraversion-introversion, locus of control, and authoritarianism.

These characteristics have been chosen for several reasons. They account for much of the variance in individual behavior and have immediate relevance to how people behave in organizations. Also, they are currently attracting the attention of researchers and teachers in the fields of organizational theory and management.

L.W. Porter, E.E. Lawler, and J.R. Hackman suggest that people need to keep in mind the average level of the variable.[1] If an organization has employees with a high level of one of these variables, its structural responses should be different from those which are appropriate when employees have a low level of the variable. Important, also, is a variable's dispersion:

> Two different organizations may have work forces that average the same degree of experience, abilities, skills, etc., but one of them may have individuals high in these qualities widely scattered throughout the organization while the other may have them concentrated in one unit or section. . . . For both organizations to adopt the same kind of structural operational features of design would appear to be inappropriate.[2]

Employees vary considerably. This makes the job of the manager or organizational designer difficult but not impossible. If a manager knows what his or her employees expect or value, what goals they have, what rewards they find reinforcing, and which personality characteristics predominate, the manager can channel the energies of the employees in organizationally desirable directions. The rest of this article describes how to use this information to design organizations in ways that effectively recognize and cope with the highly diverse nature of the human element.

DESIGN RESPONSES TO THE HUMAN CONSTRAINT

There obviously are many human characteristics that affect organizations' abilities to accomplish their goals. They cannot afford to presume that their members leave all of these characteristics outside when they come to work. Individual differences are major sources of complexity and uncertainty for organizations. As J.D. Thompson, R.K. Merton, D. Katz and R.L. Kahn, and others have made clear, reducing this complexity and uncertainty is a fundamental organizational imperative.[3]

There are several reasons for the lack of success of the traditional, bureaucratic structure mentioned earlier in reducing environmental and human uncertainty:

- It is too mechanistic; it ignores major facets of human nature.
- It is too rigidly structured to adapt to change.
- Its reliance on directives and procedures hinders communication.
- Its rigidity inhibits innovation.
- It rewards the job, not the person.
- It relies on coercion to maintain control.
- It fosters job-defensive behavior, which encourages make-work activities.
- Its goals are often incompatible with those of its members, and it contains no ready mechanism for resolving this incompatibility.[4]

The mechanistic design is out of date. It ignores the needs of many organization members and is inadequate in bringing forth their interests so they may perform at a high level at work. Many organizations or parts of organizations require more democracy, more participation at lower levels, decentralization of decision making as far as possible, less emphasis on hierarchy and authority, and less narrow specialization in order to tap the vast potential available in much of today's human resource.[5]

These pressures for change can be accommodated in two broad ways: by altering the source of the pressures (by changing the people in the organization), or by modifying the target of the pressures (by designing the organization to meet the pressures). In either case, employees should understand the designs (such as goal setting and performance evaluation procedures and their ensuing goals and expectations) as well as have some influence on those designs.[6]

Given the need for more careful organizational response to its members, what are organization designers to do? Should they change their organization's personnel? Change the organization? Should they change the organization's mix of employee abilities or its members' motivations? Should change efforts be focused on individuals, groups, or on the whole organization?[7] The designers' task is further complicated by changes in employees during their socialization into the values of the organization. Any favorable outcome from a particular design change may be short-lived, as employees adopt new and unanticipated values, attitudes, and behavior.

There are several alternatives that organizations have in designing a structure that recognizes the nature of the human constraint (see Table 1):

• Changing the people.
• Changing the organization.
• Changing the interface between people and organizations.
• Individualizing the organization.

Table 1.   People and Design Variables and Organizational Responses

Employee Characteristics	People-Related Design Variables	Organizational Design Responses	Organizational Outcomes
1. Biographical	1. Personnel systems	1. Change Personnel	1. Effectiveness
2. Work values and motivation	2. Work groups	a. selection	2. Climate
3. Life and career stages	3. Feedback and reward systems	b. training/development	
4. Commitment	4. Tasks	c. socialization	
5. Personality variables	5. Organizational structure	d. performance reviews	
a. emotionality	6. Physical settings	e. contingent rewards	
b. activation	7. Management systems	f. individualized reward systems	
c. extraversion-introversion		g. life and career stage-specific assessment and development	
d. locus of control		2. Change the organization	
e. authoritarianism		a. modify goals	
		b. modify structure	
		—reduce need for information processing	
		—increase capacity to process information	
		c. modify technology and tasks	
		—job enrichment	
		—hours of work	
		—entrepreneurship	
		—flexible physical settings	
		3. Change the interface between people and organizations	
		a. management development	
		b. contingent leadership	
		c. OD	
		d. MBO	
		e. institutionalized participation	
		4. Individualized organizations	

CHANGING THE PEOPLE

One design alternative is to try to control the nature of the human element. Different organizational structures require different types of people to function effectively.[8] Organizations attempt many approaches to this, including the following:

Personnel Selection. One of the first options available to the organizational designer is to select personnel to fit the organization. The choice as to the fit of individual to organization can be made by individual or organization. Individuals can select themselves "out" of the organization when being recruited for a position, or they can fit themselves into their organizations by personalizing their jobs. Organizations can try to select through recruiting and "testing" procedures employees who fit their needs. If this option is to work, selection procedures must meet certain criteria:

- People must differ in meaningful ways.
- Valid data about the characteristics of people must exist or be able to be gathered.
- Valid descriptions of job requirements must exist.
- People who are suited to the open jobs must be recruited and apply.
- A large number of qualified applicants must apply.
- The selection criteria must be validated by correlating them with performance data.[9]

When the "selecting in" process fails, organizations still have the option of "selecting out." Forced turnover of employees gives organizations the final option in controlling the match between employee and employer.

As N.R.F. Maier, A.K. Korman, and D.A. Nadler and E.E. Lawler point out, there are a number of intervening variables between employees' abilities —presuming these can be measured and matched to job requirements—and their job behavior.[10] Ignoring the legal necessities (such as the demonstration of the relationship between a firm's ability measurements and later employee performance levels), differences in experience, ability to learn, motivation levels, and desired organizational outcomes confuse the picture. The complexity and interactions of these variables suggest that managers should look for ways to improve existing employee abilities through training and development, rather than treating ability as fixed and immutable, identified and set at job application time.

Training and Development. Once individuals have been hired, the organization has numerous options for training and developing its employees to meet its requirements. Formal and informal training procedures, such as on-the-job training, coaching, and classroom presentations, are frequently used for new employees in entry-level positions at lower levels of organizations. Higher-level employees, particularly managers, are trained with these techniques plus developmental job assignments, study groups, and counseling by superiors. (Management development is discussed later.)

Socialization.   Organizational members come to their jobs with relatively well-established work and occupational attitudes that come from their education and types of experience.[11] Training and development processes tend to be for the purpose of increasing job-related skills. Organizations also work at producing attitudes which meet organizational needs. As C. Perrow says, "People's attitudes are shaped at least as much by the organization in which they work as by their pre-existing attitudes."[12] Socialization is the name given the process of the individual taking on the organization's goals as her or his own.[13] There appear to be a number of stages involved in socialization, and the organization must vary its approaches according to the stage in which it finds the employee.[14]

- The first stage is one of "getting in." Realistic job previews aid the employee in finding an organization where attitude and expectation differences are minimized. Flexibility in job assignments and consideration of the employee's needs and desires also aid in the integration of the employee into the organization.
- The second stage involves "breaking in" the employee. Orientation and structured training programs, effective performance feedback systems, and allowance for personalizing of work tasks help build acceptance, competence, and accurate role perceptions.
- The "settling in" stage involves the employee's resolution of conflict between his work and outside life as well as the resolution of conflicting work group demands. Counseling, flexibility, and mutual influence of and by co-workers aid in this final stage of socialization.

When successfully socialized, the employee will have internalized his or her work motivation and job involvement, a result of obvious benefit to the organization.

Reward and Feedback Systems.   One of the more powerful design tools available to managers is influence over the feedback systems of an organization. Describing for employees the goals of the organization, the behavior required to reach the goals, and the rewards available (ensuring that those rewards are desirable to the organization's members) for putting forth this behavior to reach the goals will go a long way toward producing the desired behavior and achieving the goals.[15] Self-feedback of performance levels, participation in goal setting, face-to-face and problem-solving performance reviews, rewards contingent on goal achievement, and rewards matched to individual employee needs and desires improve the efficacy of the overall reward and feedback systems.[16]

Assessment and Development of Life and Career Stages. The stage of life or career in which an individual finds herself or himself also influences the attitudes and needs that person has. It makes sense for organizations to try to work within the constraints of this reality. The following few paragraphs and tables summarize this complex subject and describe the options organizations have for dealing with employees at differing life and career states.

The organization must integrate its career development activities with its manpower planning. This means meeting the equal employment opportunity needs of all employees, majority and minority. It means planning and monitoring internal mobility and career paths. It means providing cross-functional moves, downward transfers, fallback positions, and organizational tenure in stable or contracting organizations. It also means the effective dissemination of career option information, inclusion of career counseling in performance appraisal, support of educational training activities for all employees, job posting, career development workshops, flexible reward and promotion systems, and accommodation of shifting employee needs through sabbaticals, flexible working hours, and other off-work activities.[17]

D.T. Hall and M.A. Morgan outline a number of ways that organizations can match design actions to the specific stages in which employees find themselves.[18] Table 2 summarizes the varying training needs for different career stages, and Table 3 outlines organizational actions for facilitating overall career development.

CHANGING THE ORGANIZATION

If the differences in people cannot be eliminated or controlled through the preceding types of personnel actions, the second choice open to organization designers is to change the organization. If this becomes the direction in which an organization moves, the problems need to be dealt with as near to their point of origin as possible, a wide repertoire of behavior to achieve objectives should be allowed, the organization's social support systems need to be consistent with the designed structure, and strong focus probably needs to remain on the quality of work life of the organization's members.[19]

Modification of Goals. One organizational design action that responds to the human constraint is modification of the organization's goals. Organizational goals reflect the collective objectives of an organization's members. When the members change, so often do their collective objectives. When this occurs, organizations can take a number of steps:

• Goal displacement and succession-replacing old goals with new ones.
• The dissolution of unneeded parts of the organization.

- The modification of organizational procedures and rules.
- The modification of informal norms and staff perspectives.[20]

Modification of Structure. The second set of actions an organization can take to adapt to its human constraint is to modify its structure. In general, the organization can reduce its need for processing information about the complex and volatile people input or it can increase its capacity to process that information.[21]

To reduce its needs for processing this information, an organization can try to control its environment (by changing its people, as discussed above). It can also create slack resources to increase lead time and margin for error or create autonomous, self-contained work groups that have less reliance on external resources. This third strategy generally leads to an increased span of control, and with its flattened hierarchy, to decreased specialization, and often to decreased formalization and centralization.[22]

To increase its capacity to process this information, the organization can invest in vertical information systems. This generally refers to computerized information systems for handling more of the routine chores, allowing more opportunity and resources for innovation and planning, better feedback, and

Table 2. Training Needs within Career Stages

Stage	Task Needs	Emotional Needs
Trial	1. Varied job activities 2. Self-exploration	1. Make preliminary job choices 2. Setting down
Establishment Advancement	1. Job challenge 2. Develop competence in a specialty 3. Develop creativity and innovation 4. Rotate into new area after three to five years	1. Deal with rivalry and competition; face failures 2. Deal with work-family conflicts 3. Support 4. Autonomy
Midcareer	1. Technical updating 2. Develop skills in training and coaching others (younger employees) 3. Rotation into new job requiring new skills 4. Develop broader view of work and own role in organization	1. Express feelings about midlife 2. Reorganize thinking about self in relation to work, family, community 3. Reduce self-indulgence and competitiveness
Late Career	1. Plan for retirement 2. Shift from power role to one of consultation and guidance 3. Identify and develop successors 4. Begin activities outside the organization	1. Support and counseling to see one's work as a platform for others 2. Develop sense of identity in extra-organizational activities

Source: Hall and Morgan, 1977, p. 218.

the upgrading of jobs, and for more control at lower levels. The organization can instead choose to work at creating more effective lateral relations. This involves more direct contact through mechanisms such as liaison roles, task forces, integrating roles, greater use of teams, managerial linking roles, and matrix structures. The greater the degree of complexity and volatility in the human element, the greater the need for an organization to adopt one or more of these strategies.

Modification of the Design of Work. Many of today's employees seek greater satisfaction directly from the performance of their jobs. Enriching the nature of an organization's jobs is clearly an important design option for many situations. Only a brief summary is made here.

For the employee who is high in needs for achievement and growth and desires autonomy and greater self-control on the job, an enriched task appears to increase internal work motivation and job involvement. Enriched tasks seem to have the following characteristics:

- use of a wide variety of skill;
- high degree of task identity (requiring the completion of a "whole" piece of work that the individual can call his or her own);
- high level of significance (to job-holder, organization, society);
- large amount of freedom and discretion in job procedures;
- capacity for feedback about how effectively the job holder is performing (self-feedback).[23]

These are the traditional characteristics of an enriched task. In recent years organizations have used other, less traditional, approaches to the creation of

Table 3. Organizational Actions for Facilitating Career Development

Entry: Changing Employee Inputs	**Changing the Boss's Role** (continued)
1. Better links between school and work	3. Reward managers for employee de-
2. Training students in job-related skills	velopment
3. Realistic job previews in recruiting	**Changing Organizational Structures**
4. Better selection for person-job fit	1. Matrix organization structures
Development through the Job	2. Accounting for human resources
1. Challenging initial jobs	3. Career planning services
2. Periodic job rotation	**Changing Personnel Policies**
3. Colleague stimulation	1. Rotation of managers through "people
4. Frequent feedback and performance	departments"
review	2. Lifelong job rotation
5. Rewarding good performance	3. Downward and lateral transfers
Changing the Boss's Role	4. Tenure
1. Make bosses career developers	5. Fallback positions for promoted em-
2. Train managers in job design and	ployees
career planning	6. Support for dual career employees

Source: Hall and Morgan, 1977, p. 222.

autonomous, significant, satisfying jobs. These have included the reinstitution of older patterns of entrepreneurship through structures such as franchises, small research and development groups, and independent work teams.[24] Increasing use of contracts, joint ventures, trade associations, and service firms have also provided opportunities for enriched jobs.

There is considerable argument over whether job enrichment is for everyone. The need for organizations to be flexible and to provide alternative work designs varies, depending on the diagnosed needs of the organization's employees. Nevertheless, there is growing consensus among organizational theorists and practitioners that certain characteristics are necessary if many or most of today's organizational members are to experience meaning in their work:

- widened jobs;
- continuous learning;
- participation in decision making;
- social support;
- meaningful relation between one's job and the outside world;
- desirable future.[25]

Ideally, enriched tasks and meaningful jobs are designed to meet the needs of mature, self-actualizing employees. If not all of an organization's members are of that type, traditional, authoritarian, low-responsibility jobs are probably more appropriate and will produce better organizational results.

CHANGING THE INTERFACE BETWEEN PEOPLE AND THE ORGANIZATION

Management Development through Job Assignments.   If job moves are to be used for growth and development (and they can have a very strong impact on overall development), care must be taken to use the career-planning process effectively.[26] The following steps are important:

1. Selection of a target job, with consideration of the individual's career aspirations and values.
2. Identification of the skills and experiences necessary to reach the target jobs.
3. Identification of the necessary sequence of jobs to build the required skills and experiences.
   a. Select jobs which provide changes which are large enough to stretch the individual's skills and abilities, yet small enough to be manageable.
   b. Consider lateral, developmental, cross-functional moves as well as promotions.

    c. Allow for sufficient time to master the job but not so long that the job becomes routine.

    d. Consider jobs which complement or supplement, not merely duplicate, previous experiences.

    e. Plan alternative moves or sequences (contingency plans) since it is unlikely that all the scheduled moves will take place as planned.[27]

Leadership Styles. Leadership studies invariably conclude that leaders tend to be relationship- or task-oriented; invariably, they also conclude that a heavy emphasis on both orientations is associated with leadership effectiveness. In the belief that there is seldom, if ever, one best way, some authors have recently focused on the match of leadership style to situation. Fred Fiedler suggests that relationship-motivated leaders tend to excell under conditions in which they have moderate influence and control; and that task-oriented leaders tend to be most successful under conditions in which they exert a great deal of power and influence (the mechanistic, bureaucratic structure) or under the reverse conditions, where they have little or no power or influence.[28] P. Hersey and K.H. Blanchard have identified the maturity level of subordinates (in terms of their willingness and ability to set goals and accept responsibility for goal achievement) as the element in the environment that determines the appropriate leadership style for the manager to use.[29] Low maturity subordinates are appropriately led with autocratic, close supervision; a delegative, laissez-faire style is most appropriate for mature employees.

Organizational Development. A wide set of procedures and techniques have been developed to open an organization's work climate. Collectively labelled Organization Development (OD), they include sensitivity training, team building, T-groups, action research, diagnosis and feedback, development of interpersonal skills, and mirroring. The focus of OD has traditionally been the collective set of work values and attitudes evidenced by work groups and organizations in the way they work together, confront conflict, and cope with change. These procedures all assume that the actualizing, self-controlling nature of today's employees is normal and widespread.

Management by Objectives. The goal-oriented nature of employee motivation (and organizations) has been a major impetus to the increasing use of management by objectives. This participative process of identifying managers' operating and development objectives and, thus, their performance levels, has traditionally been identified with procedures used by effective managers and organizations. The process may be standardized, but the goals and action plans are highly individualized.

Institutionalized Participation. Since participation in organizational decision making has such a pervasive influence on critical employee attitudes like commitment and motivation, many organizations have developed ways to formalize participation. Worker-management committees, joint study groups, special collective bargaining groups, and many forms of worker management (such as the Scanlon Plan) have evolved to institutionalize the procedures for employee participation and to increase motivation, commitment, and goal-oriented performance.

INDIVIDUALIZING ORGANIZATIONS

This article has been suggesting that organizations can either try to change the nature of their employees so they will fit the organization or make internal changes to try to fit the organization to its employees. Lawler suggests that there isn't much evidence to indicate that organizations adapt very well with either strategy. Even if they are temporarily successful, changes are occurring so rapidly that the adaptations are short-lived. The option that is left is to "individualize" the organization. Since employees differ in as many ways as they do, it only makes sense to try to make the organization as flexible as possible. The more options available to the organization and the more easily these are matched to employee differences, the more able the organization is to adapt to its environment with an internally acceptable organizational climate.[30]

The following are suggested for managers who want to individualize their organizations:

- Figure out what outcomes each employee values.
- Determine what kinds of behavior the organization desires.
- Make sure the desired behavior is achievable.
- Link the desired outcomes to the desired performances.
- Analyze the total situation to eliminate conflicting expectancies (as between group norms and organizational requirements).
- Make sure that the outcomes offered are large enough to motivate significant behavior.
- Check the system of equity.

If managers in the organization can and will do these things, the pay and reward systems, tasks, and group structures can be designed to meet the many individual differences faced by the organization. "Only by treating individuals differently is it possible to get them to behave in the same way."[31]

SUMMARY AND CONCLUSION

Employees see themselves as individuals—unique, irreplaceable, with different needs, desires, and goals. They make decisions about how to act at work based on expectations that certain behavior will lead to satisfaction of their needs, desires, and goals.

Organizations see people as resources—replaceable, trainable, suitable for many different purposes. The major human problem for organizations lies at that interface between employees as humans and employees as resources. This is a particularly critical problem as people become less willing to accept roles as merely resources.

Organizations do not hire just part of a person. They do not hire just an individual's mechanical skills or decision-making abilities. They get a whole person—ethnic and family background, education, political views, culture or lack of it, self-concept, feelings about family, and all the rest. Organizations have traditionally been designed to deal with only the skills and abilities of their employees, not whole persons. Organizations must deal with all parts of their employees—their memories, motivations, expectations, aspirations, attitudes, and feelings, all of which insist on coming to work with them. There are critical differences in employee motivations, commitments, and values, and organizations have many options for adapting to those differences. Only in these ways can individuals and organizations meet each other's needs.

REFERENCES

1. L.W. Porter, E.E. Lawler, J.R. Hackman, *Behavior in Organizations* (New York: McGraw-Hill, 1975).
2. Ibid., p. 243.
3. J.D. Thompson, *Organizations in Action* (New York: McGraw-Hill Book Company, 1967); R.K. Merton, "Bureaucratic Structure and Personality," in Robert K. Merton (ed.) *Social Theory and Social Structure,* revised edition (New York: The Free Press of Glencoe, 1957); D. Katz and R.L. Kahn, *The Social Psychology of Organizations,* 2nd edition (New York: John Wiley & Sons, 1978).
4. J.E. Ross and R.G. Murdick, "People, Productivity, and Organizational Structure," *Personnel* (September-October 1973), pp. 9–16.
5. Ibid.
6. J. Todd, "Management Control Systems: A Key Link Between Strategy, Structure and Employee Performance," *Organizational Dynamics* (Spring 1977), pp. 65–78.
7. H.J. Reitz, *Behaviors in Organizations* (Homewood, Illinois: Richard D. Irwin, 1977).
8. S.M. Davis and P.R. Lawrence, *Matrix* (Reading, Massachusetts: Addison-Wesley, 1977); H.L. Tosi and S.J. Carroll, *Management: Contingencies, Structures, and Process* (Chicago: St. Clair Press, 1976); J.M. Ivancevich and J.H. Donnelly, Jr., "Relation of Organizational Structure to Job Satisfaction, Anxiety-Stress, and Pay," *Administrative Science Quarterly,* Vol. 20, No. 2 (June 1975), pp. 272–280.
9. E.E. Lawler, "The Individualized Organization: Problems and Promise," *California Management Review,* Vol. 17, No. 2 (1974), pp. 31–39; E.E. Lawler, "Individualizing Organizations: A Needed Emphasis in Organizational Psychology," in H. Meltzer and F. Wickert (eds.), *Humanizing Organizational Behavior* (Springfield, Illinois: Charles C. Thomas, 1976); and Reitz, op. cit.

10. N.R. F. Maier, *Psychology in Industrial Organizations*, 4th edition (Boston: Houghton-Mifflin, 1973); D.A. Nadler and E. E. Lawler, "Motivation: A Diagnostic Approach" in J.R. Hackman, E. E. Lawler, and L.W. Porter (eds.), *Perspectives on Behavior in Organizations* (New York: McGraw-Hill, 1977), pp. 26–38; A.K. Korman, *Organizational Behavior* (Englewood Cliffs, New Jersey: Prentice-Hall, 1977).

11. A. Etzioni, *A Comparative Analysis of Complex Organizations*, revised edition (New York: The Free Press, 1975).

12. C. Perrow, *Organizational Analysis: A Sociological View* (Belmont, California: Wadsworth, 1970).

13. J.H. Barrett, *Individual Goals and Organizational Objectives: A Study of Integration Mechanisms* (Ann Arbor: Institute for Social Research, University of Michigan, 1970).

14. D.C. Feldman, "A Practical Program for Employee Socialization," *Organizational Dynamics*, (August 1976), pp. 64–80; J.P. Wanous, "Organizational Entry: From Naive Expectations to Realistic Beliefs," *Journal of Applied Psychology*, Vol. 61 (1976), pp. 22–29; J.P. Wanous, "Organizational Entry: Newcomers Moving from Outside to Inside," *Psychological Bulletin*, Vol. 84, No. 4 (July 1977), pp. 601–618; R. Presthus, *The Organization Society*, revised edition (New York: St. Martin's Press, 1978).

15. W.C. Hamner, "Reinforcement Theory," in H.L. Tosi and W.C. Hamner (eds.), *Organizational Behavior and Management: A Contingency Approach*, revised edition (Chicago: St. Clair Press, 1977), pp. 93–112; W.C. Hamner and E.P. Hammer, "Behavior Modification on the Bottom Line," *Organizational Dynamics*, Vol. 4 (Spring 1976), pp. 2–21.

16. S.F. Carroll, Jr., and H.L. Tosi, Jr., *Management by Objectives* (New York: Macmillan, 1973).

17. D.T. Hall and F.S. Hall. "What's New in Career Management," *Organizational Dynamics* (Summer 1976), pp. 17–33; J. Van Maanen and E.J. Schein, "Career Development," in J.R. Hackman and J.L. Suttle (eds.), *Improving Life at Work* (Santa Monica, California: Goodyear Publishing, 1977), pp. 30–95.

18. D.T. Hall and M.A. Morgan, "Career Development and Planning" in W.C. Hamner and F.L. Schmidt (eds.), *Contemporary Problems in Personnel* (Chicago: St. Clair Press, 1977).

19. A.B. Cherns, "Can Behavioral Science Help Design Organizations?" *Organizational Dynamics*, Vol. 5 (1977), pp. 44–64.

20. Z.F. Gamson, "Organizational Responses to Members," *The Sociological Quarterly*, Vol. 9, No. 2 (Spring 1968), pp. 139–149; P.N. Khandwalla, *The Design of Organizations* (New York: Harcourt Brace Jovanovich, Inc., 1977).

21. J.R. Galbraith, "Organizational Design: An Information Processing View," *Interfaces*, Vol. 4 (1974), pp. 28–36; J.R. Galbraith, *Organizational Design* (Reading Mass.: Addison-Wesley, 1977); Davis and Lawrence, op. cit.

22. W.B. Brown, "Systems, Boundaries, and Information Flow," *Academy of Management Journal*, Vol. 9 (1966), pp. 318–327; Gamson, op. Cit.

23. J.R. Hackman and E.E. Lawler, "Employee Reactions to Job Characteristics," *Journal of Applied Psychology*, Vol. 55 (1971), pp. 259–286; and J.R. Hackman, G. Oldham, R. Jansen, K. Purdy, "A New Stategy for Job Enrichment," *California Management Review*, Vol. 17 (1975), pp. 57–71.

24. Brown, op. cit.

25. F. Emery and E. Thorsrud, *New Designs for Work Organization* (Oslo, Norway: Tannum Press, 1969).

26. D.E. Berlew and D.T. Hall, "The Socialization of Managers: Effects of Expectations on Performance," *Administrative Science Quarterly*, Vol. 11 (September 1966), pp. 207–223; Hall and Morgan, op. cit.; E.E. Jennings, *Routes to the Executive Suite* (New York: McGraw-Hill, 1971); Van Maanen and Schein, op. cit.

27. Hall and Morgan, op. cit.

28. F. Fiedler, *A Theory of Leadership Effectiveness* (New York: McGraw-Hill, 1967).

29. P. Hersey and K.H. Blanchard, *Management of Organizational Behavior*, 3rd edition (Englewood Cliffs, New Jersey: Prentice-Hall, 1971).

30. Nadler and Lawler, op. cit.

31. Lawler, "Individualizing Organizations," p. 202.

SECTION IV

THE "WIN-WIN" MANAGER

INTRODUCTION

That management is a vital element in any organization is a reality with which few can disagree. The leadership of an organization, sometimes referred to as the managerial subsystem, is at the hub of all organizations. Management is the single most important factor influencing an organization's entire operation. While it is obvious that budgetary restraints, economic conditions, and even certain factors outside the control of an organization can have a serious impact on an organization, it is, nevertheless, accurate to stress the critical organizational role of management.

In the previous section there was some discussion of an organization's climate, culture, or personality. It is the management of an organization which is the most dominant influencer of the organization's personality. Effective managers must realize the serious responsibility they have—a responsibility which transcends the serious responsibility they have for productivity or making a profit. Let there be no misunderstanding; productivity, achieving results, "the bottom line" are essential in any organization—especially in "win-win" organizations. But what is being suggested here is that managers expand their definition of their role to be aware of the important part they play in establishing the overall tone of their organization. Managers set the tone, influence the organization's personality, and that tone permeates the organization.

With an awareness of this expanded responsibility, and an understanding that the tone set by management directly influences productivity, managers will appropriately give thought to their managerial style. These "win-win" managers will realize that they must communicate more; that they must establish a bond of trust throughout the organization; that people inside and outside their organization want to be treated with dignity; that non-managers want to be engaged in work which has meaning for them. "Win-win" managers will know that although there may be a broad range of personality types with whom they are working, this open, trustworthy, concerned style of management is appropriate in almost all circumstances.

The case for the kind of "win-win" management which is being advocated is creatively made by Perry Pascarella in his "Humanagement" article. Combining the word "human" with the word "management" is a unique way of bringing to the attention of managers the need to recognize the human dimension while managing their organizations. Pascarella simply suggests that management in the 1980s will have to deal more effectively with people. In his article he indicates that executives can be more effective by becoming more humanistic and people-oriented. He says that following this humanistic approach involves some potential risk, but that not to do so will render the manager obsolete.

Harold White has engaged in research which documents that participative leadership is the management style which best leads to group productivity and individual satisfaction. There appear to be certain personal characteristics held by managerial leaders who are the most effective. White's research indicates that the more effective manager is more likely to have trust and confidence in non-managers, widely shares information, is supportive of people in the organization and aware of their problems, and emphasizes positive reinforcement as a motivational tool. His article concludes that there is a direct relationship between a manager's leadership style and the performance of his subordinates.

With concern for the very important question of motivation, Bernard Rosenbaum's article presents five practical principles for managers to use. These principles will not only help managers to stimulate motivation within the people with whom they work, but also help them to deal more effectively with people generally.

Echoing a theme expressed by a number of people who advocate "win-win" management, Marsha Sinetar states that organizational members want to be treated with dignity and respected for their individuality. Her article appeals for a "New Age" type of manager who recognizes that people have this need. These managers will work cooperatively with people throughout the organization thus creating a more prevalent attitude of mutual trust and respect among managers and non-managers.

In accord with Sinetar's "New Age," Jim Bruno and Paula Lippin demonstrate that there is a "New Trend: Nice Guys Finish First." Their article, in contradiction to the notion that one must be ruthless in order to climb to the top of the corporate ladder, presents an extensive study demonstrating that high achieving managers are those who are truly concerned about the people they manage.

Robert Silverman and D. A. Heming suggest in their article that contemporary organizations require a new type of leadership. They say that traditional bureaucratic management, seeking mainly to preserve the status quo and regarding innovation and creativity with suspicion and hostility, is no longer accepted by the new generation of employee. They argue that the conforming stereotypical "organization man" must be replaced by professional "win-win" managers.

While most of the literature discussing "win-win" management appears in business-related publications, Harlan Cleveland remains an effective advocate for this type of management in the public sector. Appearing in *Public Management,* his article, adapted from a speech he delivered at the annual conference of the International City Management Association in 1980, discusses the local government manager's role in promoting new ideas, initiatives, and leadership.

The experience of the authors whose articles appear in this section is diverse, and yet they all arrive at the same conclusion. They all articulately posit the position that "win-win" management is a requisite for an effective organization.

HUMANAGEMENT

Perry Pascarella

The people who have managed American business developed an arsenal of skills that made the U. S. system a world giant in the generation of wealth. But this economic success has fostered a society that now clamors for changes in its economic goals, and for the satisfaction of non-economic needs. Because it has proved to be a successful vehicle for delivering the goods, the business corporation is being challenged to deliver solutions on a far broader scale.

This turning point in corporate history necessitates a change in attitudes and style for those who exercise those management skills. It suggests, perhaps, that the business executive's role will take on "superhuman" dimensions.

New objectives for the corporation are not being laid down in a rational, cohesive pattern. The expectations levied on today's corporation take executives into areas which were traditionally of secondary concern or of no concern at all in terms of getting their job done. Economic and social objectives are being dictated to the corporation in such detail and with such speed that it seems impossible to attain any of them. They jeopardize the life of the corporation.

Response to these demands calls for remarkably capable people to fill the ranks of management. The ideal manager of the future will have to be quite different from his or her predecessor. He or she will have to be sensitive to shifting demands and answerable to new constituencies.

The challenge from without, however, may be offset by a challenge from within. The need for a more humanistic corporation may be offset by the changes in what managers themselves want to invest in their work and to derive from it. They, too, will pressure for change. The external and internal forces, then, may hold the corporation together so that it can fulfill its broader role.

Reprinted by permission of the publisher from Pascarella, Perry, "Humanagement," *Industry Week*, Vol. 204, no. 1, January 7, 1980.

What appears to be a superhuman job for executives may be quite the contrary. The corporation and its managers are not growing beyond the abilities of man but are *expanding to* the human scale. The managerial role will call for people to unleash more of their talents and realize more of their humanness. The manager who would not allow himself to be crammed into corporate boxes will find that those boxes are collapsing.

The manager will find that his job will require, not the accumulation of greater power, but the sharing of power. It will reject loftiness in favor of greatness in human terms. The manager will be able to bring more of his human capabilities to the job and feel free to admit his limitations. He will be less compelled to confine himself to limited objectives and cloak himself in a mantle of perfection. A pivotal factor in determining the viability of the future corporation will be the ability of the manager to employ his humanity and his interpersonal skills to direct the corporation toward new objectives—both economic and social.

Public instrument.   The expectations demanded of today's corporation are virtually all based on the assumption that the corporation is a permanent institution. It is expected to provide a form of socialization by insuring income stability, pensions, and health care. It must work toward social objectives by providing equal opportunities for employment, training, and advancement. It must be sensitive to the political ramifications of its dealings with other nations and institutions. As the corporation is broadened in terms of its objectives as well as in its ownership base and geographic reach, it becomes a public instrument.

Not only corporate objectives, but the means by which they are pursued, are subject to challenge today. Inside the company, workers want more than a day's pay for doing what they're told to do. They want rewarding work, a sense of community, and an opportunity to participate in the decisions that affect them. Outside the company, countless individuals and groups employ various tactics for influencing the ends and the means of corporate activity.

Some managers regard these pressures on the corporation as an attempt to destroy the private enterprise system. But surveys show again and again that most Americans have a high regard for the system. They are, however, not fully satisfied with the performance of those who operate the system. Their expectations have been elevated, and they express their confidence in the system by turning to the corporation to provide them what they want. Since the corporation has generally not taken the initiative in satisfying each of these demands, individuals and groups prod the corporation. The more they prod, the more they hobble the corporation with conflicting demands, and the more they have to prod.

This pushing and resisting intensifies the public's impression that the corporation lacks the soul required to take a leadership position. It reaffirms the notion that managers may not be competent to manage our institutions since they have, after all, concentrated on the financial or technical aspects of running a business.

The corporate manager likes to think of himself as an agent of change. But change, till now, has been limited to playing by the economic rules to succeed in economic terms. He is now faced with a fundamental change in the definition of what he is to do and how he must go about it. The manager has two alternatives: resist the demands placed upon him and hope to turn back the tide of change, or welcome the added challenges and see in them hope for a better lot for himself.

Favorite feuds.   People outside the corporation may hold little hope that any change in the right direction will come from within. This country has thrived on adversary relationships, and the manager-nonmanager feud is a favorite. Many people are not sure what a manager really is or what he does, but they have an endless supply of terms for managers: "big shot, fat cat, big cheese, wheeler-deeler." Most of the terms and images fall short of being complimentary, to say the least. They tend to set managers off from "the rest of us."

These images do not serve us well. They color all managers the same lifeless shade. For every wheeler-dealer or fat cat, there are many managers who get the goods produced and still serve the community. While some managers may be detached from the outside world, there are thousands who play key roles on the boards of schools, hospitals, and churches. Business executives head Boy Scout fund-raising drives, and thousands of managers lead troops on campouts or coach Little Leaguers.

Because of the power that goes with being a manager—and remembrances of what that power once was—it's natural for a manager-nonmanager power struggle to exist. After all, a manager can hire and fire, determine how much a worker will be paid, what the worker will do, where he will do it, and when he will do it. The worker continually tries to whittle away at this power, attempting to gain more control over his life.

In varying degrees, the manager has been separated not only from others but also from his own emotions, the morality of the society in which he lives, and even his personal values. These things have traditionally been irrelevant to fulfilling the corporate role. In exchange, he was able to derive a sense of belonging and identity from the organization that employed him. But this Faustian bargain does not have the appeal it once did.

The changing role of business may be relatively easy to observe. Less obvious, however, is the change in the managerial role that is likely to be demanded by managers *themselves.* The manager is affected by the social changes that are taking place. He is driven by society's rising expectations— and also by his own. His expectations of his job, his life, and the corporation are changing. He welcomes a broader range of objectives and new techniques for managing.

The new breed, of all ages, sees the opportunity to find more meaningful work and lead a more integrated life. Today, a manager may take a broader view in his search for identity. He finds the identity derived from position or company affiliation too confining. He wants to relate himself and his organization to the rest of the world and its needs. He needs something to believe in beyond his traditional job accomplishments. What he does, how he does it, with whom he does it, and how it relates to his whole life have become important considerations for him.

There are three reasons why management is adopting a highly experimental stance. First, organizations are swamped by the demands being thrust upon them. Second, productivity improvement is not adequate to offset inflation or to beat foreign competitors. Third, managers themselves are bringing new perspectives to their work. Increasingly, they reject the model of single-minded individuals for whom profit or product is the be-all and end-all.

Because many of today's managers demand satisfying work and opportunity to achieve, they can appreciate others longing for the same things. They are experimenting with new methods of communicating, decision-making, and working together. For example, the lateral relationship approach repeatedly shows that it can work better than the militaristic hierarchy and often produce better-informed decisions and better follow-through as well.

Middle management and professional people want "more interesting and vital work and more of a chance to find a commitment they deem worthy of their talents and skills," says social analyst Daniel Yankelovich, president of Yankelovich, Skelly & White, Inc., a public opinion research firm. He places about one out of every six workers in this college-educated, whitecollar category. They are the "most willing to sacrifice either money or job security in order to fulfill these needs."

For some managers, work is not only fulfilling—it is exciting. Strapped and wired into a flight simulator for the space shuttle, George W. Jeffs, a vice president of Rockwell International Corp. and president of its North American Space Operations, checked the progress on the construction of the vehicle designed to make repeated trips into space. Speaking of the project he was captaining, the graying, 52-year-old executive said: "We put the reputation of our company, of ourselves personally, our organizations, our people on the line every time we do something that is significant. The rewards for this are certainly not in the profits. Our profits, compared with those of commercial industry, are probably about half—at best. The thing that we're most concerned about is the success that we want to see out of our efforts. We're all in it to make a living, of course, but I think, fundamentally, that we're in it for the satisfaction of doing something different, something that hasn't been done before."

Effective arm waving. Effective managers are driven by the desire to achieve—but in a special way. Unlike other achievers, they want to perform work through others. The scale of what they want to accomplish is such that they cannot work alone. It's the difference between a violinist, let's say, and a conductor. Both are achievers. Both are highly motivated by their work. Both have talent—but a different talent. To oversimplify, one makes sounds, the other waves his arms. If we see the manager only in terms of waving his arms, we might question his contribution. But, if we look deeper and see that he interprets, directs, and coordinates, we can better appreciate his role.

In traditional corporate structures, power and authority go with certain positions. They are the tools for getting things done. But for some managers power is an end in itself. Ralph may want to be vice president of his company, but not because he wants to guide it into new markets, meet social needs, or improve the profit position; he may want more pay, more recognition, more people reporting to him, or fewer bosses to report to.

There are wheeler-dealers in management ranks, too. They concentrate on stocks, bonds, tender offers, and proxy fights, moving companies in a bigger-than-life chess game. Unfortunately, these people—along with those who are just struggling to hang onto their positions—make the best material for novels and movies.

Sometimes even effective managers can get too caught up in short-term, narrowly defined objectives. They unintentionally become allies with the power grabbers, status quo proponents, and wheeler-dealers in resisting or ignoring the pressures for change.

The corporation, then, can rely on relatively few members of its management team for adaptation to a changing world. These agents of change continually seek new goals as they attain others. Although they are part of the organization, they are willing to challenge it. They operate by the rules, but they will change the rules when these get in the way of reaching goals or establishing new goals.

Social analyst Mr. Yankelovich asserts that the middle management group is not finding satisfaction in its work. These people, he says, are the "hungriest for responsibility, challenge, autonomy, informality, and less rigid authority in organization structure." They possess the "strongest creativity and achievement needs" of any workers, but incentive systems based on money and fear don't draw the best from these people, says Mr. Yankelovich. We could extend that line of thinking to justify the need for revising job content and corporate structure.

Even "successful" managers sometimes find that work isn't paying off in terms that are fulfilling to them. They hunger for something in the job besides money or status. Incentives and structures could be changed to give such people what they want and to benefit the corporation by a greater investment of talent. At a time when coercion and artificial enticements aren't effective with the new workforce, the corporation needs managers who can operate with a less precise definition of responsibilities and authority and who can bring people's personal goals into harmony with those of the organization—and vice versa. These managers may bring to the organization both a greater responsiveness to the outside world and an improvement in productivity.

No scorekeeping.   Management is a relatively new concept. Industry and the organization of work as we know them do not date back to early civilization. The Industrial Revolution of some 200 years ago established the general shape of today's business. The manager was the owner. He hired people to work for him, telling them what to do and how to do it. Then came the hired manager to whom the owner delegated specific responsibilities; he learned his craft on the job. Early in this century, some of the skills of engineers and accountants were carried over into management, giving it scientific techniques. Management became increasingly scientific. The human factors were ignored —or deliberately eliminated—in an attempt to quantify everything possible, break jobs down into simple repetitive tasks, and improve efficiency. The early management theorists believed that organizational efficiency rose in proportion to the displacement of individual values with interchangeable functions.

Since managers generally don't own the company or even a large percentage of the shares in it, profit doesn't come directly to their pockets. But it does serve as a measurement of their performance. Some are doubly rewarded when they achieve something that they deem worthy in itself and, at the same time, earns a profit for the company. Profit reflects the fact that what you accomplished has value to someone else. The increased value of the company's stock indicates that you have built a wealth-producing organization in which others want to share ownership.

A manager can be carried away by this scorekeeping, however. By concentrating too heavily on the numbers, he may miss the intangibles that are causing a bad situation, or he may not appreciate some of the positive intangibles that will be disturbed by his efforts to bring the numbers into line for a better score. Watching the scoreboard while ignoring the members of his team, his opponents, and the officials, he may lose the game.

The standards for measuring a manager's performance are neither universal nor permanent. At times they may point to maximizing sales growth, or profit growth, or profit as a return on investment, or a gain in the price of the company's stock. At other times, or in other societies, they may emphasize the maintenance of an organization for the long term. They may—and this is increasingly true today in the U.S.—point to serving a variety of society's needs such as the creation of employment, providing equal opportunities for employment, cleaning up the environment, and conserving resources.

Management functions such as sales, finance, and production—which have a good array of statistical measurements—have been the traditional routes to the top of corporate hierarchy.

Today, however, most of the problems facing the corporation are beyond definitive measurement. They involve people's values and feelings. The corporate doors have been opened wide, and what was once a private institution has, for all practical purposes, become a public one. It therefore deals more and more in people relationships. That is why we have begun to see the rise to prominence of such managerial functions as employee relations, public relations, and government relations.

In 1977, IW recognized this trend when it began its annual series of awards for excellence in management. An outstanding chief executive has been named each year in each of four categories: community relations, government relations, industrial relations, and explaining the private enterprise system to the public. The awards represent a deliberate attempt to draw attention to new yardsticks for performance.

Some of the companies that have achieved the best financial scores in this awards campaign are also the most people-oriented. (Or they have the best scores *because* they are people-oriented.) It makes sense. Managers who are concerned with employees' well-being, customers' needs, and the welfare of the public tend to the things that ultimately maximize sales, minimize costs, and generate a good "score."

People count. The rules that once worked for attaining financial success are losing their effectiveness today. Early in this century, Taylorism erected a milestone in scientific management. It advocated analyzing jobs and breaking them down into simple, repeatable tasks so as to maximize efficiency. This mechanistic approach to work created a machine-like routine for millions of people. The concept fitted well into hierarchal structures.

Today, however, industry is trying to undo this approach. Because of people's changing expectations, attempts are being made to put jobs back together again. Some managers are trying to reconstruct work in the context of people. You hear them speak in terms of "job enlargement," "job enrichment," and "humanization of the workplace." They are convinced that better worker relations and improved productivity will have to come through the workers' own motivations. They will get more out of people, they believe, by letting workers put more of themselves into the job.

The genuinely humanistic style of management begins with the attempt to understand what people want. Both workers and managers yearn for a better work situation, more freedom in the workplace, and a greater say in decisions that affect their jobs. This is not a revolution brought about by the so-called younger generation. The trend has swept up people of all ages and positions.

At the same time, the lack of opportunity to find rewarding work situations has turned off many workers. They haven't lost the will to work, but neither are they interested in accepting work as it has been packaged nor in making personal sacrifices as a term of employment. They express their frustration through demands for more time off, better pay, or other means of compensating for work that is not meaningful to them.

Critics of workplace humanization efforts say these attempts are merely new tactics for manipulating people to keep them in the hierarchy. Their accusations are sometimes correct. Some managers are genuinely interested in people *per se* and their humanization efforts are aimed at establishing jobs and relationships that provide meaningful, inner rewards. But others twist the concept into a device for improving the quality or quantity of work performed. As they attempt to superimpose the techniques on their basically negative view of people, they miss the essence and the program fails.

There is a history of using the behavioral sciences to develop new tools for improving worker output. After World War II, management turned its attention to the people factors of production and tried to apply scientific techniques there, too. Applications of science to the management of people have generally treated people as response mechanisms. Little has been done to study and respond to people's inner motivations. In fact, managers often speak of "motivating" workers, ignoring the evidence that motivation comes from within the individual—that the task of management is to present the factors to which the worker's motivations will respond.

Not all managers are concerned with the people factors in production. "There is great resistance in top management circles, once you get beyond lip service, to the idea that human resources are a key to improving productivity and competitive effectiveness," says Mr. Yankelovich. They think that capital investment, technology, and management systems are more important. Mr. Yankelovich's explanation for that: "Many of the people in top management are trained in finance or engineering or production. They are not as comfortable with intangibles of human behavior as with the more tangible areas of business. Also, in the past, technology and capital investment *were* the key factors—and were, in addition, easier to deal with."

Managers, understandably, stayed with what they knew best. But today they are being forced to consider the people aspects of managing as the old concepts of work and organization fail to produce satisfactory results. The systems to which people refuse to conform will have to be adapted to the irrationalities, emotions, feelings, needs, and wants of the managed and the managers.

"The essence of good management is the art of knowing, understanding, and fulfilling human needs," says one corporate vice president. "For if only the manager is getting his needs fulfilled at the expense of his people, and they are getting little, if any, satisfaction, it's only win for him and lose for them. This is not only unhealthy, it's stupid, for people won't put up with a losing situation for very long."

A computer can make a decision for you. But, as a manager you have to provide the heart to execute that decision. You most make the value judgments to ensure that what may be right economically and technically is also "right" with people—that what is about to be done will fit the moral and ethical climate. You must sense and solve the many human problems involved in carrying out that decision. And you have to have the guts to live with your decision.

Managers who are high achievers are as concerned about people as they are about production, finds Teleometrics International after a study of 16,000 managers in 50 organizations. Analyzing the managers themselves and the perceptions of their subordinates in its five-year project, Teleometrics concluded that high achievers differed from other managers in their search for personal satisfaction in the job and in their effort to provide the opportunity for their subordinates to do so, too. They actively communicate—sending and receiving—with their associates, and they involve their subordinates in decision-making.

The ultimate style.   The pressure for humanistic management applies to more than managerial relationships with employees. Giving the worker what he wants depends partly on how he perceives his company relating to society in terms of product, social concern and involvement, and environmental impact. The manager's effectiveness is influenced by the whole context in which his company operates. It is determined, too, by his concept of himself. He has to understand how his actions affect workers, shareholders, customers, the public, and himself.

The character of management in the years ahead might better be described by the term "humanagement." That would remind us what it is that is managed, for whom, by whom, and in what manner. Humanagement will represent change across the entire continuum of the manager's role.

The successful corporation of the future will:

- Deal with all aspects of the business in ways that reflect appreciation for people as whole persons.
- Find ways to enable the worker to put more of himself into the job and derive meaning and personal growth from it.
- Appreciate the human relationships within an organization and between the organization and the outside world.
- Take an optimistic view of people, building on cooperation rather than conflict.
- Permit the manager to reveal himself as a human being with fears, wants, and the need for growth.

Humanagement may sound like a soft style of managing—or not managing at all. This could not be further from the truth. Responding to people is far more difficult than following rules that treat them as simple response mechanisms. Acting as a complete person and regarding others as such is far more demanding than settling for distant relationships with two-dimensional figures.

With the addition of the people factors, the managerial function increases exponentially. Managers will have to master the very factors they have been taught to ignore. Many are already aware that the emotional content of their relations with others is critical to their performance. They can see that screening out human values— their own and others'—raises the odds for making a bad decision.

Humanistic as a manager may have wanted to be, he has been taught to leave that part of himself outside the plant or office. Now, that quality is becoming central to the managerial role. Organizations built on depersonalizing relations will now have to humanize them.

Rather than mastering people and resisting change, the manager must now master change and resolve people's many needs. This does not mean yielding to every request or pressure; it requires awareness and involvement in order to determine which issues to respond to and which to oppose. As the old concepts of hierarchy and domination crumble, the manager's authority comes not from his position so much as from his knowledge and his effectiveness in dealing with people.

The manager of the future will see beyond these difficulties that surround his role. He will find increased opportunities to express himself at work and to derive more satisfaction in it. He will bring the technology of his job together with his own humanism, welcoming the opportunity to play a broader role for he, too, has been the victim of Taylorism. Beneath the trappings of his office, there has always been a person with wants, needs, fears, weaknesses, and aspirations. Now he can admit that he is human. In fact, he had better reveal his humanity if he wants to succeed.

The ascent of humanagement does not signal the end of scientific management. That would entail an unlikely and undesirable loss of valuable tools for accomplishing work. Today's effective managers are already pointing the way to combining scientific techniques with humanistic behavior.

It is now possible—and necessary—for a manager to be both efficient and human at the same time, says Dr. Frederick Herzberg, distinguished professor of management, University of Utah, and the father of job enrichment. Dr. Herzberg, who is also an IW contributing editor, writes: "We must reverse the fragmentation process inherent in our post-industrial society and strive to bring a wholeness back to the individual."

Humanagement will be the mastery of organizations built of whole people serving whole people.

PERCEPTIONS OF LEADERSHIP BY MANAGERS IN A FEDERAL AGENCY

Harold C. White

Management includes the functions of planning, organizing, staffing, directing, and controlling. Leadership, considered as being synonymous with directing, is the concern of this report. Leadership may be defined as the act of providing incentives to motivate others by satisfying their needs to perform in some desired manner.

In his book, *Human Relations at Work,* Keith Davis says: "Leadership is something a person does, not something he has." R. Tannenbaum and W. Schmidt, in their article, "How to Choose a Leadership Pattern" (*Harvard Business Review,* Mar.-Apr. 1958), have suggested the variety of behavior patterns a manager may perform as a leader. These behaviors can range from one extreme by which the manager makes all decisions and announces them to the subordinates in the form of an order (autocratic leadership), through increasing amounts of subordinate involvement, to a point where the subordinates make decisions jointly with their manager on topics which affect them.

Experienced managers, when considering various alternative leadership styles, typically recognize that they have used a variety of styles, and have observed their fellow managers using them, at one time or another. They have concluded there is not one right way to lead effectively. Rather there is the appropriate way to lead, depending on the circumstances. The challenge for the manager is to identify accurately which leadership style is most appropriate for a given set of variables.

Personnel Administration and *Public Personnel Review,* July–August 1972, 1(1) 151–56.

PARTICIPATIVE LEADERSHIP

However, it is participative leadership that is most supported by research reported in the literature. The participative manager, when faced with the responsibility for making decisions which affect his subordinates, identifies objectives and establishes guidelines. Within these constraints he includes his immediate subordinates in the problem-solving and decision-making process. It is group, not individual, decision-making.

In actual practice, as contrasted with the autocratic manager, the participative manager displays consideration for the feelings, attitudes, and needs of his subordinates, supervises less closely, and spends a greater amount of time increasing his subordinates' feelings of freedom and self-responsibility.

Where it can be applied, participative leadership is most effective—is most motivating—because it is more likely to provide satisfaction of the needs of the greatest number of employees. The need for security may be satisfied by keeping the subordinates informed and by allowing them to be involved in decisions which affect their own work. Social need is satisfied because the participative process is social in nature. Decision-making is a team effort. There is status satisfaction in having one's ideas sought by an organizational superior and by having those ideas presented and discussed. There is personal growth (self-actualization) in being made aware of the total situation, in solving problems, and in carrying out decisions one has been involved in making.

The purpose of this study was to discover what leadership style, autocratic or participative, was viewed by managers as being most effective.

THE RESEARCH

Selected managers from one federal agency are the source for the data in this study. The agency employs approximately 20,000 persons: 1,000 in the national office and the remainder in offices in nearly every county in the United States. The study was conducted prior to an extensive management training program within the agency.

One group of respondents was composed of both line and staff personnel, mainly GS 12–14, located in the national office in Washington, D.C. The other group, GS 9–11, was composed of county office managers of a state in the Rocky Mountain region, each supervising from one to a dozen employees. The majority of managers in both groups supervise mainly office employees; work in the county offices involves considerable contact with the public.

Thirty-three questions were asked of each manager, a selection of which is summarized in the follow tables. Each respondent selected the most *effective* manager he personally knew in the agency and answered the questionnaire with that manager in mind. Next, each respondent answered the same questions for the *weakest* (least effective) manager known personally, in the agency. Neither the terms "effective" nor "weak" were defined. Each respondent was required to base the selection of managers evaluated on criteria he considered appropriate.

Each question contained three possible answers, which, in turn, were divided into three units, providing a nine-point scale. On the questionnaire, scales were alternated from right to left and left to right at random to reduce the possibility of a pattern developing in responding. For purposes of clarity, all scales on the following tables read from left (least desirable, 1) to right (most desirable, 9).

Numbers above the scales in the tables refer to responses of managers from the national office (indicated by an N to the left of the scale); numbers below the scales refer to the responses of the county office managers (indicated by a C). Numbers on the scales preceded by E refer to mean (average) responses for effective managers; numbers preceded by a W refer to mean responses for weak managers. The differences in responses between effective and weak managers are significant to at least the 5 percent level of confidence.

ATTITUDES OF SUBORDINATES

Approximately half the questions dealt with attitudes and behaviors of the subordinates whom the evaluated managers supervised. The results will not be discussed in depth here, but a summary of the responses is of interest.

As perceived by the federal managers completing this questionnaire, the effective managers, compared to the weak managers, supervise employees who:

1. Have more favorable attitudes toward other members in their own work unit and toward the organization as a whole.
2. Cooperate more effectively with other employees.
3. Communicate more effectively with other employees.
4. Have a greater feeling of responsibility for reaching organizational goals.
5. Have greater trust and confidence in their manager.
6. Are more accepting of information from their manager.
7. Feel greater freedom in discussing job-related problems with their manager.
8. Are more accurate in reporting their performance.

Employees of effective managers were perceived as performing effectively on most or all of the items measured; employees of weak managers tended to display inappropriate behaviors on most items.

LEADERSHIP STYLES

It might well be pointed out that a manager who supervises employees possessing appropriate behaviors and attitudes is more likely to be effective than a manager who supervises employees with inappropriate behaviors and attitudes.

However, there is evidence to suggest that this is not accidental, or luck. It is the leadership style of the manager that influences the attitudes and responses of the subordinates—a cause and effect relationship exists. Subordinates of effective managers possess attitudes and behaviors that are more desirable than subordinates of weak managers because the leadership style of the effective manager is more appropriate.

Table 1 provides information on the responses related to the leadership styles of effective and weak managers. Autocratic leadership is associated with the left-hand portion of each scale; participative leadership with the right-hand portion.

Question 1: Obtains unit members' ideas on job-related problems.

Question 2: Uses special knowledge of unit members in making decisions.

EFFECTIVE MANAGER

The effective manager, more than the weak manager, is perceived as seeking ideas and recommendations from his subordinates, and is more likely to use their ideas and special knowledge in making decisions. Encouraging upward communication is a rather continuous practice of the effective manager. The weak manager utilizes the ideas and special knowledge of his subordinates on a much more infrequent basis. Subordinates of effective managers are, therefore, more inclined to feel their interests are being considered and that the final decision of the managers will be fair and appropriate. They are more likely to develop a commitment to, and contribute effort toward, the success of the decisions.

Question 3: Aware of unit members' problems before making decisions.

Respondents perceive the effective manager is well aware of his subordinates' problems. The weak manager is frequently unaware. The effective manager is effective, perhaps in part, because he is better informed as to the needs and problems of his subordinates before making decisions.

Question 4: Adequacy and accuracy of information for unit members to make decisions.

Question 5: Shares information with unit members.

COMMUNICATION

Not only is the effective manager more likely than the weak manager to encourage upward communication from his subordinates, he is more likely to practice downward communication through keeping his subordinates informed. Such communication is seen as being both accurate and adequate. At best, the weak manager provides only partial information to his subordinates.

Typically, the manager, more than anyone else in the unit, by his own practices establishes standards and patterns of behavior for other members in the unit. If the manager communicates openly with his subordinates, they are more likely to be open with him.

Question 6: Provides support to unit members.

Table 1. Perceived Behaviors of Effective and Weak Managers

		Never	Occasionally	Always
1. Obtains unit members' ideas on job related problems	N	W3.2		E7.6
	C	W3.7		E7.4

		Seldom or never	Little	Completely
2. Uses special knowledge of unit members in making decisions	N	W4.2		E7.8
	C	W4.2		E7.4

		Seldom aware or totally unaware	Occasionally not aware	Well aware
3. Aware of unit members' problems before making decisions	N	W3.2		E7.7
	C	W3.8		E7.4

		Mostly inaccurate and inadequate	Partially accurate and adequate	Mostly accurate and adequate
4. Adequacy and accuracy of information for unit members to make decisions	N	W3.9		E7.5
	C	W3.8		E7.3

		Little or not at all	Provides minimum the manager feels they need	Shares most or all
5. Shares information with unit members	N	W3.6		E7.5
	C	W4.1		E7.5

		None	Occasionally	Completely
6. Provides support to unit members	N	W3.9		E7.7
	C	W4.1		E7.5

		Little or none	Some, not complete	Complete
7. Trust and confidence in unit members	N	W3.7		E7.1
	C	W3.9		E7.5

		Fear, threats, punishment	Rewards, some involvement, some punishment	Rewards and involvement
8. Means of motivating unit members	N	W3.9		E7.3
	C	W3.9		E7.3

		For policing, punishment	Policing, little punishment, emphasis on rewards	For unit members as a form of guidance
9. Use of control measures as productivity, costs, etc.	N	W3.8		E7.1
	C	W3.7		E7.0

N = Responses from selected managers in the national office

C = Responses from selected county managers in one state

E = Effective manager
W = Weak manager
Number of respondents: N = 38, C = 41

SUPPORTIVE ATTITUDE

One of the strongest behaviors of the effective manager is his supportive attitude toward his subordinates. The weak manager is perceived as providing only occasional support. Support comes from a variety of sources, such as the feeling of freedom to discuss problems openly with their manager, and from the practice of the manager of asking for advice and suggestions (questions 1 and 2).

Question 7: Trust and confidence in unit members.

Respondents perceive the effective manager as having considerably greater confidence in his subordinates than does the weak manager. This factor could explain, in part, the greater willingness of the effective manager to share information with his subordinates and to seek their ideas. The manager who displays a trusting attitude is more likely to receive trust in return.

Question 8: Means of motivating unit members.

REWARDS AND INVOLVEMENT

The effective manager is more disposed to motivate his subordinates through rewards and involvement thereby developing their interest in the job. The weak manager uses fear as a motivating force to obtain performance and punishment in response to poor performance. Emphasis of the effective manager is on positive motivators; emphasis of the weak manager is on negative motivators.

Question 9: Use of control measures as productivity, costs, etc.

Consistent with the mode of motivation is the use of control measures. The effective manager is more ready to reward desirable performance and is more likely to use reports of poor performance as a basis for instruction and guidance for improvement rather than as a basis for punishment. Although the weak manager may offer some rewards for desired performance, he is inclined to impose punishment for poor performance.

Additional observations: From additional data not shown on Table 1, it has been found that effective managers, as a group, are more similar in their leadership practices than are the weak managers. The effective managers tend to be participative in all behavior measures. While weak managers tend to be autocratic generally, few of them are perceived as being autocratic in all their practices. However, as the averages on the scales suggest, they are not consistent among each other as to which practices they have chosen to be participative.

DECISION-MAKING

As noted in Table 1, effective managers tend to display behaviors which are characteristic of the participative leadership style. Weak managers tend to display characteristics more associated with the autocratic leadership style. Further analysis is called for. The truly participative manager permits, indeed encourages, his subordinates to share decision-making with him. Table 2 is concerned with the amount of subordinate decision-making permitted by the managers.

Question 1: Decisions made in the unit.

Effective managers are perceived as sharing decision-making with their subordinates more than that permitted by the weak manager. Most weak managers make all decisions themselves. It is to be noted, however, that while the effective manager is more participative, he does not share all decision-making with his subordinates.

Question 2: Goal-setting.

The effective manager does not appear to be as reluctant to share goal-setting as he is to share decision-making. Nonetheless, goal-setting is not completely shared by all effective managers. They do tend, however, to seek information and ideas from their subordinates before establishing goals. It is in goal-setting that the average weak manager is the most autocratic. The average responses for the weak manager are lower for this question than for any item in either Tables 1 or 2.

Question 3: Concentration of review and control functions.

The effective manager generally limits the sharing of reviewing work and establishing controls. He does tend to delegate at least some of the functions. By comparison, the average weak manager tends to hold all such functions to himself with no delegation.

Table 2. Perceived Participation Permitted by Effective and Weak Managers

		By manager only	Mostly by manager, some by unit members	Fairly equally shared by manager with unit members
1. Decisions made in unit	N	W3.5	E5.9	
	C	W3.7	E5.5	
		By manager only	By manager after questions and comments by unit members	Mostly jointly by manager and total unit
2. Goal setting	N	W3.2	E6.5	
	C	W2.8	E6.6	
		Highly concentrated in the manager	Mainly with the manager, some delegated control	Shared equally by manager and unit members
3. Concentration of review and control functions	N	W3.6	E6.1	
	C	W3.4	E5.6	

N = Responses from selected managers in the national office
C = Responses from selected county managers in one state

E = Effective manager
W = Weak manager
Number of respondents: N = 38, C = 41

FINAL DECISIONS

Additional observations: All average responses for effective managers in Table 2 are lower than all average responses in Table 1. Even though these managers are more sharing and open with their subordinates, they have retained most of the final decision-making to themselves. It is important to note, however, that the weak managers tend even more to make all final decisions themselves.

Again, while not shown on the Table, the range of responses for both effective and weak managers is much greater for the questions in Table 2 than for those in Table 1. That is, some effective managers are perceived as being fairly autocratic even though most tend to be more participative. Also, there are some weak managers whom the respondents perceive to be tending toward participation even though the majority are highly autocratic.

SUMMARY

In general the federal manager is perceived as being more effective through:

1. Seeking ideas and knowledge from, and understanding the problems of, his subordinates, and utilizing this information in his decision-making process.
2. Sharing information with his subordinates.
3. Providing support to his subordinates.
4. Displaying trust and confidence to his subordiantes.
5. Using rewards and involvement as incentives for motivation rather than fear and threats; emphasizing corrective measures rather than punitive measures.

Effective managers, on the average, however, are not completely participative in decision-making, goal-setting, or in establishing of control. The explanation may be that complete participation is not appropriate in the governmental agency surveyed. Another explanation may be that even some of the more effective managers may not be aware of the potential available through even greater participation by their subordinates.

It is important to note that these managers, although employed in the same agency, are at different levels in the organization, are assigned different duties, and are separated in location by nearly a continent, have provided responses for which the means on almost all items are nearly identical. By their own experience and observation, they have identified *effective managers* as being relatively *participative* in their leadership style and *weak managers* as being relatively *autocratic.*

UNDERSTANDING AND USING MOTIVATION

Bernard L. Rosenbaum

A supplier has delivered the wrong merchandise for the second time. When the customer discovers it, he telephones the factory. "Who's running things there—the Marx Brothers?" he asks.

The customer, a busy executive, has successfully gotten across the fact that he is angry. Blowing off steam has relieved some of his tension, but he has failed completely to accomplish what his call was meant to do—improve operations. Why? Because he does not understand the basic principles of motivation that successful people-handlers use.

Industrial psychologists have identified at least five important principles of motivation. Many successful managers employ them instinctively; others may agree with them in theory but ignore them in practice. Still others, like the angry executive confronting his supplier, deal with people in ways that accomplish the opposite of what was desired. Mastering these five principles can help you be a more effective people-handler—whether the people be your superiors, subordinates, co-workers, friends, or relatives. Let's look at these five principles.

1. BUILDING SELF-ESTEEM

The first is based on the proven fact that the more confident people feel, the better they perform. If the angry executive understood this, he would have tried to maintain the self-esteem of the factory personnel by giving them confidence that they could satisfy him. Instead, his harshness probably made them feel defensive and think his demands unreasonable and unable to be met,

Reprinted by permission of the publisher from SUPERVISORY MANAGEMENT, January 1979, © 1979 by AMACOM, a division of American Management Associations. All rights reserved.

no matter how hard they might try. The executive's mistake was focusing on the two or three items in the order that were shipped in error. He should have focused instead on the 20 that were received as specified and then gone on to complain about the others.

Other examples of the positive approach: One of your field people is late with a report that you need for a meeting. Begin by commending the thoroughness of his reports, then subtly mention that it was late. Or one of your security officers has overstepped his authority. Recognize his diligence, then define the limits of his role.

Most people tend to fulfill the roles to which others assign them. If you expect the best from someone, and you let him know that you expect it, you have a better chance of getting it than you would otherwise. This principle is tested regularly and often yields dramatic results.

2. FOCUS ON THE PRINCIPLE

To illustrate the next principle, let's take another hypothetical case. One of your employees is absent repeatedly. You may be tempted to say, "You used to be interested in this job. Now you don't seem to care may more." But it is better if you focus on the problem rather than your assessment of the employee's attitude or personality. Tell him he has been out four times this month, and ask him if there are any job-related problems that you can help him with. You and he can then objectively discuss the problem.

What would have happened if you had followed your first instincts? Chances are the individual would have become defensive, and the discussion would have quickly deteriorated.

Another reason why attention should be focused on the problem and not on attitudinal or personality questions is that statements about the latter tend to be vague and are often misinterpreted. A vice-president for sales was conducting a performance appraisal with one of his regional sales managers. The vice-president told the regional manager that he must be more "aggressive," so the regional sales manager promptly hired two additional district managers. The vice-president had merely meant that his subordinate's sales goals were 8 percent less than he thought they should be. "Raise your sales goal by 8 percent" would have been far better communication than "be more aggressive."

3. REINFORCEMENT

The technique of reinforcement encourages desirable behavior and discourages undesirable behavior. It does this by conditioning the other party to expect a positive response to his desirable acts and a negative response or no response at all to his undesirable acts.

For example, when a salesperson's sales continually increase, he gets a raise, so he works even harder because he wants to elicit management's favorable response (giving him a raise) again. Or a more subtle example: a division manager who is constantly being criticized for spending by his superiors manages, by year's end, to stay within budget. Management responds by giving him a freer hand with spending. It has encouraged desired action with a positive response—this time by removing an unfavorable condition.

The most common form of reinforcement practiced is responding negatively to undesirable action—punishing the other party. Unfortunately, this is the least effective. The other party may become defensive, irrational, hostile, and prone to resume the behavior as soon as punishment stops. He may permanently adopt the desired behavior and use it at the wrong time to get even.

Rather than use punishment routinely, ask yourself if the other party will be adversely affected by a lack of reaction on your part. This is almost always the case if the other's action was intended to evoke a response from you. In such cases, taking no action may be the best response. For example, you might fail to return a phone call or acknowledge a request.

The technique of reinforcement is a powerful motivator and it is used with consummate skill by the great people-handlers in management, government, and other fields. Unfortunately, many managers pay too little attention to systematically responding so as to shape the behavior of others. Often they unthinkingly respond in a way that motivates others to do precisely what they do not want.

A chairman drones on endlessly wasting valuable time. The committee members are annoyed, but following tradition each one congratulates him when the meeting ends. The committee has followed an undesirable act with a positive response, encouraging the chairman to do the same at the next meeting.

A young employee comes in late on the day of a blizzard, and he explains to his supervisor that he had to dig his car out of the snow. He anticipates commendation, but his supervisor merely shakes his head at the lateness. The supervisor has given a negative response to desirable behavior. What will happen is that during the next snowstorm the employee will stay home.

A no-response would also have been wrong in that situation. Failure to praise good performance is management's most common mistake. Almost without exception, good performance that goes unnoticed deteriorates.

Here are some tips to help you motivate using reinforcement.

- Respond to both small and large instances of behavior. Begin with the first sign of desirable or undesirable behavior rather than wait for a trait to be repeated or become pronounced.

- Apply more reinforcement at the outset since it is harder to initiate a change in behavior than keep it going.
- Respond immediately following the other person's act. If you wait, your response may be confusing to that person.
- Make certain that your positive and negative responses are seen as such by the recipient. An employee was docked for three days due to an act he felt was justified. When the union representative had the docking reduced from three days to one day, the employee threatened to leave the union because he saw the docking as a reward for taking a stand on something he believed in.
- When it comes to supervising people, rarely is there too much positive reinforcement. Managers who encounter undesirable behavior should ask themselves when and in what way the desired behavior was last reinforced.
- In almost any supervisory setting, it is most effective to reward every improvement in performance until the desired performance level is achieved, then gradually—but not abruptly—reduce the reinforcement schedule, applying positive reinforcement intermittently.

4. ACTIVELY LISTEN

Here's an example of the fourth principle of motivation at work.

A plant manager slams his palm down on the conference table. "You give me impossible schedules, and you don't pay overtime. Am I supposed to work miracles?"

The vice-president for manufacturing nods sympathetically. "You feel we're asking too much. You're angry because we don't seem to recognize your problems or care about them," he says.

The vice-president is practicing active listening, feeding back the information he has been given and the feelings expressed. Active listening assures the other party that you understand him, and it is a necessary part of any exchange if you hope to motivate. It is especially valuable in emotional exchanges, defusing the situation because the other party can hardly argue with someone who seems sympathetic. Remember to convey both the content and the feelings the other person has expressed. However, do not include your own opinion at this point.

"This is the third price increase in two years," a jobber executive said to a manufacturer. "Our salespeople won't even display your merchandise. They'll promote items from the other divisions. At the rate we're going, we'll never match last year's sales."

The manufacturer replied, "You think our pricing isn't realistic, so your salespeople won't even try to sell our line. You're discouraged because you're afraid this might hurt your sales."

Satisfied that he was being heard, the jobber executive was open to the manufacturing executive's explanation about the price increase.

5. SET SOLID GOALS

The fifth and final principle of motivation is tied to maintaining open channels of communication. Say you've held a meeting to discuss plans for improving quality control. The meeting is over, but the process of motivation has only begun. Before you leave, make certain that you have an agreement. Set specific and clearly understood goals. Don't say, "Let's get together again in a couple of weeks." Instead, set a date for the follow-up meeting. Keep in touch, and keep analyzing and reviewing the problem.

The goals you set should be somewhat hard but achievable. Goals that are too simple or too difficult demotivate. Be wary of those who suggest goals that are too ambitious in an attempt to please. People with a history of failure usually tend to set unachievable goals.

Since people live up to their self-perceptions, your most important contribution will be building the other person's confidence that the goal can be met. Remember, nothing succeeds like success, and nothing fails like failure.

Many major corporations such as Exxon, Westinghouse, and Union Carbide are teaching managers to utilize effectively these motivational skills through a process known as behavior modeling. Specially constructed videotapes show the company's managers successfully using these motivational principles in a variety of managerial situations. Participants view the models, identify with the problems and situations since they are representative of those at their own company, rehearse the behaviors under the coaching of a trainer (usually a line manager), and transfer the skills back to the job. This training design has met with outstanding success in teaching these five key principles of motivation. If you haven't access to such programs, the task of developing these skills can be more difficult, but the results are well worth the effort. Once you've developed the skills needed to motivate people, you truly are on your way to becoming an effective manager. After all, managing is defined as getting things done through people.

MANAGEMENT IN THE NEW AGE: AN EXPLORATION OF CHANGING WORK VALUES

Marsha Sinetar

Nothing is worth having in this sphere unless it comes from the inside of you.

E. F. Schumacher

The management practices which characterized the '60s and '70s will not do for the 1980s. People have changed. They've changed too deeply, too significantly, over too large a cross-section of our country to ever again wholeheartedly accept the ground rules and attitudes by which management has been playing. In fact, even the best management techniques of earlier decades have done little more than lay a foundation for this emerging era. Furthermore, we've so swiftly entered what author Mark Satin calls a "New Age" that all but the most progressive organizations may have already felt their collective heads swimming when trying to figure out what to do to assuage labor's demands for better working conditions.

REVOLUTION CHANGE AND HEALING

What is this New Age? How has it come about, and how has it affected our organizational life? In his book, *New Age Politics,* Mark Satin describes the emergence of a new political system within all our socio-economic systems, one which brings about both radical change—and healing. A look at that radicalism shows us that it is:

"Management in the New Age: An Exploration of Changing Work Values," by Marsha Sinetar, copyright September 1980. Reprinted with the permission of *Personnel Journal,* Costa Mesa, California; all rights reserved.

... less interested in standing up for alternative ways of doing things than in standing up for appropriate ways of doing things ... a radicalism that understands that the real problem is not how to get people, groups and governments to agree on the "one best way" to do things, but how to get all the different ways, all the old political "isms" to agree to live and work synergically* together.... [I]t is a radicalism that asks: what are the specific ethics and political values that must be shared by everyone in order for everyone to survive, flourish, grow?[1]

[*Defined by Satin, "synergically means: so that people, groups and governments can get more done by cooperating together than they can by competing against one another."]

At this point, it would be useful to examine some of the specific values and ethics which are cropping up in this New Age and to pose a framework in which management can begin to work synergically with everyone in its organization. Let's start by tracing some of the more noticeable changes which have affected us in the last decade, and then use those tracings as a means of viewing the revised ethical constructs of the New Age, again with some help from *New Age Politics.*

Among other matters, Satin points out the newness which dominates so many areas of life today:

- **New Problems,** including nuclear threat, overpopulation and energy mismanagement (erroneously called "scarcity")
- **New Technologies,** such as those affecting transportation, communication, the military and science
- **New Consciousness** of individual and community rights, with more vocal minorities, a more involved citizenry (resulting in tax, legislative and consumer revolts), and an emphasis on individual growth and spiritual renewal.

In other words, we've made a radical break with the way things used to be and are searching—some of us desperately—for a more satisfying replacement. We are doing so in the midst of an "instant culture": instant foods; instant celebrities; instant cures; instant pleasures; instant creation; and instant obsolescence of not only consumer products, but language, ideas, behavior systems and even whole communities.

Appropriately enough, we are also growing more self-aware by leaps and bounds, aided by a looming "experiential" technology in the form of cults, drugs and mass tools for human development—spiritual and philosophical commercialism. Transience surrounds us, as is clear from our endangered institutions (e.g., marriage; the nuclear family; various urban, suburban and organizational life-styles) and our endangered resources (wildlife, energy, the human resource).

Novelty in life-styles, products, ideas and behavior is the New Age status quo. Its effects on living, breathing human beings are profound. In order to maintain equilibrium amidst all this change, we look inward, rearrange our priorities, and search—formally and informally—for answers in order to stabilize ourselves so that we do not fall out of balance with the world as it shifts. In the process, we grow more aware. Behaviors change: We become more cognizant of our "adaptive range" and learn to use it as a means of continually adjusting ourselves to changing life-styles.

This New Age has also resulted in an altered way of seeing the world, as well as an altered manner of behaving in it. Various ideas and movements over the last 10 years have literally transformed the way growing numbers of people perceive reality. These movements are important to business. Every activist group—whether feminist, antiwar, progay, human potential, ecological, black or Chicano—has helped redefine what is, and what is not, acceptable treatment of life on this planet. In their struggle for acceptance and dignity, these groups have radically altered our collective consciousness and widened the participation of people in their own destinies. This includes their working destinies.

WELLNESS, CONSCIOUSNESS

It may have been psychologist Abraham Maslow who most dramatically influenced the trend toward increased health when in the 1950s, he selected the self-actualizing personality as the object of his research. Subsequently, our attention began to focus on wellness, drifting away from the preoccupation with neurosis. Growth was explained as a natural thing. We learned about unused potential, about how smoothly a healthy being could sail through life, and many of us wanted to be like that healthy, self-actualized person we were reading about. Our concept of our own potential expanded, and self-development became a new goal for many Americans as they began to question the materialistic, outward-directed goals of earlier years and looked instead toward their inner needs.

When a variety of behavioral sciences, philosophies and practices became available, promising to unlock that plethora of talent which Maslow had been writing about, countless individuals took advantage of them, gradually revising themselves and their ways of looking at life. From the hippies, from Eastern gurus, from behaviorists came various ideas and systems which filtered into our traditional value structures. A new language developed, marked by phrases such as "human potential," "consciousness raising," "self-esteem," "alternative life-styles," "job enrichment," "career pathing," "strength assessment" and "human resources." These eventually became more than cocktail party buzz words and even infiltrated the agendas of organizational-planning sessions. Although not yet universally accepted, this new vocabulary has initiated the ground rules for managerial activity in the New Age.

THE DAILY QUALITY OF LIFE

The New Age is one in which we have become more aware of change and, in our examination of those changes, more concerned about the quality of life, again including working life.

There was a time when the quality of life was not a subject to be considered in our daily activities. We simply did what we had to do: smoked as much, drank as much, and worried as much as needed in order to do the "necessary" things. We lived up to the cultural definitions of our roles. We "fit in."

However, it is unlikely that human beings in the New Age will continue to accept fitting in as a satisfactory way to spend their lives. With our growth of awareness has come a general desire for a more satisfying level of experience. There was a day when we performed, and accepted, any objective set for us by family or organization or country: men went to work and to war, women stayed at home, minority groups knew their place. The young did as they were told, and the elderly, not wanting to inconvenience anyone, obediently went off to rest homes. People did not easily question the way it was supposed to be, the way it had always been. While some of us still go along with that attitude, larger numbers are questioning more institutions more often.

There now appear to exist both an examination and an attempt at integration of life—an audible, grass-roots voice. This voice is telling business, schools, government agencies, the armed forces, prisons and even churches that they must respond in new ways when problems arise. The people who work for and are served by these institutions have changed. They want different things from their organizations.

Humans today want more than to survive: they want to flourish. They want their institutions, their governments and their work places to be responsive to this need, to assist them in their flourishing, to assist them in becoming whole.

THE NEW AGE AND MANAGEMENT

So this New Age has affected people in two basic ways: we are questioning the basics of our lives, and in doing so, we are gaining a larger sense of ourselves.

The interplay of these two characteristics is now making increasingly strong demands on organizations. Management is expected (and in some cases, even expects itself) to have a different, more democratic relationship with labor. We in management are beginning to realize how effectively we've cut ourselves off from various sources of personal satisfaction at work—all by failing to establish a network of cooperative communication and mutual support with our colleagues and employees.

This network personifies an emerging value system whose components deserve closer examination here.

Increased Communication Needs: It is astounding that with all the talk of communication inprovement, so few exemplary programs come to our attention. Communication is vital to the success of any work group, since its main values are the improvement of management-employee relationships and enhanced productivity. A smooth, two-way information flow is essential to effective human functioning. Yet even in organizations which experience high turnover, job transfers and changes in work groups, the evaluation of communication effectiveness is often either a neglected issue, or one that is left to internal departments lacking both technical knowledge and objectivity about this exploding field of human behavior.

As organizations develop a New Age mentality, the concept of wholeness will become more important. With a growing awareness gained from physics about how significantly various parts of a system affect the whole, management will find it increasingly desirable to have a sense of relatedness to all the various parts of the organization.

Relatedness does not come about by handing down edicts from some top perch to some lower rung. New Age management, rather than seeing communication programs as a waste of time, will increasingly view interactive, effective communications as an opportunity to assemble the bits and pieces of organizational diversity into a more strongly solidified whole.

A New Age premise is that truth is kaleidoscopic. People see things from their own point of view; they are not necessarily "wrong." Vertical communication groups will thus become "situations" in which we will each be able to hear one another and our respective points of view. While in the past, there seems to have been a lot of energy taken up with the notion of two camps (i.e., management and labor), perhaps now each will be able to see things with an awareness of the other's needs and convictions.

The Need for Satisfying Work: In the New Age, both management and those managed will find they have an increasing need to experience work as something that is satisfying on a deep and intrinsic level.

A recent article on the Bolivar quality of work life experiment reveals that the project's principal goal was not to increase productivity, but rather to make work more satisfying.[2] The Bolivar experiment was a cooperative organizational change effort between an automotive manufacturer and the United Automobile Workers. The very design of the project acknowledged workers' need not only to participate in the cooperative design of their working environment, but also to earn a fulfilling livelihood. The project authenticated the idea that quality of working life and organizational effectiveness are two sides of a single coin.

It is important that management appreciate the ideological framework of the New Age as it addresses itself to this issue. Perhaps no writer more sensitively describes the intrinsic satisfaction of working at what one enjoys than Michael Phillips:

Right livelihood is something I learned from Dick Baker, a Zen Buddhist Roshi. . . . Please don't take me too literally—this is not a typical *Cosmopolitan* questionnaire to measure something like whether you're gay or straight sexually. It is simply a way to give you a perspective on what right livelihood is. First, do you think you can undertake your work for a long time? Right livelihood could be spending a whole life as a carpenter, for one of the qualities of right livelihood is that within it, within the practice of it, is the perfection of skills and qualities that will give you a view of the whole world, in a sense similar to Hemingway's story of *The Old Man and the Sea.* . . . Aging works for you in right livelihood. It's like a good pipe, or a fine violin; the more you use it the deeper its finish.[3]

This may not really be too foreign to someone sitting impatiently behind a desk, wondering when it will be time to go home, puzzling over the fact that time goes so much more quickly when one is engaged in pursuits that are inner-directed. Richard Bach says it well, "The more I want to get something done, the less I call it work."

Certainly, we find ourselves entering an age where salary and fringe benefits do not seem rewarding enough to growing numbers of workers. They just will not "stay put" when other elements of their work are unsatisfying or constricting. It used to be that when an organization hired a person, it simply set out its performance expectations and then acknowledged that employee on one of two occasions: when expectations were exceeded and when they were not. But in the New Age, the shoe will be on the other foot. Organizations are likely to come under employee scrutiny (either openly or covertly), and when management comes up short, turnover will increase, and grievances or inertia will sap and corrupt productivity. During the next 5 years, it is estimated that 350 out of every 1,000 people employed will change jobs, despite management's efforts to make working life more financially rewarding. People are simply demanding more today from all aspects of life, and working life is no exception.

A bank vice president complained to me while I was doing research for this article that the bank's turnover rate was higher than it had ever been. When I inquired if they'd looked at the cause, I was told that there wasn't money enough to do that (despite the fact that it takes two people to do the job of one person who has been on the job for a long time and so developed a sense of loyalty and an understanding of what makes the organization tick).

A more specific example: A personal friend, once head of marketing for one of the largest California banks, recently resigned to become a private consultant. He confided that there was no job which had any meaning for him at the bank—this, in spite of the fact that he was well paid and had plenty of authority and status. Organizations who are experiencing higher turnover at any level would be well advised to survey who is leaving and their characteristics. In the New Age, it will no doubt turn out to be the more self-sufficient, creative individuals who sever ties with a secure weekly paycheck. It is this talent loss which will prove to be most costly in the long run to organizations who fail to meet their workers' human needs. Job enrichment will thus surely turn out to be an active ingredient in managerial planning, with objectives such as increased worker productivity hinged to such goals as increased job satisfaction; improved supervisory-subordinate relationships; better communication; and a creative, perhaps individualized, redesign of working methods and schedules.

The Demands of the New Work Ethic: Management will also want to acknowledge and deal with an entire cluster of values which Albert Dunn has termed "the new work ethic." All levels of organization may soon be questioning how well they accept employees and peers whose values conflict with traditional working ground roles.

In a recent *Harvard Business Review* article, Dunn vividly describes a case study of this clash of two generational value systems, the old and the new, and calls it the "management problem of our time."[4] I happen to think the management problem of our time is on a somewhat deeper level, but would agree that as new work ethics come into conflict with traditional viewpoints, lowered morale, poor performance, lower productivity and disloyalty can result.

Broadly described, the new work ethic is one in which an employee becomes more inner-directed about all aspects of work. Such things as work schedules, budgets, priority setting and standards of personal conduct are all screened through an inner filter of what one wants and does not want to do. In line with the whole surge of awareness that characterizes the New Age, employees are taking the position of "the company doesn't own you," and are quite willing to take responsibility for the outcomes of their actions. A certain sense of social responsibility comes into play here, whether it's an individual taking full responsibility for his or her choices, or an employee group examining company policies prior to accepting any as "law." This attitude is a far cry from the traditional view, which was externally directed, materialistic and almost passively obedient to objectives set by the organization.[5]

Mark Satin quotes New Age economist E. F. Schumacher in this regard:

> I believe that it is everyone's personal task to try and demonstrate in some way, by word or deed, what [he or she] considers to be true, adequate, right, etc., and not look over his shoulder whether people follow [his or her] example or believe what [he or she] says. . . . It is not so easy to maintain this sturdy attitude. In India, they call it "karma yoga"; you just do what you consider right and you don't bother your head with whether you are successful or not, because if you don't do what you consider is right, you're wasting your life.[6]

The Meaning of Interrelationship: We are moving toward a "you and me" world view, away from the "you or me" perception of things which so dominated our earlier behavior. "You and me" has these significant features:

1) **It is a contextual shift** from "What do I need to do to survive?" to "What do I need to do to make my life work for me and the people around me?" The latter question is grounded in the belief that people are interrelated, that what happens to one person ultimately happens to all people.

2) **"You and me" is a perspective** that asks each of us to look at how we can make a contribution to the lives of others, rather than examining how we can exploit others to get status or power. It is a perspective that gives potency to life, and is an important part of the value system of the New Age.

We do, in fact, seem to be moving nearer a behavioral mode that is based more on cooperation than competition. This is a radical new understanding of the interrelationship of life and may take some time to filter into organizational planning, but its influence is unmistakable.

Barbara Ward describes not only the world's economic interconnectedness, but also how the "have nots" may agitate the rest of us into paying attention to them, into giving them a larger share of industry and more favorable access to developed markets.[7] She also gives us a framework by which we can see that those "have nots" within our own organizations (those who are not given communication access to management; those who are unacknowledged for their work, problems, successes or needs) are also in a position to sabotage the plans and goals of those in power. One group which has helped bring this issue to our attention is the secretaries and clerical workers. Although the professional literature is just starting to acknowledge the developmental needs of office and secretarial personnel, a recent article in the Los Angeles *Times* expresses the "have not" situation of this *key* working group quite well. Columnist Letitia Baldrige reports:

> The executive secretary—that person who is secretary to the chairman of the board, the president, vice chairman or the important vice presidents of the company—is incredibly important to the success and happiness of the executive he or she serves, as well as to the image of the company in the outside world, and to the overall success and profitability of the organization.
>
> These are skilled executives themselves, although sometimes their paychecks and their perks do not reflect that. . . .
>
> . . . They objected to being referred to as "my boss' right hand." One woman remarked, "To me this is the equivalent of saying 'my maid' or 'My cook'—domestic, rather than professional status."
>
> . . . I feel personally that top management secretaries should eat in the executive dining rooms and be accorded the same perks junior management receives. Many of them are on an upward track within the organization, and all the talented ones are invaluable to the work of the company and its successful image.

I know a few executive secretaries who are brighter than their bosses. Don't you?[8]

Although recent world events have brought this "you and me" idea home in a hurry, the interrelatedness of organizational life was pointed out by Douglas McGregor as early as 1960, in *The Human Side of Enterprise:*

> In considering the psychological environment of people at work, one thinks first of the relationship between superior and subordinate. This relationship has been the subject of intensive research for several decades, and a good deal is known about it today.... A central characteristic of this relationship is the interdependence of the parties. Since each of the parties in an interdependent relationship affects to some degree the other's ability to achieve his goals or satisfy his needs, major difficulties are likely to arise unless both have positive expectations that the relationship will further these purposes.[9]

McGregor also points out that while conventional organizations give recognition to the dependence upward, they fail to recognize the significance of interdependence (even of dependence) downward. New Age management will acknowledge such interdependence and will make management-labor interrelatedness a part of official organizational policy. This process hinges on power—an element of management we have been loathe to share. We are all too slow to learn that shared or delegated power is one way of strengthening group responsibility, commitment and enthusiasm for work. New Age management may find that by "giving away" its power, it gains more: more loyalty, more employee energy and better focus on tasks at hand.

SELF-ESTEEM AND SELF-ACTUALIZATION

The values described above are those of wholeness and integration. Two key employee needs in the New Age are a part of this value construct, and are also related to Maslow's hierarchy of needs: need for the esteem of others and need for self-actualization.

The first of these emerges as a continual demand within an organization by all personnel for improved communication systems, for more effective "talking-it-over" skills, for a vehicle through which workers can be heard by management. This need now begins to show itself among secretarial pools, factory workers, bus drivers and garbage collectors. People simply want to be appreciated. They want more dignity, more say in what happens, clearer communications when things aren't going well and even when they are.

It appears that legislation will support this need. Recent articles on arbitration trends point out that management now finds it profitable to work within the labor contract, and that legally they may be found negligent when employer-employee communications have been unclear. Previous warnings for an

Management in the New Age			
Traditional Work Values		**New Age Work Values**	
Basic Needs:	Management Practices/Attitudes	Basic Needs:	Management Practices/Attitudes
Security, approval of others, control, status, power, and "agreement" with external world.		Self-esteem, relatedness to others, self-definition, self-actualization, personal power, utilization of own talents, directives, responsibility	

	Egocentric Frame of Reference	Object Orientation	Synergic Frame of Reference	Human Orientation
Motivating Questions	"Whom do I need to impress?" "What's in it for me?" "Who's in charge?" "What do I need to do to make it?"	Worker and self as an object, a number, a means toward an end. Impersonal quality between levels of organization. Communication: one-way, downward. Attitude of: "They're dependent on me (us)," "I'm responsible for everything around here." Fragmented awareness: departments, functions, policies considered in isolation.	"How can we get all the diverse elements here to contribute to things working out as much as possible for everyone?" "What can I contribute?" "In what ways is this activity useful?" "What is the communication format that will allow things to work?"	Worker and self as a human being, respect for others' individuality. Sense of relatedness between all levels of organization. Communication: two-way. Attitude of mutual trust, mutual respect, mutual cooperation.

	Work as a Source of Power, Safety, Status	Power Orientation	Work as a Path to Self-Fulfillment	Holistic Orientation
Motivating Questions	"How safe is it to do this, to think, to act this way?" "What will people say . . . ?" "What does the boss want me to do?" "How can I get 'mine' out of this?" "Who makes decisions around here?"	Accumulation of material symbols to represent satisfaction. Policies and work problems linked to "survival." Relinquishing power, authority, linked to loss of safety.	"How does ths work contribute value and satisfaction to my life?" "What is the quality of well-being I get from being around here?" "What is the quality of work life, and how does it affect me?" "Which of my talents am I using?"	Health seen as a function of participation with others. Development of the individual will promote the development of organization. Cooperative decision-making programs.

offense must be made clearly and specifically. Company rules should also be clear, reasonable and carefully communicated to the employee. In another effort to improve trust and communication, one of my more enlightened corporate clients has just revised their performance appraisal system, so that subordinate sits with superior during the yearly appraisal and has an opportunity to voice agreement, raise questions or disagree.

The raised level of satisfaction which management experiences when communication systems work goes without saying. What is worth stressing is how managers themselves gain in awareness, in job satisfaction, in knowledge of the full spectrum of human concerns when they take the time to sit down and talk things over. When working conditions are impersonal, computerized and bureaucratically cut-and-dried, dissatisfaction clearly mounts, and with it, managerial anxiety. In an interrelated world, when one group is unhappy, all groups suffer.

Enhanced communication systems and democratic practices are essential to meet the human needs of this New Age. However, the most important of these needs is more personal and highly complex: this second basic employee concern manifests itself as a desire within each person, blue and white-collar worker alike, to be true to his or her own nature. It means working at tasks that come from some inner portion of the self, working at one's own pace, and being more of what one really is. How management deals with this need for self-actualization, is, as I see it, *the* central management issue of the 1980s. How we address this human requirement will ensure organizational health or disease, and it is to this issue that enlightened management must turn its attention in the new decade.

The drive to self-actualize is present in all human beings who have passed through other stages of development. Although this desire expresses itself in many different, unique ways, as Toffler points out, it can be heard simply as a plea for more knowledge, for a fuller intellectual experience of one's life. Toffler describes an old, white-haired man who attended a class of his on the sociology of the future. Most of the class participants were corporate executives, staff members from planning institutes, and research center heads. In "cracked yet eloquent English," the elderly man told the group why he had attended the seminar:

> My name is Charles Stein. I am a needles worker all my life. I am seventy-seven years old, and I want to get what I didn't get in my youth. I want to know about the future. I want to die an educated man.[10]

Each of our organizations is full of men and women like Charles Stein. Each of us wants to know more and be more. We want to use up our lives in tasks that have meaning for us. If the tasks at which we work are dull and meaningless, we at least want to be treated as living beings. In the past, organizations have seldom been sympathetic to this issue, but in the New Age, more and more people, managers and workers alike, will openly express their conviction that work can provide great intrinsic rewards.

This conviction may be misinterpreted as job dissatisfaction, perhaps as negativism. Certainly, there is no clear-cut formula for identifying and dealing with this most personal need of the New Age. It is evident, however that management must become more aware of our era's changing values and, having become more aware, must do more to meet the expanding needs of the human resource.

REFERENCES

1. Mark Satin, *New Age Politics* (New York: Delta Publishing Company, 1979), p. 9.
2. Barry A. Macy, "A Progress Report on the Bolivar Quality of Work Life Project," *Personnel Journal,* Vol. 58, No. 8(August 1979): 527–530, 557–559.
3. Michael Phillips, *Seven Laws of Money* (Menlo Park: Word Wheel/Random House, 1974), pp. 8–9.
4. Albert Dunn, "The Case of the Suspect Salesman," *Harvard Business Review,* Vol. 57, No. 6 (June 1979): 38.
5. For a keen description of the traditional work ethic, see William Whyte, Jr., *The Organization Man* (New York: Simon & Schuster, 1956).
6. Satin, *New Age Politics,* p. 232.
7. Barbara Ward, "Progress for a Small Planet," *Harvard Business Review,* Vol. 57, No. 5 (May 1979): 89.
8. Letitia Baldrige, "Executive Secretaries Sound Off," Los Angeles *Times,* December 21, 1979, p. 33.
9. Douglas McGregor, *The Human Side of Enterprise* (New York: McGraw-Hill Book Company, 1960), p. 133.
10. Alvin Toffler, *Future Shock* (New York: Random House, 1970), p. 427.

NEW TREND: NICE GUYS FINISH FIRST

Jim Bruno and Paula Lippin

Successful managers do not 'look out for number one.' Instead, they align their subordinates' needs with organizational goals, a critical factor in motivation.

UP THE CORPORATE LADDER—the great American dream—is achieved through successful management. Quite simply, a successful manager is one who 'gets the job done.' How he goes about accomplishing this will determine his degree of success.

Most managers reach their position by being good at their job. Yet, most employees who aspire to managerial responsibilities are not prepared to make the transition from staff to management. It is difficult to accept that a manager's prime responsibility is to motivate and develop subordinate personnel, who make up the great majority of the workforce, instead of digging in and doing it 'himself.'

The question is, what makes a good manager? What are his innate qualities and how can certain techniques be utilized to make him an achieving manager?

Despite the commonly accepted image that the climb to the top of the corporate ladder is usually accomplished by the ruthless disregard of others, studies have found that the high-achieving manager tends to welcome the input of subordinates and to be concerned over whether they are being personally fulfilled in their jobs. In short, achieving managers are 'nice guys.' This statement is in direct conflict with the widely held belief that 'nice guys finish last.'

Republished with permission from *Administrative Management* (June 1979), copyright © 1979 by Geyer-McAllister Publications, Inc. New York.

According to the findings of an extensive study by Teleometrics International, a Texas-based firm specializing in applying behavioral science to organizational dynamics, success in management begins with an understanding of Maslow's concept of the five levels of human needs which are motivational forces: basic creature comfort, safety, social, ego-status, and self-actualization. In order to achieve the first three levels, an employee strives to *avoid* dissatisfaction. The last two levels, ego-status and self-actualization, are the prime motivating factors that lead an employee to seek satisfaction. The need for self-actualization is the dominant motivational influence for high achievers, while average achievers are mostly driven by ego-status needs.

It is generally accepted that motivation is something the person brings with him to the organization, that managers cannot really instill motivation into their employees. The best a manager can hope for is to accurately identify the incentives under his control which coincide with his subordinates needs. However, the manager's view of motivation—of what is important to his subordinates and of what is possible in the way of satisfaction within the organization—is a critical component of the motivational process. It is essential for the manager to identify his employee's capabilities and needs and to try to structure the job around the employee's strengths and interests whenever possible.

In reality, the manager's personal theory of motivation becomes a powerful force in the workplace, shaping and facilitating subordinates' expression of some needs and blocking or denying that of others. High achievers place major emphasis on actualization and result in creating a climate that causes their subordinates to strive on the same level. In other words, high-achieving managers create high-achieving subordinates.

"There is a similarity between a manager's personal motivation and his feelings about what motivates others," noted Jay Hall, president of Teleometrics International. "The research results indicated that high-achieving managers are concerned with those aspects of the job that provide a sense of personal fulfillment. They tend not only to talk about these things with their subordinates but attempt to structure the work situation so that subordinates can get personally involved and find the same kinds of fulfillment as the high-achieving managers."

Participative management is a viable and feasible technique for organizational effectiveness and can be directly linked to individual career accomplishment and managerial achievement. It is founded on the belief that people directly affected by a decision should participate in making that decision. The emphasis is on joint decision-making about events which have future implications for the parties involved, and over which they can realistically exert a degree of influence.

This technique was originally embraced as a mechanism for countering the unilateral decision structure and authoritarian values often found in traditional organizational theory. Participation positively affects loyalty and creativity. It is now found that it distinguishes between those who achieve managerially and those who do not. According to the Teleometrics survey, it has been found that the amount of participation is directly correlated to the personal responsibility, commitment, and pride of authorship. Its effectiveness varies with the amount of mutual confidence found in the manager-subordinate relationship. Participatory management will only be effective and successful when employees and managers are trusting and open, and problems can be approached in a spirit of joint inquiry, resulting in a consensus being worked out.

Interpersonal competence plays a vital role in the successful use of participative methods. The following have been put forth as the outcomes of interpersonal competence:

- Greater awareness of relevant problems among parties to the problem-solving relationship.
- Increased problem-solving accuracy in that problems remain solved.
- Decreased likelihood for the problem-solving process to be negatively affected in any way.

In order to assist a group of people in getting the job done, you must be aware of the problems they may encounter and, if possible, pave the way for them by opening doors and soliciting cooperation from other people or departments. By being aware, you can eliminate roadblocks to the problem-solving process and also increase the accuracy of the solution.

A manager can achieve interpersonal competence through such behaviors as *owning up* to or accepting responsibility for his ideas and feelings, *being open* to his own thoughts and those of others, and *experimenting* with new ideas and helping others to own up, be open, and experiment with their concepts and attitudes. The interpersonal competence of one's subordinates is a direct reflection of the manager's achievement. A collaborative and participative managerial style typifies high achievers.

From a motivational standpoint, the achieving manager needs to find meaning in his work and strives to afford such meaning to others. His technique is to employ an integrative style of management. In this style, people are valued just as highly as accomplishment of production goals. The atmosphere would be one where candor, openness, sensitivity, and receptivity make-up the rule in interpersonal relationships, rather than its exception, and participative practices are favored over unilateral directive or lame-duck prescriptive measures.

To achieve, one must employ the practices mentioned and eschew self-serving defensive, self-authorized techniques. The manager must acknowledge that his subordinates possess interest and expertise. He must then create openings for their expression, incorporating them into the work flow. He must be receptive to innovation, sensitive to the dynamics of relating, and willing to take risks. And finally, ever conscious of his role as norm setter, the manager who would achieve must look to his subordinates for his reflection—truly achieving managers produce achievers.

Unfortunately, just as high-achieving managers breed high-achieving subordinates, low and moderate achievers "create subordinates in their own image," according to Hall. "Low achievers tend to avoid meaningful communication as much as possible. Instead of listening for new ideas, they quote policy and the procedure manual." Quite often their only major contribution to communications with subordinates are "reasons why something cannot be done."

Moderate achievers, on the other hand, usually listen closely only to superiors. In their dealings with subordinates they are preoccupied with their own ideas, and tend to think that showing interest in a subordinate's idea is a sign of weakness.

Although the expression 'looking out for number one' has carried a negative connotation, it can also be applied in a positive manner. A manager can accomplish this by providing his subordinates with the atmosphere that will foster achievement thereby 'getting the job done.' When the job gets done well, the manager has taken care of number one. It gives him the opportunity to move up and ahead, taking on new challenges and responsibilities. In the process, his work is delegated to his subordinates, thereby allowing them the same growth.

In actuality, by developing his staff the achieving manager is developing his potential replacement. Although this may be threatening to some, if handled properly, the manager himself grows en route, opening up new horizons and broadening his job responsibilities in the process.

And he can still be a nice guy.

EXIT THE ORGANIZATION MAN: ENTER THE PROFESSIONAL PERSON

Robert Stephen Silverman and D. A. Heming

During the fabulous fifties, William H. Whyte, Jr. captured the profile of a working person and turned it into a best seller: *The Organization Man.* According to Whyte, a body would leave home—spiritually as well as physically —and sell his mind and soul to the organization. Today, enlightened organizations relegate the Organization Man as an anachronism—a thing of the past. No longer do most working people feel a sense of dedication and belonging to any one organization. Why should they? Exit the Organization Man; enter the Professional Person—the best prepared man or woman any society ever produced.

The Professional Person has a much higher level of needs, values, awareness, consciousness and sensitivity than the Organization Man. Unlike the Organization Man, he belongs chiefly to himself: an individual motivated by competency and personal growth. His loyalty and commitment belong first, to his profession; and second, to the organization for which he may be working, at any particular time. He feels uncommitted to any one organization but willing to deploy his individualism, knowledge and creative abilities to solve problems with resources provided by the organization. Committed to self-actualization, but with the full expectation it will mesh successfully with required organizational roles. The Professional Person appears willing to take risks in asserting his individualism even in large organizations. He looks upon himself as an individual marketing three interrelated products: his knowledge, his skills and his competencies.

"Exit the Organization Man: Enter the Professional Person," by Robert Stephen Silverman and D. A. Heming, Copyright March, 1975. Reprinted with the permission of *Personnel Journal,* Costa Mesa, California; all rights reserved.

Conflict exists in many present organizations between the leadership needs of the Professional Person and the traditional leadership behavior of organizational bureaucrats, who seem to thrive on the decline of innovation and creativity. Traditionally, bureaucratic leaders cannot tolerate risk-taking because their value systems normally revolve around the preservation of the status quo. The traditional principles of management involve organizing, planning and controlling to preserve the status quo. Human relations, to many bureaucrats, have relevance only because they ensure the proliferation of the status quo, at the expense of individuality, if necessary.

THE NEW CONSCIOUSNESS

The Professional Person has a give and take attitude in relation to organizations and, therefore expects something from it. Once this restructuring of self-consciousness has occurred, a gap opens up between The Professional Person and those who have not changed. When the restructured consciousness of The Professional Person encounters the traditional status quo manager, an Organization Generation Gap results.

Without recognizing the realities of the organizational problems surrounding them, the older generation manager has had to fumble with solutions based on outdated organizational principles. The older generation manager interprets the behavior of The Professional Person in terms of his own frame of reference. The Professional Person represents the vanguard of the new consciousness in organizations, but he finds himself in social structures unwilling or unable to reshape and renew themselves.

As expectation levels and need patterns change, upper management levels respond accordingly. When upper management fails to respond, organizational rigidity and stagnation, coupled with an increasing level of frustration, isolation, and alienation, sets in. The Professional Person encounters isolation and alienation from administrative and control mechanisms inherent in bureauracies, such as the federal public service. Within bureaucracies, interrelationships, have lost much of their direct, honest and human quality and have instead assumed a rather plastic character saturated by the spirit of indifference. Relationships between men then assume the character of relationships between things. Before upper management levels can respond positively to the concerns and philosophies of The Professional Person the new need patterns and value systems of these individuals will have to be discerned.

THE EMERGING NEW NEED PATTERNS AND VALUE SYSTEMS

The Professional Person assumes responsibility for making his job a constructive vehicle for innovative and creative self-expression. He fulfills himself not only by contributing to his particular organization, but also to the larger world around him. Wanting to contribute his skills and talents to society in general, he brings with him the capacity for developing a learning continuum. He sees education as a life-long process. A practitioner and student simultaneously, he realizes that new knowledge constantly makes previous knowledge obsolete.

The Professional Person won't allow the galloping bureaucratic system to change him from a committed, idealistic individual into another member of the apathetic herd. No educational cripple, he won't sink into intellectual apathy due to lack of challenge and incentive. He traces much of the intellectual sterility and apathy that is evident today in organizations to managements handing down objectives and decisions to individuals in lieu of first hand experience. Meaningful, productive and challenging work, together with recognized achievment, motivates the Professional Person. But to accomplish the output requirements of his position, he requires performance-oriented, dynamic organizations rather than authority-oriented, bureaucratic organizations—organizations with definite centers of accountability, managed by objectives rather than bosses.

The Professional Person needs achievement, recognition and responsibility; a widening range of responsibilities and a broadening control over these responsibilities. He needs to operate in his own way without interference, bringing only exceptional situations to the attention of his superior. In this way, he feels important, needed and trusted to do his best. This style of management permits him to utilize, in a synergistic fashion, his experience and total knowledge.

The Professional Person needs the tangible participation in the organization, achieved by creating decentralized organizational units, in order to manage within the control of the overall organization or by establishing task team, temporary work assignments and other ad hoc groups. Fast moving, dynamic thinking proves alien to some present day federal public service managers, who find it difficult to share authority, responsibility and accountability. The Professional Person will eventually alter traditional organization structures drastically by the temporary task team approach which cuts radically across functional divisional and departmental lines. Most federal public service managers process an academic understanding of the participation ideology, but mistake human relations for participation. To the Professional Person, good human relations exist when management treats each individual as a unique entity and when the organization does everything possible to create conditions in which each individual can use his capabilities to the fullest.

The supervisor only can give a worker self-respect, and no one else can deprive him of it as easily. Without self-respect, employment in large organizations: i.e., the federal public service, will become an increasingly empty and unrewarding experience; regardless of fringe benefits. And without self-respect, work gradually deteriorates from an opportunity to discover one's own potentialities into a breeding ground for frustration, conflict, grievances and appeals. When management promises more than it can deliver, the conflict in approaches to participation and human relations precipitates an expensive loss of talent. In large organizations such as the federal public service the very people able to contribute to the broad social aspects of bureaucracy will leave in quest of self-actualization.

The Professional Person doesn't seek to dictate organizational policy, but merely to contribute to the decision making and policy formulation processes. He believes that, as a member of the organization, he should have some voice in making decisions that affect him and the results of his labor. He seeks to serve as catalyst, in emphasing that organizations should not wait until problems become major crises before introducing change. Trapped in an ineffectual bureaucracy, the Professional Person views himself an inert component of a group, not a participant in any significant way—simply carried along with the crowd.

The Professional Person believes that all organization members should have the opportunity to participate in the formulation and execution of plans, policies and objectives. He thinks that traditional management should cast aside any preconceptions about employee-employer relations and introduce a viable system of communication and participation that will allow him to contribute his knowledge and expertise to solving organizational problems.

MANAGEMENT BY CREATIVE OBJECTIVES

Traditionally, federal public service management styles have emphasized decision making at the highest level, and then implemented the decisions by working through other people. The Professional Person needs a new style of management and leadership because he reacts to creative ideas rather than to ideologies, precedents, policies and orders. Some Bureaucrats argue that the Professional Person has little, if any, respect for authority. Quite the contrary, he does respect authority, the type of authority earned through competence, performance and leadership ability, rather than merely position. Competent leadership, stressing performance and creative organizational objective formulation, coincides with the philosophy of The Professional Person. Under effective management, the leader stimulates the group to high levels of performance by instilling a sense of competency motivation. The Professional Person accepts responsibility and the accountability for its risks and results.

The recent trend in the federal public service towards Management of Objectives illustrates the growing pressures from both inside and outside government organizations for more creative management. Unfortunately, too many public service managers attempt to integrate Management by Objectives into management systems presently in use, rather than implement it as a completely new way of managing. Today, no federal public service manager has any real chance of maintaining a level of credibility with his subordinates, peers and perhaps his superiors, unless organizational objectives tune in to the needs, abilities, values and personal aspirations of the achievers of these objectives. By failing to include appropriate objectives within the ambition and capability of a manager's staff, the organization risks losing capable and ambitious people.

By working under a system that forces leaders and followers to work together on the establishment of individual and organization objectives, the intellectual atmosphere needed for situational sensitivity is provided. When intellectual sterility sets in, due to objectives imposed by a rigid bureaucratic approach, the most productive and creative people will leave. If they don't actually leave, one can expect continuous conflict. The Professional Person needs an environment in which he can identify his effectiveness areas and standards. There, he can attain a realistic sense of involvement and participation in the establishment of creative objectives. Management by Creative Objectives requires openness, trust, a sharing of responsibility; it allows the individual to function as a whole person within the organizational context.

INDIVIDUALISM

The Professional Person, by seeking participation and creative objectives, finds personal expression within his organization. He chooses to act as himself, not as the organization would prefer him to act.

Most modern bureaucracies do not foster or reward people for unorthodox or individualistic behavior. The Professional Person, however, demands relevance, responsibility and individualism in his job. The intellectual and awareness gap which exists between younger and older subordinates and managers, will continue as each new generation experiences a technologically, intellectually and emotionally different world. The problem is to find acceptable means of reaching mutually acceptable organizational and individual objectives. The Professional Person will respond positively to managers, who have an informal managerial style and a direct honest approach that recognizes him as an individual and equal—even though less experienced person. Ideally, organizations should create atmospheres in which the experience of the older generation meshes with the knowledge and enthusiastic individualism of the younger generation. When the organization does not run smoothly, the status quo manager traces a failure in communication. In many cases, however, the message has reached the Professional Person clearly, but has been found unacceptable. When an organization becomes too tightly integrated and preempts all available resources and methods with policies and procedures, then it fails to provide a margin of spontaneity and individuality that makes growth possible for the Professional Person. Stifling formality drives the Professional Person from the organization due to apathy, lack of incentive and withdrawal of commitment.

Justification for too many organizational formalities is found only in their continued use. Silence and conformity provide the illusion of tranquility. Loss of inner self, on one hand, and outer conformity on the other create a lulling and discontinuous organizational atmosphere, in which mediocrity flourishes and individual initiative evaporates. The Professional Person has launched a quiet revolution to gradually change the face of organizations. When armed with situational sensitivity, management skills and style flexibility, the Professional Person fulfills the measurable, time-bound output requirement of his position without relinquishing his personality. And that has made all the difference.

THE PUBLIC EXECUTIVE: A SENSE OF RESPONSIBILITY FOR THE WHOLE

Harlan Cleveland

Of all the professions that profess to "get it all together," you who manage our urban life are the most self-consciously professional. A profession is marked partly by specialized skills, but mostly by general attitudes. Some years ago, at a smaller ICMA convention, I listed four attitudes as indispensable to the management of complexity. I think they are still indispensable, and your survival in the world's toughest profession suggests that you do too:

- The notion that crises are normal, tensions are promising, and complexity is fun;
- A realization that paranoia and self-pity are reserved for people who *don't* want to be public executives;
- The conviction that there must be some more upbeat outcome than would result from the sum of available expert advice; and
- A sense of personal responsibility for the situation as a whole.

Hubert Humphrey, the great American in whose honor I am now privileged to work, was the very model of the situation-as-a-whole person. He felt personally responsible for growing more food, manufacturing useful goods, making our cities more livable, distributing wealth fairly, creating better jobs, delivering public services, combatting inflation, and ensuring the common defense and keeping the peace. We need a million more Americans with a similar sense of responsibility for the whole, and ICMA is certainly doing its part to recruit, develop, and encourage them on their way.

Reprinted from PUBLIC MANAGEMENT, December 1980, by special permission, © 1980, of the International City Management Association.

FINDING THE REAL LEADERSHIP

As I get around the country this year, I find my fellow-Americans not so much overwhelmed by the problems we face, as underwhelmed by the leaders who are urging us to face them. I think there is something that you and I can do about this mood.

That isn't because we are wiser than the people at large. It's because the people at large are already beginning to sense that they are going to have to lead their leaders out of the wilderness.

The American people have had quite a lot of practice, in the 1970s, getting out ahead of our leaders. The federal government was the last to learn that the war in Vietnam was over. President Nixon and his staff were the last to realize that Nixon was through. The tidal movements of social change in the past 20 years—environmental sensitivity, civil rights for all races, the enhanced status of women, recognition of the rights of consumers and small investors—were not generated by established leaders, but boiled up from the people at large.

But as we now look down the long murky tunnel of the '80s and '90s, it is clear that the American people (who will continue to make U.S. policy) still have a very long way to go in thinking through the contradictions of inflation and recession, growth and environment, defense and detente, work and welfare, resources and restraints, enterprise and planning. The people who make the policy are going to need help—help in peering into the middle distance, beyond this year's election and next year's balance sheet, help in analyzing alternative futures, help in seeing the inter-connections of their microproblems with the macroproblem, help in reconciling special interests with the general interest-help, that is to say, in "getting it all together."

Where is the help going to come from? Not, with painfully few exceptions, from the prominent leaders of the great established institutions—the federal government, business, labor, universities, or foundations. Those leaders are, ironically, too responsible to take the responsibility for change—until the direction of change is widely accepted and it thus becomes more dangerous to stand there than to move on. For the leaders of record, it's just too scary to be the first birds off the telephone wire*—until they're sure the rest of the flock will follow.

That's why the new ideas, the practical initiatives, and most of the real leadership in promoting new policies come from people like you: activist citizens, managers who (as ICMA's Committee on Future Horizons put it) know how "to lead by being led," men and women who are not preoccupied with formal power or getting their names in the newspapers—people whose concern exceeds even their confusion.

You are the shock troops of the get-it-all-together profession, and the

---

*Thanks to John Gardner for this image.

get-it-all-together professionals have to keep getting out ahead of the publicity heroes that *People* magazine still thinks are our leaders.

It's an exhilarating profession, but also a vulnerable one. The first reaction to your new idea may recall that pungent line from a Damon Runyon story: " 'Shut up,' my father explained."

The resistance to what's never been done before may remind you of Peter Ustinov's claim that one of his grade school teachers wrote on his report card, "Peter shows great originality, which must be curbed at all costs."

The first birds off the telephone wire need the spunk and persistence of that courageous and original lady who was arrested on a one-way street for going the other way. "Officer," she said, "has it occurred to you that that arrow may be pointing the wrong way?"

Each of us who presumes to this kind of leadership—the kind of leadership that shows but doesn't show off—has to try hard to think about the situation as a whole. I mean that quite literally. None of us can expect to *act* on more than a tiny corner of the great complexity. But in our interrelated society, itself part of an uncompromisingly interdependent world, we have to *think* about all of it in order to act relevantly on any part of it.

"If we are to retain any command at all over our own future," says John Gardner, "the best people in every field must give thought to the largest problems of the nation. They don't have to be in government to do so. But they have to come out of the trenches of their own specialty and look at the whole battlefield."

If you believe that's too tough an assignment, don't blame the messenger who brings the news, blame the complications and dynamics of social reality. And if you can't bring yourself to fall in love with the complexity and revel in the dynamism of our time and place, you can always stay on the telephone wire and wait to see where the other birds are going next.

But for the next few minutes, I'm going to assume that the birds in this aviary are itching to take off for the future—if they can just figure out where that is.

WHAT IS LEADERSHIP?

The indispensable quality of leadership—the get-it-all-together function in a complex system—is breadth. Breadth is a quality of mind, the capacity to relate disparate "facts" to a coherent theory, to fashion tactics that are part of a strategy, to act today in ways that are consistent with a studied view of the future.

People are forever saying that leadership is an art, not a science or technology—a matter of instinct, not the product of thinking. The classroom is indeed an unlikely place to learn charisma. But leadership is the art that determines the social fallout of science and points technology toward human purposes. The information to understand our tools and our purposes, and especially to relate them to each other, is not carried in our genes. It has to be learned.

We have the beginnings of a general theory of leadership, from history and social research and above all from the ruminations of reflective practitioners such as Moses, Pericles, Julius Caesar, Jesus Christ, Martin Luther, Niccolo Machiavelli, James Madison, and in our own time such disparate sources of wisdom as Mahatma Gandhi, V.I. Lenin, Winston Churchill, Charles De-Gaulle, Dean Acheson, Mao Tse-tung, Chester Barnard, John Gardner, and Henry Kissinger, who have very little in common except that they have not only been there but tried with some candor to speculate on paper about it.

From folklore and observation, then, we know that leaders are physically strong and abnormally hard workers. They are the strategic thinkers, more inclined than their followers to relate things and people to each other, to project patterns of collective behavior, to keep trying to see the situation whole. They are unusually curious about issues and methods outside the specialties in which they got their start. They are more preoccupied with values and purposes than their contemporaries and former fellow-specialists; that is, they are most likely to cut through the forest of how-to questions and ask "Why?" They are the optimists, the visionaries—the people who, confronted by the gloom and reluctance that are the hallmarks of expertise, are most inclined to ask "Why not?"

THE DANGER OF DOING NOTHING

The beginning of wisdom is to take the forecasters, and their forecasts, with a shaker of salt.

The get-it-all-together people in any enterprise are surrounded with gloomily reluctant experts, bidding their leaders to study the problem some more and then do nothing, cautiously. The most breathless and computerized of these Cassandras seem very often to be wrong, and I have puzzled a good deal about the abnormal frequency of predictive error. Sir Isaiah Berlin (in one of his *Conversations with Henry Brandon*) gives us the clue:

> *As knowledge becomes more and more specialized, the fewer are the persons who know enough ... about everything to be wholly in charge ... One of the paradoxical consequences is therefore the dependence of a large number of human beings upon a collection of ill-coordinated experts, each of whom sooner or later becomes oppressed and irritated by being unable to step out of his box and survey the relationship of his particular activity to the whole. The experts cannot know enough. The coordinators always did move in the dark, but now they are aware of it. And the more honest and intelligent ones are rightly frightened by the fact that their responsibility increased in direct ratio to their ignorance of an ever-expanding field.*

"The experts cannot know enough." Keeping up with trends in one's own field is difficult enough, and the expert is almost bound to assume that the factors he does not have time to study will cancel out the factors he has studied but does not understand. That leaves only his own golden line of extrapolation from the corner of the complexity he really does know something about—and each specialized projection, carried far enough into the future, leads to the Apocalypse.

The demographers, who underestimated the effects of development of world population growth and, in the United States, overestimated the need for school buildings and tickets of admission to higher education, are only the most obvious practitioners of that original statistical sin, which is to assume that what you know will not be stood on its head by what you do not know.

The get-it-all-together person, on the other hand, knows by instinct what the souls in Dante's *Inferno* learned to their sorrow: they could see clearly what lay far in the future, but things blurred as they drew nearer. You learn to mistrust predictions, especially when they are so long range that when the eventual disaster is due the forecaster—and, if his prediction is correct, his readers, too—will be dead. Or, if not dead, the forecaster might at least hope to be retired, preening himself on his long record of accuracy like that ancient retiree from the research department of the British Foreign Office who served from 1903 to 1950 and boasted thus at his retirement ceremony: "Year after year the worriers and fretters would come to me with awful predictions of the outbreak of war. I denied it each time. And I was only wrong twice!"*

You'll remember that Mark Twain was also hard on the extrapolators. "In the space of one hundred and seventy-six years the lower Mississippi has shortened itself 242 miles," he wrote. "That is an average of one mile and a third per year. (So) any person can see that seven hundred and forty-two years from now the Lower Mississippi will be only a mile and three quarters long. "There is something fascinating about science," he went on. "One gets such wholesale returns of conjecture out of such a trifling investment of fact."

WHERE WE ARE NOW

Instead of trying to predict the unpredictable, let's stare hard at where we are right now. People in every generation think they are living in a time of transition, and of course they're quite right. But I think we can claim to live at the confluence of more historic transitions at once than any of our ancestors.

Think comprehensively, for a moment, about the macrotransition we are in. It comprises a variety of changes in beliefs, loyalties, fears, aspirations, doctrines, and assumptions about personal and national futures. The transition simultaneously reflects changing concepts of security, changing concepts of growth, and changing concepts of equity (or "fairness").

---

*Thanks to Thomas Hughes for this relevant recollection.

"Post-industrial," the sociologists call the society we are becoming. I find that too retrospective a tag for so different and exciting a future, and too economic a name for a period in which the analysis of political, cultural, and psychological dynamics will be at least as important as economic analysis to an understanding of what is going on. Besides, if we are to set our compass by where we have been, I could add at least nine other equally backward-looking nicknames for the Eighties and Nineties. We are emerging into a post-New Deal, post-Keynesian, post-discriminatory, post-centralized, post-automatic, post-nuclear, post-military, post-national, and post-scarcity era.

These nicknames tell us where we're coming from. But they also tell us something about where we are going. Let's try them on for size.

We are moving, it seems, from concepts of *noblesse oblige*, charity and government largesse *to* doctrines of rights and entitlements. Public policy is already graduating out of minimalist notions like social security, unemployment insurance, public housing, and the "welfare state", graduating to a greater emphasis on productivity, full employment regardless of age, and universal entitlements to be educated, to earn, to contribute, and to participate. From Franklin Roosevelt to Lyndon Johnson we thought that if there was a problem, another government agency and a larger appropriation would help solve it. In the 1980s and 1990s, we are still going to want more governance, but we're going to want it with less government.

- We are moving *from* a Keynesian science of business cycles, in which you could depend on inflation and recession to remain at opposite ends of the cycle, *to* an economics of human purpose, in which need (not purchasing power) is the measure of demand and capacity (not production) the measure of supply. And this in turn is part of a larger shift: *from* an ethic of quantitative growth (measured and symbolized by that grotesque index, GNP) *to* an ethic of quality and sustainability and control of one's own destiny.
- We are certainly moving *from* a man's world *to* equality of the sexes—and as a second approximation, to self-selected differentiation of functions by sex. We are moving, not quite so fast, *from* an era of accepted racial discrimination *to* a climate in which equal opportunity and affirmative action become the norm and discrimination the exception. Worldwide, the achievement of racial equity and cultural pluralism still awaits a very long footrace between feudalism and fairness.
- We are moving *from* doctrines of centralized power *to* notions of decentralization, devolution, separatism and broadened participation. Central economic planning, popularized around the world by industrial democracies that do not practice it themselves, is everywhere in disarray.

Power is leaking out of national governments to local communities determined to exercise more jurisdiction over their own destinies. The formulation of public policy is increasingly done by nongovernments (profit and nonprofit) which can more easily think farther ahead, and experiment more flexibly, than governments can. And the yen to participate keeps spreading—through what the Communists call collective leadership and the Japanese call consensus and we call committee work—so that the key dilemma of the new era is how to get everybody in on the act and still get some action. In consequence we seem to be moving beyond "planning" viewed as scientific management or management engineering (which brought us PPBS as the *reductio ad absurdum*), to a concept of planning as a dynamic flow system.

- We are moving *from* notions like the "inner logic" of technological change and the "invisible hand" of the market *to* social direction-setting for new technologies and political bargaining as the dominant force in the market place. The 1970s were a watershed decade, in which the pretenses of automaticity were stripped away. The decisions not to deploy an antiballistic missile system, not to manufacture a supersonic transport, and not to develop the B-1 bomber were straws in a new wind. So were the dwindling enthusiasm for nuclear energy as a way to make electricity, the tightening regulation of carcinogenic foods and drugs, and the new caution about technological marvels like genetic engineering and weather modification. During the same decade, the rugged automaticity of the market was shoved aside whenever an important enterprise proved to be insufficiently enterprising; the efforts to rescue Lockheed, Chrysler, and the steel industry bear witness.
- We are moving *from* a conventional balance of international power based on certainty, *to* a nuclear balance of power based on uncertainty. We seem to have invented the ultimately unusable weapon, the weapon that cannot even be effectively brandished. (The last good brandish was Khrushchev's threat to "incinerate the orange groves of Italy and reduce the Acropolis in Athens to radioactive ash," which only served to galvanize Italy and Greece as loyal members of the NATO alliance.) Strategic nuclear weapons are useful, it seems, only for mutual deterrence. The Soviets don't know what we would do *if,* and their uncertainty is soundly rooted in our own: we don't know what we would do *if,* either. Our uncertainty is therefore credible, and that's the deterrent.
- At the same time, we are moving *from* concepts of national security as military defense based on complex weapons systems, *to* concepts of security as including oil, environmental risk, nuclear proliferation, population growth, unsafe streets, Islamic revolutions, and a global epidemic called inflation. The most frightening security nightmare of the 1980s may not be the familiar mushroom cloud but the unfamiliar and unsettling collision of modernization with resentments about future fairness and resentments about past traditions—which are producing not only the Irans but the Lebanons,

the Cambodias, the Northern Irelands, the El Salvadors, and who knows how many other future examples of the incapacity of national governments to cope.

- We are moving *from* local and national technologies *to* inherently global technologies (for weather observation, military reconnaissance, telecommunications, data processing, resource sensing, orbital industries, etc.) and as a result, we seem to be moving *from* concepts of national ownership, sovereignty, and citizenship *to* ideas such as the global commons, international monitoring of environmental risks, and "the common heritage of mankind."

- We are moving away *from* our early-1970s preoccupation with "limits to growth," based on an assumption that the world's key resources were nonrenewable, *to* a much more sanguine attitude about physical scarcities—with a new emphasis on recycling, on biological resources (because they're renewable) and on information as a nondepletable, expandable resource, a resource that is not subject to the law of conservation of energy.

THE POST-SCARCITY WORLD

The prospect of a post-scarcity world merits more discussion because it has such large and intriguing implications for the future of management.

It is clear enough now that the race between world population and world resources won't look nearly so scary in the 1980s and '90s as it did in 1970.

What used to seem an exponential explosion of population is now beginning to resemble the familiar biological S-curve. Only a few years ago, demographers could snatch headlines, sell books, and be taken seriously if they predicted the world's population would grow to 7½ or even 8 billion by the year 2000. The current United Nations median projection barely reaches 6 billion by then.

The forecasters had once again mistaken current trends for human destiny. They were mousetrapped by countervailing trends: development, chemicals, women's instincts, and hope. All proved hard to fit into a computer program.

I don't want to be misunderstood about this. Population growth is still the primary engine of world poverty. Two billion more mouths to feed, three-quarters of a billion jobs to create—these are still massive assignments to tackle in one short generation. But the task might just be manageable. By contrast, the assignment implied by the earlier projections seemed unmanageable— looked so discouraging, in fact, that we were all exposed to that popularized nonsense about lifeboats and *triage*.

On the resources side of the equation, we have also gained in knowledge, insight, and wisdom during the 1970s. The early '70s panic about limits to growth was a useful wake-up tonic. But it soon became evident that the "problematique," as the Club of Rome called it, was not a shortage of physical resources as such but a shortage of political will to control our human selves in using the biosphere's rich and versatile endowment.

Even nonrenewable resources, the familiar fossil fuels and hard minerals, would present no real supply problem over the next generation—*if* conserving attitudes, research-and-development on petroleum substitutes, and international cooperation don't continue to be in such short supply.

Beyond the nonrenewables lies a hugely underutilized biomass (one fifth of it microorganisms, an inconceivably numerous army of workers now underemployed in making cheese and sauerkraut and fermenting beer and wine), plus a supply of solar radiation which is for practical purposes infinite. And these renewable resources are disproportionately available in the world's tropical regions, which are home for most of the absolutely poor.

Beyond the physical and biological resources, *information* has in the 1970s come to be regarded as a resource, too. It's not marginal; Peter Drucker says information is now the key resource in our business economy. It's not depletable; John McHale taught us that information expands as it is used. It's not scarce; Lewis Branscomb says information "is in quantitative surplus. To be sure, there are great gaps in human knowledge that have yet to be filled by research and study. But the yawning chasm is between what some have learned, yet others have not yet put to use."

Taken together, the computer, the satellite and the silicon chip are historically comparable to the invention of steel and the steam engine—if not to the discovery of fire and the invention of the wheel.

The implications of putting more emphasis on bioresources, and on information as a resource, do not leap to the eye. But if you think hard about them, as I have been trying to do, you may conclude (as I have) that, compared with the resources associated with the age of physics and geology, they encourage:

- "extensive" rather than "intensive" systems ("extensive" in terms of geography, capital, and labor);
- economic, social and cultural patterns that make interdependence, not independence, the law of life (for nations, for groups, for individuals);
- the spreading of benefits rather than the concentration of wealth (biomass is more equitably spread around the world than petroleum or uranium);
- the maximization of choice rather than the suppression of diversity (it is harder to regiment farmers and intellectuals than assembly-line factory workers or members of a government bureaucracy);
- the diffusion of individual responsibility rather than hierarchical command and control.

In a world depending less and less on the allocation of scarce (because nonrenewable) resources, more and more on biological and informational (that is, renewable and expandable) resources, management is bound to have a different "feel" to it:

- cooperation not coercion;
- more "sharing" transactions and fewer "exchange" transactions;
- more "positive-sum" games, fewer "zero-sum" games; and
- horizontal not vertical structures.

With nobody in general charge but everybody partly in charge, more participatory decision making implies a need for much feedback information widely available. That means more openness, less secrecy—not as an ideological preference but as a technological imperative.

In such a management environment, "planning" cannot be done by a few leaders as experts with detailed blueprints. "Planning" has to be dynamic improvisation by the many on a general sense of direction which is announced by "leaders" only after genuine consultation with those who will have to improvise on it. Maybe that is the updated definition of democracy.

BROADENING OUR VISION

My effort to sketch the macrotransition is only a very primitive start. Each of you can—indeed, you had better—develop from your own experience and study your own analysis of the macrotransition we are in. But for our present purposes my point is this:

If you chart the direction of all the conceptual changes I have mentioned, you find a common characteristic; our concepts are all *lengthening* and *widening* to include what used to be regarded as "externalities"—a fancy academic word for factors that don't fit into a traditional discipline or profession or analytical system, yet seem to be disturbingly relevant all the same.

We are coming to realize, whenever we make avoidable trouble for ourselves, that Abe Lincoln and Walt Kelly were right in their different formulations to finger as us the enemy. We—you and I, not merely the other guys—have often found it seductively comforting to tunnel our vision, focus too sharply on one issue at a time, neglect to ask the questions that illuminate the ways in which, as the study of ecology has now taught us, everything really is related to everything else.

We plunged into the use of nuclear power for electricity without asking the hard questions about the back end of the nuclear fuel cycle—about safety, about waste, about proliferation. We pursued growth without asking "growth for what?" and "growth for whom?" we were persuaded by narrow-gauge, straight-line extrapolations that we were running out of resources, when we were mostly running out of imagination. We applauded a goal of national energy independence when the problem was the management of international energy interdependence. We produced new gadgets and only then inquired about their consequences. We built highways and discovered only later their effect on urban living. We built on land without asking how the nearby weather would be thereby modified. Some corporations neglected their social responsibilities, induced consumer outrage expressed in government regulation, and then wondered how that army of regulations happened to become so intrusive and so burdensome.

In international affairs the effect of tunnelling our vision, working hard on the detailed tactics and neglecting to project a strategy that relates the disparate parts of our foreign policy to each other, is even more serious. We have had far too many object-lessons in the decade just past, from our invasion of Cambodia in the spring of 1970, through the collision of human rights with arms control, to the hostage politics of the 1980s.

Just now there is an extraordinary vacuum of general strategy—a larger vacuum than I can remember in a generation mostly spent observing and practicing diplomacy. Historians may say of the 1970s that in the first part of the decade there were leaders in Washington who did bad things on purpose, and in the latter part of the decade there were leaders in Washington who did good things and didn't relate them to each other—and that worked out almost as badly.

I will, therefore, make one prediction: that, along with the scholars in every discipline and the practitioners of every profession, every public manager will find it imperative to be more and more interdisciplinary, interprofessional and international—because otherwise we'll be out of touch with the reality we are presuming to manage.

MORE GOVERNANCE WITH LESS GOVERNMENT

The macrotask ahead of us is to manage a worldwide transition from indiscriminate and wasteful growth to purposeful, efficient, and compassionate growth. It is to enhance the human environment within perceived energy and resource constraints, minimize the damaging side effects of development, and guide the growth of the presently richer societies to allow "growth with equity" in the presently poorer societies. This task has to be undertaken in a world where no one race or creed or nation of alliance can (or should) arrogate to itself the function of general management; in other words, a pluralistic world society.

A tidal change of values is already well under way; I have suggested this morning some of its surface manifestations. The main obstacle to converting these new values into politics, practices, and institutions is not limits to physical resources, even water, or limits to the capacity of the human brain. It is the limits, even more recently discovered, to government.

If we are going to work out ways of governing ourselves without inflating our governments more and more, those with public responsibility for action are going to need continuous access to the best thinking of those who, because, they are not publicly responsibile, can more readily convert into suggested public policy the interest of the general public in getting that macrotask performed. And those of us who are privileged to think freely because we are not burdened with formal responsibility must be the first to widen our perspective and lengthen our view. Thus can the nonresponsibles·be partners with the responsibles, in the governance of a nobody-in-charge system.

The reactive mode of modern government requires that most new ideas originate outside government. An interesting division of labor results, between nongovernmental experts, thinkers, and advocates on the one hand, and government officials and legislators on the other. The nongovernments in our society can do some things better than governments can:

- They can work, ahead of time, on problems that are important but not yet urgent enough to command political attention;
- They can shake loose from conceptual confines and mix disciplinary methodologies;
- They can think hard, write adventurously and speak freely about alternative futures and what they imply for public policy today;
- They can generate discussion among people in contending groups, different professional fields, and separate sectors of society who might not otherwise be talking to each other; and
- They can organize "dialogue" across local, state, and national frontiers on issues not yet ripe for more official "negotiation."

I do not suggest that nongovernmental organizations are universally or even usually effective in compensating for the rigidities of responsibility. But the opportunity is there, and is reflected in the rapid growth of nongovernmental enterprise working under such rubrics as policy analysis, futures research, humanistic studies, environmental action, public interest law, energy conservation, technology assessment and (in my case) "public affairs."

There is even a rough and ready test of relevance for nongovernments: Are they working on issues that are still too vague, too big, too interdisciplinary or too futuristic for governments that are too busy, too crisis-ridden and too politically careful to tackle?

To ICMA's perceptive prospectus, "New Worlds of Service," I would therefore add only a greater emphasis on the public manager's responsibility to include the nongovernments in a wider concept of governance. The key dilemma of the 1980s can be expressed (like most truth) as a paradox: How are we going to get more governance with less government?

The Chinese, as usual, said it best a long time ago. "Ruling a big country," said Lao Tse, "is like cooking a small fish"—that is, too much handling will spoil it.

SECTION V

APPLYING THE "WIN-WIN" CONCEPT

INTRODUCTION

The concept of "Win-Win" has been presented; the concept must now be applied. There is little need in the management and administration fields for new theories to stand in some kind of academic isolation. The theories must have practical applicability, and the concept of "Win-Win" most assuredly can be applied.

Contemporary organizations, while in many cases doing reasonably well, can be more productive. Most private sector organizations could increase their profits. Most public organizations could provide services more effectively and efficiently. Most organizations could be more satisfying places in which to work. Many industries could make a better quality product. Many organizations could be more pleasant places with which consumers or citizens do business. Applying the "Win-Win" concept can achieve these results.

Serious managers, whether in a profit-making organization or in a governmental agency, know that in their organization there is room for improvement and are open to new ideas and concepts. While the concept of "Win-Win" may not be a particularly new idea to many managers, the presentation of the concept in this format may stimulate some new thought. For a number of reasons the "Win-Win" concept makes sense, and the articles in this section open the door to thinking about how to apply the concept.

Even though human resources accounting may not be a specific activity engaged in by many of today's organizations, its potential value still exists. The article by J. Carroll Swart somewhat deals with this activity, but goes quite a bit further to make the case for humanistic management as a way to apply the "Win-Win" concept. Documenting his thesis with a variety of realistic examples of concrete situations in which new ideas have been tried, Swart demonstrates that humanistic management is highly successful in a wide variety of organizations. Establishing a climate of caring and trust—humanistic management and all which the term represents—may very well be the first step toward achieving "Win-Win" in any organization.

Recognizing the importance of humanistic management, Letty Cottin Pogrebin in "The Working Woman" makes points which are not unique to women. Her brief article, published in a popular periodical, raises a number of valid organizational concerns which are applicable for men and women. Suggesting that how one has to do their job can cause unhappiness, Pogrebin presents several examples of how employers are increasing their worker's happiness—and productivity—by humanizing their working conditions.

Humanistic management means participative management to Dale McConkey. The concept of participative management is one with which enlightened managers have been familiar for some time, and McConkey's article serves as a realistic demonstration of its viability as a way of applying the "Win-Win" concept. The article provides a practical guide for implementing participative management, and McConkey argues that if the concept of participative management is properly understood and applied, it can be highly effective in an organization.

Participative management may be considered as the forerunner of what is currently referred to as "Quality of Work Life." The absence of detailed research examples to support his position does not diminish the value of Edward Glaser's article. In his article, based on a paper he presented at the annual convention of the American Psychological Association in 1979, Glaser finds mounting evidence pointing to the impact of an organization's quality of worklife. Where this quality is high, improvement in job satisfaction—and productivity—are usually among the desirable results.

With reference to a specific example of the implementation of a Quality of Work Life program in private enterprise, Robert Guest succinctly defines what Quality of Work Life means. Cooperation, openness, and sensitive concern for interpersonal relations are necessary characteristics of a successful Quality of Work Life program. Guest indicates that the Quality of Work Life movement is spreading and represents a significant change in the way management and labor view their respective roles.

It is not suggested that the articles in this section represent the totality of ideas for applying the "Win-Win" concept. It is hoped, though, that these articles serve to begin the process of increasing the dialogue. Consideration of the concept, by managers in any organization, will surely have a positive impact on anyone who is touched by the organization.

THE WORTH OF HUMANISTIC MANAGEMENT

J. Carroll Swart

Humanistic management, often called job enrichment, is a new way to cope with old problems—motivation, work satisfaction, morale, and productivity. The author presents concrete situations in which new ideas have been tried among white-collar and blue-collar workers. Many companies—banks, insurance firms, manufacturing and industrial plants—have applied behaviorist theories. Removing time clocks and putting everyone on a salary are two measures adopted by several companies. Involving the workers in decision making is also becoming more widespread. One corporation, General Foods Corporation in Topeka, has based its total organizational system on humanistic management. To date, its operations have been highly successful, and the plant in many ways is a working laboratory to test behaviorist theories.

If you have a Mickey Mouse job and you put a good man in it, the odds are that you will wind up with a Mickey Mouse man.

In 1922 Henry Ford I said, "The average worker wants a job in which he does not have to put much physical effort. Above all, he wants a job in which he does not have to think." Henry Ford was a giant in the auto industry's early years, and a number of his ideas are valid to this day. On the other hand, greater numbers of executives believe that this automotive pioneer's philosophy concerning worker attitudes is not valid in 1973. Many businessmen have modified their attitudes concerning the relative importance of employee needs and values, and think that the behaviorists may have something when they talk about upgrading the work force and giving people a greater sense of responsibility. In short, to use the vernacular, in the past fifty years "we've come a long way, baby."

Reprinted from *Business Horizons,* Volume 16 (June 1973), by permission of the publisher.

This article is not intended as a discussion of humanistic management in the abstract. Rather, the author's purpose is to describe actual business situations where modifications were made in work content, employee responsibilities, and the work environment—with targets being higher motivation, morale, satisfaction, and productivity. Although job enrichment—essentially job enlargement—is proving to be an important means for achieving these four goals, it is not the only way.

Currently there is some controversy as to exactly what job enrichment encompasses. For the purposes of this paper the human element in organizations is discussed within a framework formally labeled humanistic management. It is hoped that the presentation of concrete examples will be informative and helpful to businessmen and students actively interested in the topic. Obviously, theories in humanistic management will not solve every problem of motivation, work satisfaction, and productivity. The reader is asked to answer for himself the question: What applications of humanistic management, if any, might be appropriate in the organization where I work? No pious value judgments are intended by the author.

LOGICAL OR BIZARRE?

The battery division factory of Matsushita Electric Company in Osaka, Japan's largest home appliance firm, contains "self-control rooms," where many a worker attempts to relieve himself of pent-up tensions. On approaching the control area, a worker first observes a number of concave and convex mirrors. The immediate reaction is that he is likely to laugh at seeing his own distorted image. Next he enters a gymnasium equipped with punching bags and an assortment of exercise equipment, a place where he warms up for the main attraction.

Then he moves to the central control room containing life-size dummies seated on knee-high platforms. The worker is provided with a bamboo stave (a club-like weapon) and, yelling and cursing, he clubs, swats, and slashes a life-size dummy to his heart's content, keeping in mind the one (a boss, probably) who is the object of his blows.

After his aggressive behavior is spent, he listens to one of a series of tape-recorded speeches by the board chairman himself, Matsushita, urging harmony and meaningful relationships. Should these activities not satisfy the employee, a counselor is standing by in an adjacent room.

The innovative employer also might want to consider applying a lunar cycle theory to his work force. A Japanese firm, Ohmi Transport Company, takes into account each man's lunar cycle, the few days each month when, according to some physiologists, the employee functions below par in a manner comparable to that of a woman during her menstrual period. To keep depressed workers clear of danger, Ohmi does not assign a man to a hazardous job during his lunar cycle. The firm claims a 30 percent drop in its accident rate since the program went into effect.

Most readers probably feel that the two illustrations are ludicrous and far-fetched methods of attempting to improve employee satisfaction and productivity. I suggest that you may have to think open-mindedly about the two methods described. If, after a complete reading of this article, all other methods discussed seem bland and unworkable by comparison, then in aiming to improve the workers' lot at your organization you may want to try the Japanese style.

WHITE-COLLAR APPLICATIONS

A Banking Firm—The New York Chemical Bank deliberately made a number of jobs more complicated. Targets were higher worker satisfaction and greater productivity. The bank previously had had a production line setup for a segment of its check sorting operations. One group of women took checks out of envelopes; another group encoded the checks; another put entries in proper accounts; another stapled checks; and the last group enclosed checks in envelopes to be returned to customers.

A decision was made to abolish the production line concept. Individual employees were given responsibilities for handling a series of tasks from start to finish for specified accounts. In effect, each woman knew what accounts she was working on. In turn, the account owners, in this case commercial banks, knew—or could find out—which bank employee was handling their business. The result, according to bank officials, was that the women handled more total volume more efficiently than they had before. As a specific example, one can cite the experience of Mary, a female bank clerk:

> My job was to pull invoices and checks out of envelopes and stack them into three piles: one under $10, another between $20 and $25, and a third over $25. Then I'd pass the piles on to the next person. After two months I was so bored I would have quit within another month.[1]

After New York Chemical applied job enlargement concepts, Mary handled all the processing for twenty-two corporate accounts, from crediting payments to returning unsigned checks. She said that handling her own accounts was a lot more interesting, and it gave her feelings of accomplishment. In Mary's department, in the four years prior to job enrichment, turnover averaged 59 percent a year, nearly double the bank's overall rate of 30.9 percent. After job changes were introduced in 1970, the turnover rate in Mary's department plummeted to 24 percent. According to an assistant vice-president, the impact of boredom on productivity had out-weighed the benefits of extreme specialization.

---

[1]Roger Ricklefs, "Boredom Fighters Put Variety in Many Jobs," *Wall Street Journal,* August 21, 1972, p. 1.

An Insurance Firm—Account supervisors at Travelers Insurance Corporation at Hartford formerly spent about 35 percent of their time answering questions from subordinates and 45 percent doing production work—essentially handling clerical tasks when clerks ran into snags. In applying humanistic management the clerks were delegated more authority as well as encouragement to solve more problems on their own. Some significant results: the two functions together consumed only 25 percent of the account supervisors' total time; the clerks were more satisfied with their jobs; and account supervisors were able to devote more time to planning and budgeting.

A Brokerage Firm—At Merrill Lynch, following work modifications, seventeen clerks were able to do the work that a year earlier had required twenty-five employees. In addition, the worker error rate was reduced from 4 percent to 1 percent. Improvements were accomplished mainly by stimulating interest and making fuller use of potential. Previously, the clerical supervisor was spending four hours a day on the phone answering questions from brokers. The processing of stock certificates was broken down into so many tiny tasks that only the clerical supervisor could handle a question about end results.

After job tasks and relationships were reorganized, each clerk was assigned to handle all of the office work on a certificate and to take responsibility for it. In the processing of stock certificates the new requirement was that each clerk sign her name and phone extension on the paperwork. Also, the company specified that clerks had to be able to handle incoming phone calls from brokers, and to convey to brokers the accurate stock certificate information. One effect was that the clerical supervisor's phone time with brokers was reduced by 70 percent. According to company spokesmen, overall results were positive in terms of employee satisfaction and productivity.

A Private Utility—Utilization managers for the American Telephone and Telegraph Corporation, at the urging of the personnel director for manpower, initiated job improvement programs at some 400 locations. At Indianapolis, female employees once compiled telephone books by working on specific information pieces. After job enlargement concepts were applied, employees had the responsibility of putting together all the white pages, for example, of a phone book for a specific city in Indiana. If a city is large, that city's phone book would be assembled by a team.

As another example within the AT&T System, the manager of the commercial division at Pacific Telephone in Los Angeles increased the service representatives' responsibilities and their authority to make decisions. The results were better customer service, more job satisfaction, and higher productivity. Turnover was reduced from 62 percent in 1969 to 48 percent in 1970. The company saved $3,800 in training costs for each service representative who was retained instead of replaced.

A Commercial Airline—In St. Louis, American Airlines improved the commitment and morale of twenty of its agents who handle flight boarding.

Two agents had been assigned to each flight, under the direction of a supervisor. In redesigning the relationships of responsibility and authority, one of the agents was designated as flight coordinator and given the responsibility for getting the flight off the ground. It was necessary for him to clear only the most unusual decisions.

One flight coordinator delayed a takeoff to accommodate twenty passengers from a competing airline that had canceled its flight. The coordinator judged that the additional revenues would justify the delay.

A Manufacturing Firm—In Washington, W. Va., the Marbon division of Borg-Warner Corporation applied job enrichment ideas to the sales force. In 1972 the plastic products division assigned its more productive salesmen to plan the national sales meeting, develop a training program, and even develop marketing plans for a given product.

The division also was considering reducing each salesman's paperwork and expanding his authority to arrange prices. The manager of markets for the division was trying to make the sales job rewarding enough in its own right so that people would look at it as a career rather then as a stepping-stone.

An Industrial Firm—Humanistic management also is incorporated in management training programs. At General Electric, for example, about 2,000 foremen and supervisors have participated in role playing sessions. In the GE program, managers are encouraged to use an alternate way in dealing with workers.

A foreman playing the role of a worker may act out a situation in which a workers is called in by his superior to discuss a problem—anything from absenteeism to poor work habits. The action is videotaped and shown to supervisors, who engage in lively discussions and critical analyses concerning the particular role playing exercise. According to a GE personnel research executive, most men who have gone through the sessions go away with the feeling that they can be more effective in their jobs if they put aside the image of a tough guy.

In one GE electronic components plant, a group of supervisors went through the training. Ten weeks later, the workers they were supervising were performing at a level 20 percent higher in production efficiency. A GE research officer said, "We're not trying to change a foreman's behavior with a lot of theory. We're saying that there is more to his job than just clobbering people when they get out of line, which is the way a shop has traditionally been run."[2]

A Footwear Manufacturer—The R. G. Barry Corporation, a shoe manufacturer in Columbus, Ohio, has been attempting to measure the human element through human resource accounting. Working with researchers from the University of Michigan, the firm is one of a handful of enterprises trying to assess, in an unconventional way, how effectively their investments in human resources are being used.

---

[2]"Management Itself Holds the Key," *Business Week* (September 9, 1972), p. 146.

Barry has incorporated human resource measures in its past three annual reports to stockholders, side by side with conventional accounting measures. The firm calculates the investment it makes in hiring and training new managers and in developing the abilities of existing managers. Then it amortizes this investment over appropriate periods. The Barry Corporation's innovative format is illustrated in the accompanying table.

Robert N. Anthony, a faculty member in the Harvard Business School, is of the opinion that human resource measures may be extremely important for service and professional businesses such as accounting and law firms, consultants, and medical clinics. In these types of enterprises, according to Anthony, return on investment makes no sense, either as a basis for pricing or as a method of measuring performance. "The principal resource is not the amount of capital involved but rather the skill of the professionals whom the firm has hired, trained, organized, and motivated."[3]

Possibly many readers assess human resource accounting as an ambiguous and fragmented system that will never go beyond the experimental stage. Such an assessment may be correct. On the other hand, the Barry corporation's

R. G. Berry Corporation Balance Sheet, 1971

	Conventional and Human Resources	Conventional Only
Assets		
Total current assets	$12,810,346	$12,810,346
Net property, plant and equipment	3,343,379	3,343,379
Excess of purchase price over net assets acquired	1,291,079	1,291,079
Net investments in human resources	1,561,264	
Other assets	209,419	209,419
	$19,215,487	*$17,654,223*
Liabilities and Stockholders Equity		
Total current liabilities	3,060,576	3,060,576
Long-term debt, excluding current installments	5,095,000	5,095,000
Deferred compensation	95,252	95,252
Deferred federal income taxes based upon full tax deduction for human resource costs	780,632	
Stockholders equity		
Capital stock	1,209,301	1,209,301
Additional capital in excess of par value	5,645,224	5,645,224
Retained earnings		
Financial	2,548,870	2,548,870
Human resources	780,632	
Total stockholders equity	10,184,027	9,403,395
	$19,215,487	*$17,654,223*

Source: Business Week (September 9, 1972), p. 137.

---

[3]"A Better Basis for Better Decisions," *Business Week* (September 9, 1972), p. 139.

conventional and human resource balance sheet is indicative of that firm's sensitivity to the human element, and of its open-minded approach to ways in which it might be measured.

APPLICATIONS IN THE FACTORY

Salary and Time Clocks

For most employees there is more status associated with salary than wages. Salary compensation also suggests more regularity in the paychecks received, and, in turn, promotes feelings of security. Companies might anticipate more contract talks that include the salary demand. This desire will be initiated by more unions in the 1970s, including the United Auto Workers.

In France, Renault has agreed to give monthly pay status to workers in 1973. Following Renault's lead, the Patronat, the French employers association, has reached an agreement with unions that will put almost all French industrial workers in the status of monthly personnel by 1975. President Pompidou suggested that the change would go a long way toward ending the working class stigma for those now paid on an hourly basis.

Closely allied to the salary issue are company policies regarding the use of time clocks. Although this is atypical, some firms have removed time clocks. In doing so, a number of companies retained the wage form of compensation, while others initiated salary pay. A few firms that have done away with the time clocks are Corning Glass, Texas Instruments, Alcan Aluminum, Donnelly Mirrors, Motorola, Eaton Yale & Towne, and R. G. Barry. According to a Motorola Corporation spokesman, "Taking out the time clocks was a sign we wanted to treat our employees like adults, not control them like children or mechanical devises."[4] Frederick Herzberg, the contemporary father of job enrichment, says:

> How motivated would you be if your job consisted of tightening five bolts with a torque wrench a thousand times a day, and if, in addition, mechanical devices called time clocks and whistles told you when to work, when to eat, when to stretch your legs and when to use the bathroom.[5]

Herzberg's contention is that most production jobs provide so little satisfaction that they should be automated out of existence. Or, where such a transformation is not economically feasible, an honor system that eliminates time clocks helps improve worker motivation and satisfaction.

Redesigning Jobs and Building Teamwork

Corning Glass—The plant at Medfield, Mass. employs about 100 people. In 1967, with absenteeism and turnover running at high rates, the company

---

[4]James MacGregor, "The Honor System," *Wall Street Journal,* May 22, 1970, p. 1.

[5]McGregor, "The Honor System."

decided to make some major changes. Privileged parking spots for executives were removed, jobs were redesigned to make them more interesting and challenging, and employees were given a greater voice in setting and meeting their own work schedules. Increased responsibilities enabled the plant to operate with two fewer managers.

Today, employees meet monthly with department heads to discuss production goals, and twice a month teams of employees confer with the plant manager in sessions officially called "coffee with the boss." The workers participate in decision making. When an inventory buildup occurred in 1971, the majority of workers suggested that the firm go temporarily on a three-week month to slow production without laying anyone off. After consideration, the plant manager agreed with the proposal.

Donnelly Mirrors—The firm at Holland, Mich. had sales of $14 million in 1969, and has raised its profits roughly 20 percent since 1952. A few years ago the Donnelly Corporation removed its time clocks, put everyone on salary, and turned a large number of shop-floor decisions over to its employees.

Today, about 500 workers are assigned to task-oriented teams under foremen, who in turn are members of a team of foremen. Workers are paid on a salary basis with a bonus tied to production. Workers can decide how much of a salary increase they will receive; however, they must find ways to pay for it through higher productivity, cost reduction, and elimination of needless jobs. Quality also is a factor in the bonus calculation.

Alcan Aluminum—At the rolling mill in Oswego, N.Y., automation started plant officials to thinking about ways to improve morale. At a $90 million installation having a work force exceeding 600 people, some problems were especially costly. When a bored or disgruntled worker pulled a wrong lever somewhere along the 600-foot-long hot rolling mill, often the whole mill had to stop for repairs.

The plant removed time clocks and took steps to permit employees to determine their own break and lunch times. Job rotation also was introduced. With appropriate training, workers began relieving each other until most men knew one or two other jobs in addition to their own. For example, a cutting machine operator also learns to drive a forklift truck, and the forklift truck driver becomes competent in running an overhead crane. When a man becomes eligible for a better job, it is possible that he already has done it. In effect, the versatile person is in a better position to know if he wants a particular job on a permanent basis. Because some employees can do several jobs, total employment at Oswego is as much as 100 men fewer than under standard union job definitions (there is no union at Alcan).

The company guarantees full pay for time off for urgent business—with one day's notice. There is also full salary for up to twenty-six weeks to an employee idled by layoff; however, the plant has not had a layoff since it was built in 1963. On days when no production is scheduled, workers pull out brooms or paint brushes for plant cleaning.

Alcan is the only nonunionized plant in the Oswego area despite a pay scale slightly lower than the industry average. In 1970 absenteeism was running at about 2.5 percent, compared with an industry average of about 10 percent. At Alcan, according to one worker, it is a lot easier getting up in the morning to go to work.

TRW Corporation—The Cleveland-based firm has used a heavy dose of job enrichment with both salaried and hourly workers in attempting to create a climate in which workers can share their ideas and get them through the system. According to a top executive at TRW, "We're convinced that in terms of productivity, the man who is most productive is the one who has a real piece of the action. He's in a job where he has control and influence, and one where he is measured on results."[6]

In 1972, in one of its manufacturing plants TRW created the semiautonomous work team. The workers were given the responsibility of assembling a product as a team rather than separately performing assembly line tasks. Once given the new assignment, team members were allowed to schedule their own time as long as they did the job.

One result was the elimination of different shifts for a given job, since it made no sense to work as a team unless its members worked at the same time. Hours of work were staggered when necessary to fit personal needs, and the firm started to see team members take on tasks formerly regarded as the company's responsibility. Older, more experienced employees were voluntarily spending time in training younger team members. According to TRW, productivity went up 15 percent.

General Electric—By forming work teams GE appears to be broadening its efforts to make jobs more interesting. The aim is to create a setting in which each member of a team can see the relationship between what he does and what has to be done. Hopefully, a worker will see himself as part of a small system which, in turn, is an integral part of a larger system. According to GE, what is important is to identify a task and then to assign a group of five to fifteen people to handle it. The key is to give the group as much responsibility as possible.

In a fabricating plant, twelve welders were given responsibility for planning and scheduling their work load. They determined, for example, how much time it would take to meet specifications on any items requiring special welding techniques, a job formerly done by a methods and standards engineer. The welders were experienced enough to decide which one would perform a specific job within what time frame. The company's interpretation is that the responsibility meant that the men had a bigger say in how they did their jobs. They became more committed to the work as team members.

---

[6]*Business Week* (September 9, 1972), p. 143.

What about the engineers? They were freed to work on new product models while the welders decided how the daily work was going to be done. Overall, both the efficiency and the quality of work improved.

A TOTAL SYSTEM

With few exceptions, humanistic management has been applied on a piecemeal basis. Examples cited in this article depict behavioral ideas applied mainly to departments, offices, and particular jobs. At one firm in particular, however, behavioral concepts have been applied over a total system. Because of its uniqueness, plus the fact that initial results are available, this section of the article is devoted exclusively to a discussion of one company's experiences.

In 1968, General Foods Corporation decided to build a new pet food plant in Topeka. In the overall design, the company desired to incorporate and apply knowledge developed by the behavioral sciences. A number of key managers were selected. For more than two years the appointed group met with behavioral science experts and visited industrial plants that were experimenting with innovative organizational methods. Recommendations of this management group were instrumental in the overall design of the Topeka plant that began operating in January of 1971. Key features are discussed below.

Autonomous Work Groups—The total work force of approximately seventy employees is organized into six teams. On any one shift, three teams are at work, each covering an entire phase of the plant's operation: processing from the raw material to the end product, packaging and shipping, and office work. A team is comprised of from seven to fourteen members (operators) and a team leader. Assignments of individuals to sets of tasks are subject to team consensus. Although at any given time one employee has primary responsibility for a set of tasks within the team's jurisdiction, some tasks can be shared by several operators. In addition, tasks can be redefined by the team in light of individual interests and capabilities.

Other issues that fall within the scope of team recommendation or decision making include: temporarily redistributing tasks to cover for absent workers, coping with manufacturing problems that occur within or between the teams' areas of responsibilities, selecting team workers to serve on plant-wide committees or task forces, screening and selecting employees to replace departing operators, and counseling those who do not meet team standards.

Integrated Support Functions—Most staff units are eliminated. Activities typically performed by quality control, maintenance, custodial, industrial engineering, and personnel units are built into an operating team's responsibilities. Complicated electrical maintenance is one exception. Team members maintain the equipment, "housekeep" their areas, perform quality tests and ensure quality standards, and screen job applicants.

Challenging Job Assignments—Every set of tasks is designed to include functions that require definite responsibilities and specialized abilities. The integrated support functions provide an important source of job enrichment. Also, plant technology is designed to eliminate dull jobs as much as possible. But some nonchallenging yet basic tasks still must be compensated for. For example, the forklift truck operation is not technically challenging. Therefore, the team member responsible for it is assigned other, more mentally demanding tasks, such as planning warehouse space utilization and shipping activities.

Job Mobility and Rewards for Learning—Because all sets of jobs are designed to be equally challenging, although each set comprises unique skill demands, it is possible to have a single job classification for all operators. Increases in pay are geared to an operator's mastery of an increasing proportion of jobs, first in the team and then in the total plant.

Thus, team members are paid for learning more aspects of the total manufacturing system. Since there are no limits on the number of workers that can qualify for higher pay brackets, operators are encouraged to teach each other. The old plant, in contrast, featured numerous job classifications, with pay increases based on progress up the classification hierarchy.

Facilitative Leadership—Team leaders are selected from foremen and are largely responsible for team development and group decision making. This contrasts with the old plant's use of supervisors to plan, direct, and control subordinates' work. The company believes that in time the teams might be self-directed. If so, the formal team leader position might not be required.

Self-Government—The management group that developed the basic organization plan before the plant was manned refrained from formulating any plant rules in advance. The firm is committed to letting these rules evolve from collective experience.

Congruent Physical and Social Context—Differential status symbols characterizing traditional work organizations are minimized in the new plant. There is a single entrance for both the office and plant, an open parking lot, and a common decor throughout the reception area, locker rooms, cafeteria, and offices.

In many ways, the Topeka plant is a working laboratory for testing behavioral theories about motivation, morale, worker satisfaction, and productivity. What were initial results after the first eighteen months of operations? Using standard data, industrial engineers originally estimated that 110 employees would be needed to man the plant; the actual average work force employed at Topeka, however, was 70. The safety record was one of the best in the company. Turnover was far below average. The plant's fixed overhead rate was 33 percent lower than in the old plant.

Reductions in variable manufacturing costs for example, an absenteeism rate 9 percent below the industry norm and 92 percent fewer quality rejects resulted in annual savings of $600,000. Operators, managers, and team leaders became more involved in their work and derived higher satisfaction from it.[7] One report comments as follows:

> A plant where work teams perform without supervisors, where many decisions are based on employee consensus, and where most of the staff functions are assigned to line operators—in what future organization would such a phenomenon exist? Probably in most, because such radical innovations are part of the emerging answer to alienation in the workplace.[8]

The purpose of this article is to discuss contemporary examples of humanistic management. I shall repeat a statement contained in the introductory words of this article: "The reader is asked to answer for himself the question: What applications of humanistic management, if any, might be appropriate in the organization where I work?"

Among many forms we observe that management is increasingly aware of and sensitive to issues of worker motivation and satisfaction. There is also a keen interest in studying intricacies of human behavior in the work force.[9] In the immediate future, with the availability of more information, undoubtedly we shall read that a number of humanistic work designs survived the test of time. In all likelihood, we shall also read that many designs that proved to be costly and unworkable were abolished.

What is an important purpose of humanistic management? In the words of Frederick Herzberg, "Managers must get more men going home to their wives saying, 'Honey, do you know what I did today?' instead of 'Honey, do you know what they did to me today?' "[10]

---

[7]Richard E. Walton, "How to Counter Alienation in the Plant," *Harvard Business Review,* L (November-December, 1972), pp. 70–81; also see *Business Week* (September 9, 1972), pp. 143–46.

[8]*Harvard Business Review,* L (November-December, 1972), p. 70.

[9]A number of interesting developments aimed at building worker motivation, satisfaction, and productivity are occurring (and also being planned) at the Saab and Volvo auto plants in Sweden. By 1975, with forthcoming data, a more accurate assessment of the Swedish innovations will be possible. For information concerning this matter, see, for example: *Harvard Business Review,* L (November-December, 1972), pp. 80–81; "Sweden Tests a New Assembly-Line Concept," *Business Week* (March 4,1972), p. 70.

[10]*Time* (November 9, 1970), p. 74.

THE WORKING WOMAN
Letty Cottin Pogrebin

Why do some people bounce off to work each morning while others drag their heels?

Your attitude toward your job obviously depends on many factors, among them personal problems, salary satisfaction and actual job content. It's hard to be happy, for instance, if your child is on drugs, your salary doesn't pay the rent, or if you love words and people and you're stuck working with numbers and machines. Conversely, it's easy to feel enthusiastic about a job that fits your interests, pays well and is utterly free of monotony.

Most people fall between these extremes of outright misery and perfect joy. There are niggling contradictions. The job is okay but the working conditions are out of Charles Dickens. Or the atmosphere is nice and your co-workers are great, but you feel exploited.

A change of jobs may not be necessary. The solution may be a dose of what the Work in America Institute calls "Human Values in the Workplace." Very simply, this relatively new labor philosophy recognizes the right of employees to have more control over what happens to them in the workplace. It also supports the "whole person" concept: the idea that it's impossible to divide a human being into her or his interest segments (partner/parent/-physical/cultural/leisure/work, etc); that a happier, smarter, healthier *person* is a better worker.

To innovate, to humanize the workplace and give consideration and dignity to the worker, may cost management a little money at first. In the long run, however, the new humanized work programs seem to pay off for all concerned.

SELF-SUPERVISION

Kenneth Kwiat, plant manger of Y & S Candy Company, describes the effects of "self-supervision" at his Brooklyn, N.Y., plant: "I wanted to build a rela-

---

© 1978 LHJ Publishing, Inc. Reprinted with permission of the author and *Ladies' Home Journal.*

tionship with the workers based on trust and confidence. But how could Spanish-speaking, new immigrants from South America, Mexico and Puerto Rico relate well to old-style American bosses? First, I realize that instead of expecting one hundred and fifty people to learn English, it made sense for me and our production superintendent to learn Spanish. So we did.

"Then, when one of the foremen left us. I decided to experiment with the team concept. In one department I told the people they could work at their own pace with no foreman and leave when the job was done, instead of watching the clock until 3:30. The trust was a two-way street. When they found they were finishing by 2 P.M., they asked for more work. After a year, that department's output was up ten percent. We converted the whole plant to self-supervision and productivity rose twenty percent!"

Kwiat also sponsored, and provided space for, sports activities: soccer for the men and volleyball for the women; gave English lessons in his office to those who wanted them; helped immigrants with their status problems and got quality legal counsel for those who needed it. On a rotation basis, he took groups of five or six workers out to lunch, not to talk about work but to get to know each other. And since Spanish cultures have their main, hot meal at mid-day, Kwiat rigged a steam pipe into a warming oven where workers' precooked meals of rice and beans or chicken and plantains could be heated for lunch.

Trusting his employees and respecting their ethnic heritage inspired not just friendship but loyalty. When the company moved from Brooklyn to Lancaster. Pa., eight workers moved with it—an almost unheard of phenomemon amoung non-management employees.

JOB ENRICHMENT

Workers' complaints: boring, repetitive jobs. Supervisors' complaints: low morale, high error rates, heavy backlogs. To cure both problems, companies have successfully redesigned jobs to give workers more responsibility and greater possibilities for work pride. In 1972, at Guardian Life Insurance Company, as many as eight employees handled one insurance policy, assembly-line style—each responsible for a small segment of the whole. After "job enrichment," each person was given her or his own clients, the freedom to set a work schedule and to do a "whole job" whose progress could be measured against visible objectives. After three years of "being treated like adults," productivity was up nearly 25 percent.

Job enrichment reduced clerical errors at Western Union in Philadelphia when the billing process was restructured. Instead of dividing 12 functions among 12 different types of clerks, the 12 clerks each mastered the whole variety of functions and just split the work load. Workers in the money-transfer division of Chase Manhattan Bank responded dramatically to job enrichment that included more tasks, more responsibility, teamwork and customer identification. Error rates decreased 13 percent and the bank no longer needed to pay checkers to police the workers.

CONCERN FOR THE WORKER

More than a third of the 7,300 eligible employees at Kimberly-Clark Co. in Neenah, Wisc., take advantage of a unique company-sponsored tuition plan that gives each worker a "bank account" of $480 to use for educational costs. If not drawn out, the sum reverts to the company after a year. Kimberly-Clark also offers paid sabbatical leaves of two weeks to a year for specialized, job-related education and has a special education plan to cover employees' families.

A smart mind needs a sound body, of course. A number of corporations have hypertension-detection programs that cost less than $1 per employee for the screening process and $125 to provide treatment if high blood pressure is discovered. New York Telephone Company has had such a program for more than 10 years, with a 43 percent cut in absenteeism and an untold number of prevented strokes.

Besides regular health and disability plans, progressive companies are beginning to pay attention to the effects upon workers of work-related stress. About 120 companies participate in the International Meditation Society's programs for business; hundreds more pay for executives to learn stress control, relaxation, meditation and biofeedback. A recent news article reports that industry loses up to $20 billion a year in missed workdays and early death from stress. Granted, many companies may be financing mountain-climbing, transcendental meditation retreats and smoking cessation seminars out of self-interest. But from the employees' viewpoint, these programs are life-enhancing, whatever their rationale.

INCENTIVE PROGRAMS

The Scanlon Plan (named for the steelworker who invented it 40 years ago) emphasizes three forms of worker involvement: 1) participation (you identify with the company history and goals, share in its responsibilities and decision-making); 2) achievement (your performance and ideas help increase productivity and reduce costs); 3) reward (you share the economic gains). Basic to the Scanlon Plan is a committee-style communications network between workers and managers and a system of bonuses based on productivity. During 25 years under the Plan, employees of Herman Miller, Inc., in Zeeland, Mich., have received more than $5 million in bonuses. At Dana Corporation in Edgerton, Wisc., the employees may make work-improvement suggestions to their committees, and each committee may vote to spend up to $200 to implement each suggestion on a test basis. This lets employees "work smarter rather than harder," and finances a worker's innovation with company money on the chance it will benefit both parties. About 100 Scanlon Plans are in effect nationwide.

SENSITIVITY TRAINING

The Marley sheet metal plant in Louisville, Ky., would have risked losing government contracts if it didn't fulfill its affirmative action plan and hire women. But every time a woman was hired, she left within a month because of hostility from the 275 male employees. To help women enter this traditionally-male job category, and to help men accept female co-workers, Marley brought in the Women and Employment Project (sponsored by the Louisville YWCA), which presented a "psychodrama" to the company's 25 male supervisors. The skits explored typical male responses to women's changing roles and brought the men's fears and misconceptions into the open without embarrassing or challenging them directly.

SETTING YOUR OWN PAY

Many employees receive costly benefits they neither want nor need, says Dr. Edward E. Lawler, an organizational psychologist. He reports that when a large West Coast electronics firm let 12,000 workers devise their own pay package, 80 percent changed their benefits to fit their family situations. Many took lower salaries and higher benefits. When an Oakland sales outfit let its 15 employees research the group rates and set its own wages, they turned out to be only slightly higher than union scale. Married employees often adjust the salary/fringes ratio or give themselves less vacation and more health insurance, while unmarried workers do the opposite.

FLEXIBLE SCHEDULES

The most frequently cited "quality of working life" innovations are those that allow employees' work times to be in harmony with their individual needs, family responsibilities and leisure-time interests. Studies find that the four-day, 40-hour week is preferred by 78 percent of white-collar workers who've experienced it; they like its extra leisure, the increased knowledge gained while covering for the 20 percent of workers who are off each day, and the decreased supervision that goes with it. However, nearly two-thirds said their work is more tiring—and many had trouble coordinating their lives with others.

About 13 percent of all U.S. businesses use "flexitime," a system that requires all employees to work during a "core period" (say 9 A.M. to 3 P.M.), but lets them choose when to work the remaining hours. Workers like to adjust their starting or quitting times to children's schedules, traffic flow, housework, advanced studies, civic activities and child care logistics. According to a 1977 survey of 805 executives, management likes the fact that flexitime improves morale and productivity and reduces absenteeism and turnover.

Part-time work with good benefits can be the most humane work option for women with school-age children, or for students who need to earn money —two groups who happen to comprise the total 139-member work force at Selby Bindery in St. Paul, Minn. The mothers work from 8:30 A.M. to 2 P.M. and the students from 2:30 to 5 P.M..

"Most people are less productive in their sixth through eighth hours of a day," says Richard Mangram, Selby plant manager. "We are presumably getting the best five work hours of our people's time." Mangram also gives workers a weekly profit and loss statement so there is satisfying feedback about their performance or quick correction of their mistakes. Since 1970, Selby has promoted about 150 employees to better paying, more skilled jobs—and each year more minority women and teenagers (groups with the highest rate of unemployment) gain valuable experience, employment references and good work habits. No wonder Mangram reports that the community expresses "fierce loyalty" toward the Selby plant!

PARTICIPATIVE MANAGEMENT: WHAT IT REALLY MEANS IN PRACTICE

Dale D. McConkey

Probably no other words in management jargon have been more perverted, misunderstood, misapplied, and maligned than "participative management." This confusion is unfortunate because many management authorities argue, with substantial reasoning to support them, that the participative style of managing will continue to grow in importance in the future. Participative management *can* be a highly effective, demanding, and rewarding style of managing.

MISCONCEPTIONS

Much of the criticism and skepticism about participative management appears to result from several major misconceptions about what it is and how it should be applied. There are several popular misconceptions.

- **Participative management is synonymous with "permissive" management.** Permissive management sometimes results from a misguided attempt to practice participative management. In effect, permissive management allows each manager to do as he or she wishes *without sufficient regard to the requirements or needs of the organization.*

    Participative management, in marked contrast, starts off by making it clear to each manager that the primary reason he or she is employed is to help carry out the requirements of the organization. Then, each manager is acquainted with the organization's objectives and priorities. Ideally, each man-

Reprinted from *Business Horizons,* Volume 23 (October 1980), by permission of the publisher.

ager should be provided with both long- and short-term guidance. This guidance can take the form of: the long-term plan for the organization; the short-term (annual) objectives; and areas of concentration—usually areas of problems or opportunities which lower-level managers should examine.

Providing the long-term plan is especially important to many staff managers whose efforts generally reach fruition only over a period of time, such as research and development managers responsible for new products and services and human relations managers who are concerned with bringing about behavioral change.

Then, each manager is asked how he or she can help carry out the organization's objectives and priorities. In responding to this question each manager is given the greatest possible (practical) latitude or participation in determining his or her own future within the organization which is *consistent with the requirements of the organization*. Permissive management results when managers pursue their own ideas with inadequate leadership and direction from top management.

- **Participative management is the same as "democratic" management.** Democratic management results in leaderless chaos. It requires a higher-level manager to permit subordinates to vote on all decisions and then be bound by the majority vote.

The current popularity in the literature on the Japanese approach to consensus decision-making has probably helped to promote this misconception that "participative" and "democratic" are synonymous. Those who would uphold this view would be well counseled to delve more deeply into both the Japanese management environment and what actually happens in their consensus approach. In neither case is it "democratic."

Any attempt to practice democratic management would be particularly chaotic at the present time when more and more people are demanding greater participation but are often not trained to exercise it properly.

- **Participative management replaces responsibility for individual decision making with decision making by a group.** A definite distinction must be made between participation in the decision-making process and the decision itself. For example, normally only the chief executive officer can make the final decision on strategic planning subjects. However, before he or she makes the final decision, prudent management practice dictates that the CEO secure the input and recommendations of all subordinate managers who can contribute to the quality of the decision when it finally is made.

The participation, in this case, takes place prior to the decision. The decision is made after the participation and always by the higher level manager in charge of the unit. The failure of the higher level manager to think and act in this manner usually results in the senior manager abdicating one of his/her more important responsibilities. Many of the ills of "democratic" management frequently result.

An effectively functioning participative approach requires that each manager at each level of management make the decisions for which he or she is accountable. To hold otherwise would result in destroying the individual accountability which is the cornerstone of the whole approach.

- **Once the participative style of management is adopted, it must be practiced 100 percent of the time.** Can subordinates be developed effectively if they do not participate in every decision having a bearing on their operation? Obviously, time constraints and exigencies of the moment may preclude the opportunity for participation or render it inadvisable. J. Clayton Lafferty, president of Human Synergistics, Inc., and a well-respected behavioral scientist, notes:

> "When a three-engine Boeing 727 flying at 40,000 feet loses all three engines at once (under normal circumstances the plane could glide for over 130 miles) the captain has ample time for quickly consulting with his copilot and flight engineer to get their ideas about the cause and remedy, and to discuss emergency procedures with the stewardesses.
> "However, if a similar power loss occurred at 500 feet during a takeoff climb, the captain would be ill advised to practice such participative techniques."

Dr. Lafferty's example is dramatic, but it does establish the distinction between desirable management practices to follow under normal circumstances and those that must be waived for the moment based on a higher priority and good business sense. For example, it would be foolhardy for a president to delay answering one of the company's top customers for several days just because the sales manager was in Europe and could not be reached for discussion prior to making an important decision; or for the higher level plant manager to delay shutting down a production line that was turning out rejects until he could page and locate the lower level production manager. However, in all but the most extreme cases, the subordinate's growth will be enhanced by giving him or her the maximum opportunity to help determine the course of action to be taken.

- **To be fair and equitable, all subordinates should be given the same latitude or participation.** Managers who live and work in the real world have long appreciated the considerable differences in competence and motivation that exist among their subordinate managers. This appreciation permits them to deal realistically with the varying degrees of participation they can permit their subordinates to exercise when determining their accountability. The three major degrees are illustrated by the following superior-to-subordinate comments:

Level 1. "Here are your objectives!" The boss has the full initiative and no participation is invited or expected.

Level 2. "Here are several objectives I believe are realistic for you. What do you think of them?" The boss continues to have the initiative but participation is being invited and encouraged.

Level 3. "Here are the higher level objectives and priorities for next year. Using these for guidance, let me have your recommended objectives." Now the initiative has passed to the subordinate and full participation is being encouraged.

Obviously, a management style that is preponderately participative depends on a vast majority of managers participating at or near level 3, with a much smaller number operating at level 2 and a few at level 1. Level 1 managers may be unusual, but every organization undoubtedly has a few of them.

A WORKING DEFINITION

Managers' responses to participative management vary from indicting it as a "goodie, goodie" approach to bankruptcy to staunchly advocating its many virtues. Frequently, any in-depth discussion becomes impossible because of lack of agreement as to the meaning of the words. Most of those managers who condemn participative management will candidly admit that their views are based on past experiences in which they experienced failure when trying to practice what they viewed as being participative management. I offer the following practical definition of participative management:

"A decentralized, team approach to managing in which all managers are given the greatest *practical* latitude to determine or influence their jobs as they help carry out the requirements of the organization."

In practice, this definition implies the following:

Responsibility.   Major voice in determining the job content and its scope or parameters.

Accountability.   Major voice in determining results (objectives) which must be achieved.

Planning.   Do their own planning for their units.

Authority. Major voice in determining clear-cut authority for themselves.

Decision making. Decisions made at lowest possible level at which all of the *information and competence* necessary to make the decision come together.

Supervision. Emphasis is on self-supervision with minimum from above.

Management. Wide latitude to manage their own resources.

Communications and feedback. Tailored to their individual needs on a need-known basis.

The acid test as to how extensively participative management is being practiced can be measured by determining to what degree each manager is permitted to manage him or herself—what is often referred to as "self-management."

THE REWARDS

Obviously, there are no guarantees in management. However, there are many *potential* rewards or benefits which a manager may expect from participative management when it is properly understood and properly practiced. These potential benefits include:

Major voice in determining future.
Greater commitment.
Greater motivation.
Appraisal based on results.
Rewards based on results.
Agreement on what is expected.
Know where going as a manager.
Better development.
Prepared for greater responsibility.
Better planning closer to the "scene of the action."
Less supervision required when objectives are clear.
Self-discipline.
Greater authority.
Better decisions nearer the time and scene of the action.
Greater freedom to manage resources to reach objectives.
Greater satisfaction in completing a job which manager
helped to determine.
Less criticism of matters for which manager is not accountable.

More respect from subordinates.
Better feedback and control.

THE DEMANDS

As could be expected from any situation which promises rewards to the manager, participative management also makes demands upon each manager. Participative management requires the manager to: Accept accountability for the results of the unit. Plan for the unit. Accept and carry out authority. Make recommendations relative to the operation of the unit. Make decisions as called for by level of authority. Seize the initiative in problem solving.

THE TRANSITION

No manager, regardless of his or her competence and sincerity, could implement overnight a decision to increase the amount of participation granted to subordinates.

Prior to deciding how far participative management can and should proceed in an organization, it is necessary to examine the present management style of that organization.

"What is our current style of management?" should be the first question. Once the current style has been identified, management can analyze and provide the most prudent possible answers to four more all-important questions.

The answers to these questions are criticial because each style of management rests upon a distinct foundation tailored to that particular style of management. Two different management styles, say, autocratic and participative, have different foundations or "supportive systems" including policies, procedures, authority, training, objectives, decision process, feedback, compensation, and many other factors.

Under an autocratic style of management each brick in the foundation will have been tailored to support an autocratic structure. Policies will be oriented to centralized decision making, little authority will have been delegated down the line, few managers will participate in actual planning, and feedback will be directed only to the top management.

In contrast, if a participative style of management is being practiced, policies, planning, decision making, and the like must be characterized by a high degree of decentralization . It is not possible to foist a participative style of management on top of supportive systems designed for an autocratic style, so close attention must be paid to building and maintaining the proper foundation.

To what extent does management want to change the current management style? The decision to move from one management style to another cannot be made easily or quickly. A large insurance company in the north-central United States serves as demonstrable evidence of this point. The chief executive officer had heard many favorable accounts of management by objectives. To operate successfully, management by objectives involves full scale, in-depth delegation; it is an excellent example of participative management at its best.

The chief executive decided to adopt management by objectives and brought in an outside management consultant for counseling. After talking for three days with the chief executive and his senior officers, the consultant flatly refused to have anything to do with installing MBO in light of the management style and supportive structures then existing in the organization. The company had one of the most autocratic styles the consultant had ever witnessed, and discussions with the senior officers disclosed little evidence of a desire to change it.

Confronted with the consultant's findings, the chief executive was genuinely shocked and announced that he intended to change both the style and the supportive systems immediately. Over a period of several months he issued directive after directive and held meeting after meeting, attempting to accomplish the change. The major result of his efforts was almost complete chaos among his managers. They simply were not geared to such drastic change. Instead of moving immediately to change the management style, the president should have first made a determination as to just how much change could and should be made.

This question should not be answered too quickly or taken lightly. Management history is full of examples of organizations who extolled the virtues of participative management but, at the slightest hint of an economic downturn, quickly centralized most of the decision making.

How fast can and should the change be made? Once the determination has been made about how far management wants to go in changing its style, consideration must be given to how fast the change can be made. The important factors are how fast the supportive systems can be developed to uphold the new style and how fast the support of key managers can be gained. There are no magic rules or formulas for arriving at this determination . However, the experience of many managers indicates that it takes between three and five years to move from an autocratic to a participative management style. If the management style lies somewhere between the autocratic and participative styles, as most probably do, this time estimate would be shortened.

What data and information must be decentralized to lower level managers for decision making and how fast can this be accomplished? A truism of decision-making provides that the quality of decisions cannot consistently rise above the quality of the information upon which they are based. Thus, before decision-making can be decentralized, the information required by each manager must be brought into focus for him or her. Otherwise, managers would be asked to make decisions without being in possession of the requisite information. Poor, costly decisions would result. Thus, if managers are required to plan, control, and generally self-manage, they must be given this tailored data.

To what degree can the acceptance and support of subordinate managers be gained and maintained? Many factors must be considered when management responds to this question: How well are the managers trained? Does an environment exist which promotes motivation and achievement? Does a reward and recognition program exist which encourages high levels of performance? Does top management continuously promote and actively involve itself in the participative management approach?

DETERMINING READINESS

While not intended as an all-inclusive or overly scientific test instrument, the accompanying checklist will help an organization determine its overall readiness or current posture with respect to major aspects of participative management. It will serve as a guide as to where the organization currently stands as well as the time and effort which will be involved in moving to a more participative management style. It is suggested that at least three levels of management take part in completing the checklist. Each level will be reacting from a different vantage point and with different information. Frank, candid resolution of major differences can produce better results.

Readiness Checklist

Factor	Major thrust	Little if any 1 2 3	Exception rather than rule 1 2 3	Rule rather than exception 1 2 3	Extensive 1 2 3
Support and participation by top management	Active involvement vs. lip service	□□□	□□□	□□□	□□□
Favorable environment for change	Willingness to change vs. protecting landed interests	□□□	□□□	□□□	□□□
Open, non-threatening environment	Trust and respect vs. fear	□□□	□□□	□□□	□□□
Willingness of senior managers to share authority	Secure vs. insecure manager	□□□	□□□	□□□	□□□
Quality of subordinate managers	Ability and willingness to accept responsibility	□□□	□□□	□□□	□□□
Willingness of subordinates to accept objective measurement on the job	Results vs. effort or busyness	□□□	□□□	□□□	□□□

Readiness Checklist (Continued)

Factor	Major thrust	Little if any	Exception rather than rule	Rule rather than exception	Extensive
		1 2 3	1 2 3	1 2 3	1 2 3
Willingness to comply with disciplined approaches	Planning vs. seat-of-the-pants	☐☐☐	☐☐☐	☐☐☐	☐☐☐
Environment predictable enough for planning	Stability vs. instability	☐☐☐	☐☐☐	☐☐☐	☐☐☐
Participation in objective setting	Self-management vs. dictation from above	☐☐☐	☐☐☐	☐☐☐	☐☐☐
Relationship between objectives of the organization and lower level objectives	Supportive vs. fragmented	☐☐☐	☐☐☐	☐☐☐	☐☐☐
Verifiable objectives	Measurable vs. vague/nebulous	☐☐☐	☐☐☐	☐☐☐	☐☐☐
Relationship between achievement of objectives and reward system	Results-oriented rewards vs. subjective ones	☐☐☐	☐☐☐	☐☐☐	☐☐☐
Willingness to take risks	Innovative vs. playing it safe	☐☐☐	☐☐☐	☐☐☐	☐☐☐
Free and open interdepartmental communications	Team building vs. empire building	☐☐☐	☐☐☐	☐☐☐	☐☐☐
Degree of interdepartmental coordination among managers on matters of common concern	Freedom and willingness to consult with other involved managers	☐☐☐	☐☐☐	☐☐☐	☐☐☐
Data/information in focus for decision making	Decentralization vs. centralized	☐☐☐	☐☐☐	☐☐☐	☐☐☐
Job responsibilities clearly delineated	Agreement between superior and subordinate on job scope and content	☐☐☐	☐☐☐	☐☐☐	☐☐☐
Priorities can be determined	Most important vs. less important	☐☐☐	☐☐☐	☐☐☐	☐☐☐

AND INTO THE FUTURE

Circumstances continue to emphasize the importance of participative management. Several forces in particular seem to argue most strongly for managers to sharpen their skills in this style of management. These include the rapid rate of change; the rapid increase in complexity; the breakdown in command authority; and the need for job satisfaction among managers, particularly at the middle management level.

Rapid change. Change is accelerating so rapidly that it has become necessary for statisticians to coin a new acronym—ROCOC (rate of change of change). It has and will become increasingly impossible for one manager, or even a handful of managers, to cope with this rate of change. Thus, more participation by more managers will be required.

Complexity. Change, by itself, is difficult enough to cope with. However, the problem is compounded by the increased rate of complexity which is occurring concurrently with change. Again, no single manager can hope to cope with the increased complexity; a team effort seems to be the only way.

Job satisfaction. The problem of job satisfaction among managers, particularly those at the middle level, has been documented by survey after survey and study after study. Many techniques and approaches have been advanced for lessening the problem. Experience to date in many organizations would indicate that participative management, properly practiced, would go far in providing each manager with a meaningful, challenging job and then leaving him free, within agreed upon boundaries, to "self-manage" the job.

Breakdown in command authority. Traditional power and authority relationships are crumbling. The prompt salute and "yes sir" or "yes ma'm" are fast disappearing from the military. Dogma and blind faith in one's superiors are no longer widely accepted by many levels of church management. Both students and teachers are rebelling against the traditional, all-knowing approach of school administrators. The traditional relationship between parent and child has been replaced by one less dependent on power and authority. The actions and attitudes of employees and managers, especially middle-level managers, indicate an appreciable amount of unrest and dissatisfaction with jobs in which they do not have a major voice.

These broad and sweeping departures from the past—the demand for a larger voice in self-determination by those who work for organizations—suggest one means of meeting these demands: participation designed to achieve definite, desired results for the organization and optimize these results by providing a vehicle for utilizing the talents of all managers. Participation that affords all managers a significant voice in self-determination can go far in helping to make their efforts more satisfying and rewarding.

For all these reasons, managers should complete a penetrating self-appriasal of their approach to the value and practice of participative management. They should also thoroughly understand what participative management really means in practice in the real world of management.

PRODUCTIVITY GAINS THROUGH WORKLIFE IMPROVEMENT

Edward M. Glaser

Evidence that we have a nationwide productivity problem—in both public and private sectors—has mounted alarmingly over the past couple of years. According to the *1978 Economic Report to the President,* for example, the slow-down in productivity growth in the United States is "one of the most significant economic problems of recent years."

At an October 1978 conference on productivity, President Carter's (then) Chief Inflation Adviser Robert S. Strauss said that the establishment of a Cabinet-level Council on Productivity would "provide a high-level central focus" for productivity programs in government agencies and coordinate such programs with the private sector. He also said that such a council would hopefully help increase industrial output and hold down inflation.

The (then) Federal Reserve Chairman G. William Miller agreed with Strauss, stating that "increased productivity is the best prospect for breaking the cycle of wages chasing prices and prices chasing wages."

The following month, during a forum sponsored by the National Academy of Sciences, six representatives of business, government, and academia voiced their concern about what they considered to be a crisis in America's innovative spirit. As evidence, they cited the decline in our rate of economic growth, a worsening U.S. balance of payments, the decreasing number of U.S. patents issued, and a decrease in the amount of dollars allocated by industry for research and development.

Many proposals have been offered for coping with or overcoming these problems, including massive reform of federal regulatory practices; a greater emphasis on job training, especially for young people; establishment of incen-

---

Reprinted by permission of the publisher from PERSONNEL, January-February 1980, © 1980 by AMACOM, a division of American Management Associations. All rights reserved.

tives for undertaking industrial innovation; modernizing plant, equipment, and technology; doing more basic research and development; curtailment of overall government spending; reorientation of tax laws; and review of confusing antitrust and patent laws. Conspicuous by its absence from this list, however, is the important contribution that can be made by structuring and managing work situations in ways likely to motivate employees at all levels to become active participants in problem/opportunity identification and problem solving with reference to any aspects of the work situation that were perceived to be in need of review. One way to facilitate this kind of participation is to foster, on a broad scale, improvement in the quality of worklife in American organizations.

QUALITY OF WORKLIFE—THE ISSUES

What is meant by "quality of worklife" (QWL)? Basically, it is a process by which all members of the organization, through appropriate channels of communication set up for this purpose, have some say about the design of their jobs in particular and the work environment in general. In this kind of participative and responsive organizational climate, suggestions, questions, and criticism that might lead to improvement of any kind are encouraged and welcomed. In such a setting, creative discontent is viewed as a manifestation of constructive caring about the organization rather than destructive griping. Management encouragement of such feelings of involvement often leads to ideas and actions for upgrading of operational effectiveness and efficiency as well as environmental enhancement. Increased productivity thus is likely to result as a natural byproduct.

Improving the quality of worklife is a process rather than a set of specific steps, because organizations and institutions are not all alike. That is, the QWL improvement ideas that each company evolves for its own use are based on the culture, needs, and "change readiness" in that particular organization.

Two subtle, related benefits that often result from efforts to improve the quality of worklife are an improvement in organizational communications and a reduction in the number and intensity of adversary relationships. As individuals and groups learn to agree on common goals and the means to achieve them, they become more responsible and thus require less monitoring. As a result, overhead costs may decrease significantly. To pursue productivity improvement in comprehensive ways, this goal must be thought of as more than just the increase in output of goods and services divided by the hours of work needed to get them done. Heightened management effectiveness and efficiency must also be a goal.

One authority points out that the participative style involved calls for change in the philosophy and behavior of many managers and officials—both in companies and in unions—with regard to the way human resources are valued and utilized. Allowing employees to participate in decision making that bears upon the design, structure, or organization of the work may be viewed by supervisors as an erosion of their authority. Union officials, on their part, may view such concerted action between workers and management as an undermining of their role as designated employee representatives.

From the union's point of view, the major aspect of developing a viable QWL process is to create a climate that promotes employee job satisfaction. The key focus is not on improved productivity or reduced labor costs, but the creation of an atmosphere in which workers can take part in decision-making processes on matters that affect them, and to do this in such a way that expands their opportunities for job satisfaction. From such an operating style, productivity improvement is a likely fallout. Many managers, however, feel that productivity gains should be an upfront objective along with QWL improvement, not just a byproduct.

CONDITIONS FOR SUCCESS

It should be noted that several QWL improvement experiments have failed, for various reasons. Those cases should be studied for an understanding both of the most common reasons for failure and of the conditions that seem required for success. Companies interested in undertaking such a program should keep in mind the following conditions that are essential for successful long-term results:

- Management must be committed to an open, nondefensive style of operation that includes sharing appropriate information with employees and sincerely inviting their input regarding problems, opportunities, and implementation of improvement plans.
- Employees must be given opportunities for advancement in organizational or career terms.
- Supervisors must be trained to function effectively in a less directive, more collaborative style.
- Traditional status barriers between management and workforce must be broken down to permit the establishment of an atmosphere of trust and open communication.
- Employees should receive feedback on results achieved and recognition for superior performance. Other forms of positive reinforcement, such as financial incentives should also be made available, where feasible.
- Personnel should be selected who can be motivated to strive for excellence in job performance.
- Both positive and negative outcomes of the QWL improvement program should be analyzed and evaluated, and these results used to work toward continual improvement of the system.

This type of participative management is consistent with organizational discipline and appropriately controlled operations—controlled, that is, in the interest of efficiency, effectiveness, quality assurance, customer service, profitability, and high employee morale. Managers still continue to be responsible for achieving their goals; once they realize that inviting consultation with, or tapping the collective wisdom of, their subordinates will help them achieve these goals, they become better managers.

Such an approach to improving the quality of worklife is not to be confused with an abstract sociopolitical concept of "democratic management." That is, decisions about what is to be done in the work context are not arrived at by voting. The QWL improvement process is democratic in a psychological rather than a sociopolitical sense. It invites employees from all departments at all levels to have a say in what they do, which in turn makes for a sense of "part ownership" in any change that may result and a stake in organizational success. Thus it enhances self-esteem and reduces the feeling of powerlessness that all too often arises in the organizational setting.

A caveat is needed here. While the participative principle offers an opportunity for building employee morale, it must be used appropriately. Many decisions call for the input of experts from various organizational groups and/or outside consultants, and their considered opinions may far outweigh what nonexperts may want or think about the matter at hand. Thus participative decision making is not the right vehicle for *all* problem-solving situations.

Then, too, a responsible leader or legitimate decision maker sometimes faces constraints that do not permit much active participation: the need to reconcile a problem between conflicting special interest groups, for example, or a tight deadline for making a decision. In such cases, he or she must take the position that commensurate authority accompanies responsibility, and the individual with the responsibility must act as he or she deems best, subsequently giving reasons for the decision made. If the consequences are not irrevocable, the decision can be reviewed and/or refined after a period of implementation.

QWL improvement programs are basically preventive rather than remedial strategies, yet the elements involved have been used for rescue purposes. Following is a case in point.

QUALITY OF WORKLIFE AND THE ORGANIZATION

A Midwest-based manufacturing company was experiencing labor-management friction and declining product quality. As a result, business fell off considerably, half the workforce was let go, and the company was soon thereafter sold to a Japanese firm.

The new chief executive officer immediately called a meeting of management members and union officials to discuss the situation, soliciting their questions and their suggestions on improving quality and cutting costs. He then met with the rest of the workforce and invited their ideas as well. The CEO pointed out that if appreciable sales expansion could be achieved through the ideas generated, the company would be able to rehire the laid-off employees and provide greater job security for all.

The next step involved setting up a joint labor management committee to analyze production problems, evaluate ideas for improvement, propose problem-solving actions, share in making decisions about the design and organization of work, and give employees feedback. The result: Within nine months, business improved to the point where the company was able to rehire the same number of employees it had been forced to terminate.

The dramatic turnaround in this organization's fortunes resulted from a managerial style that enlisted the cooperation of interested personnel at all organizational levels, including local union officials, in solving problems *they* helped to identify and in devising methods of capitalizing on perceived business opportunities. In addition to instituting a responsive, collaborative management/union relationship with joint participation in various types of planning, the new owners demonstrated a readiness to adopt modernizing technical changes and a willingness to invest capital in promising business ventures.

The manufacturing firm was only one of several that achieved a relatively high level of worker identification with legitimate needs for cost-effective operations and superior product quality. In the 1950s, Donnelly Mirrors, a firm based in Holland, Michigan, decided to redistribute power from the top down to all organizational levels—the goal being to tap the creative resources of the entire workforce. In addition to setting up a participative style of management supported by related organizational-development activities, Donnelly installed a cost-savings/sharing plan. Employee involvement in setting goals and in making work-related decisions is still encouraged, and the employees share in the gains that result from their efforts. Some reported results were a reduction in the price of the company's main product by 25 percent between 1972 and 1974, thus expanding their share of the market; in 20 years, productivity per person has doubled; employee bonuses have averaged 12 percent over base pay; absenteeism has dropped from 5 percent to 1 percent; quality levels have climbed from 92 percent to 98.5 percent; there has been a marked reduction in returned goods; employee job satisfaction has increased noticeably.

The total number of U.S. organizations that have achieved substantial improvements in productivity and the quality of worklife through tapping the wellspring of latent motivation of people to become ego-involved and perform is very small, compared with the number of companies that could potentially do so. This is unfortunate, in view of the dimension of our productivity problem.

THE GOVERNMENT'S INVOLVEMENT IN QWL

In late 1978, a promising piece of legislation was passed that attempts to stimulate wider implementation of QWL improvement programs in both the public and the private sector by giving companies and unions financial incentives to implement such programs.

The sponsor of the Labor-Management Cooperation Act of 1978 was Congressman Stanley N. Lundine (D-NY). The former mayor of Jamestown, New York, he served as the initiator, catalyst, and gadfly for the introduction of the Jamestown Labor-Management Committee in 1972 when the city was experiencing a severe economic downturn, a 10 percent unemployment rate, and major labor problems. Through the labor/management committee, Lundine was able to get local managers and union leaders to sit down and discuss problems, establish training programs and, in some cases, initiate cost-savings/sharing programs. Significant improvements resulted.

When Lundine was elected to Congress in 1976, he began working on his proposed bill, and in October 1978 the bill was passed as an amendment to CETA legislation. The bill's stated purposes are to:

- Improve communication between representatives of labor and representatives of management.
- Give workers and employers opportunities to study and explore new and innovative joint approaches to achieving organizational effectiveness.
- Assist workers and employers in solving problems of mutual concern not subject to resolution within the collective bargaining process.
- Study and explore ways of eliminating potential problems that reduce the competitiveness and inhibit the economic development of the organization, area, or industry.
- Enhance the involvement of employees in making decisions that affect their working lives.
- Encourage free collective bargaining by establishing continuing mechanisms for communication between employers and employees through federal assistance to the formation and operation of labor/management committees.

The Federal Mediation and Conciliation Service is authorized to enter into contract negotiations and make grants under this Act only in situations where employees are unionized. More important than the financial subsidy, however, is the potential benefit to be gained if this incentive stimulates company managements and employees to explore methods of working together toward QWL improvement objectives, and to follow through with appropriate action.

Obviously, such exploration does not require governmental assistance. Companies should and can do this on their own initiative because it makes good sense *and* is in the national interest.

QUALITY OF WORK LIFE
PROSPECTS FOR THE 80s

Robert H. Guest

Delivered at the Harvard Business School Club of New York, New York City, January 10, 1980

My recent *Harvard Business Review* article, "Quality of Work Life—Learning from Tarrytown" describes a series of extraordinary developments at the General Motors Tarrytown plant. In a period of a few years this huge plant went from one of the lowest positions in General Motors to one of the top performers among all of its plants in all major indices of performance—in terms of labor costs, quality, absenteeism, turnover, grievances—and in the speed in which it adjusted to a new production model.

The key to this amazing turnaround was a joint effort by General Motors and the UAW to involve workers and all of management in a process known as Quality of Work Life. At the heart of QWL was a fundamental acceptance by GM management and by the UAW of the idea that the ordinary workers on the shop floor had a great deal to contribute to the success of the organization that went far beyond the traditional role that was expected of them. They discovered the simple secret to success of finding a way to unlock the creative and motivational potential among its people.

I'm not going to discuss at length what happened at Tarrytown, but what did happen there is both substantive and symbolic of a movement—a quiet revolution one might call it—which is taking place in a number of companies in many places in the U.S.

Reprinted from *Vital Speeches of the Day,* March 1, 1980, by permission of the publisher, City News Publishing Co.

My central thesis is that policy makers and managers had better understand the importance of this quiet revolution and respond intelligently and with commitment in the 1980's. The Quality of Work Life movement is no flash-in-the-pan phenomenon. It is different from a lot of human relations and employee communication programs of the past. It represents a fundamental shift in the way white collar and blue collar workers view their roles in the work environment and the way management responds to these changing views.

Let's put things in perspective. Managers face a lot of critical challenges today—inflation, the energy crisis, environmental problems and, of course, the broad geopolitical crises on the world scene. But let's not lose sight of some other underlying issues—issues that any effective executive or manager can do something about—and begin right now, as hundreds of progressive organizations have done, to enrich the quality of work life itself with measurable results in the productive health of the organization.

Two arresting developments come to our attention. One is the national decline in the rate of productivity growth. The other is the increase in employee dissatisfaction in recent years. The two are related.

Productivity measures are complicated and include a variety of factors—economic conditions, technological changes, cyclical factors, etc. But the productiveness of our human resources is crucial to any measure. The rate of productivity growth since 1966 is significantly lower than it was in the previous two decades. According to the latest reports of the Joint Economic Committee of Congress, labor productivity took its steepest plunge just in the last six months; less than 2 percent growth. And unless there is a substantial change, it is not expected to increase much in the 80's. Compare this, for example, with West Germany's 6 Percent and a hefty 9.5 percent for Japan. Not only has this affected the domestic economy but foreign competition is beating us to the punch in many dimensions.

Now for the other development—the changing characteristics and attitudes of people in our offices and factories. One remarkable shift, of course, is in the lowering age levels of the work force. By the end of this decade there are expected to be 60 million workers in the 25–45 age bracket; an increase of 55 percent over the 1975 figures. The proportion of women will increase. The level of education has risen. Far more young people will have gone through high school and college. These cold statistical facts will have—and are having—profound effects on what people expect from life at work—from the quality and meaning of work itself and its rewards.

We are blind if we do not recognize the impact of the so-called youth counterculture movement of the 1960's on the attitudes of employees. There were the convulsive reactions to Vietnam and Watergate and the strong push for civil rights, personal rights, affirmative action—the whole churning of dissent and dissaffection that has had a profound influence on the way the New Breed views its role in organizational life, how they react to the intrinsic meaning of work, how their skills and their minds are used or not used, how they react to authority, how they perform. For 30 years the Opinion Research Corporation has been keeping the pulse on worker satisfaction. They demonstrate clearly that worker dissatisfaction in just about every measure has increased substantially in the last few years more than ever before (interestingly enough the opposite trend has been found among managers and executives!) The dissatisfaction is expressed equally among white collar and blue collar workers.

In our research and consulting we hear the superficial explanation for the change in employee attitudes and behavior. We hear complaints of sloppy work, absenteeism, turnover and a general don't-give-a-damn attitude. And everyone here can point to dozens of concrete examples right in his or her organization. The facts are unassailable. They are true. But to say that young people in our factories and offices are inherently lazy—"products of a permissive age" or "lacking the good old American ethic of progress through hard work" is to dodge the issue.

That's what a lot of managers were saying at Tarrytown a few years back —"This young crowd is a bunch of hippies. They only want the buck without putting in a half a day's work. They'll try to get away with anything. There's only one way to handle them—use your authority. Keep 'em in line. Give 'em the pink slip." And what was the composition of plant personnel?—a pot pourri of whites, blacks, Jamaicans, Puerto Ricans, ethnics, people from dozens of national backgrounds, men, women—even a few descendents of the early Hudson River Dutch settlers!

These same human beings, under an enlightened management and with the support of concerned union leaders, turned Tarrytown around in a few years. These same people assumed a new participatory and problem-solving role in the organization. These same people got charged up enough to make the 1980 model car changeover (the Citation), the most radical plant changeover in its history, a resounding success.

Why? Because the quality of their work lives had changed. More than thirty five hundred human beings in that plant came to feel involved, to feel they had a piece of the act in turning the plant around. They were listened to. They were trained in problem-solving techniques. Constructive ideas exploded from one end of the plant to another—and management was amazed by the creativity that had obviously been locked up for years. And this was the same group and the same union that had 2,000 labor grievances on the docket at one time a few years previously.

The people there had not changed. The environment had changed. People were allowed to express themselves in response to some basic human needs. In the behavioral sciences we have understood for a long time what these needs are, but somehow life in our giant complex pressure-ridden organizations has stifled the opportunity to fulfill these needs. What are the building blocks to psychological well-being? Daniel Yankelovich, talking about the New Breed of workers, summarized them:

— a sense of self-esteem and a conviction of one's worth as an individual
— the ability to believe that one's actions make sense to others as well as to oneself
— a set of concrete goals and values
— feelings of potency and efficacy
— enough stimulation to avoid boredom
— a feeling that one's world is reasonably stable
— an overall sense of meaning and coherence to one's life

Now do these seem strange and academic to us? Certainly not. Are these not the same positive feelings all of us enjoy when we have successfully tackled a tough problem, when we have made decisions that substantially benefitted the organization, when our bosses realize that we have made a difference, when there are spillover effects of accomplishment that give richer meaning not only to our work lives but to our family and community lives.

But somehow we do not always realize that the group of drones card punching on the tenth floor of a downtown building or the bevvy of assemblers putting widgets together in Oshkosh need the same kind of stimulation that we, the managerial elite, do. Or even if we do have some empathy we excuse ourselves and say that those working at the grassroots levels of our organizations are unfortunate victims of a system, a system that says, in the sacred tradition of scientific management and Frederick W. Taylor, that human effort should be fractionated, broken down into simple constituent motions, made repetitive, given little room for human judgment. And, of course, there must be rules, regulations, precisely-defined job descriptions and a system of authority that tells who should do what, when, and how.

Even the methods and systems experts are coming to question their own assumptions about the design of jobs. Serge Birn, one of America's leading industrial engineers confesses:

> "For years, we industrial engineers have been fragmenting jobs by pursuing the one motion/one job principle and developing the one best way to do a job. In our headlong drive to save seconds, we forgot about the much more important elements of human productivity—the proper utilization of people's abilities."

Many companies have come to question the old assumptions as to how to utilize their human resources more effectively. I would cite among others, General Motors, Bank of America, Guardian Life, Lincoln National Life, Polaroid, Cummins Engine, Harmon International, to name a few. They recognize that the work population has changed not only in demographics but in attitudes, the high proportion of more educated youth, the growing dissatisfaction about the rewards of life at work that go beyond the paycheck, nice bosses, pleasant surroundings and the coffee break. Although accepting the vital necessity of sound management practices and operating systems they recognize that the rigid application of scientific management principles in designing the way people perform work only creates dissatisfaction and trouble. All of us at times have experienced what I call the dead hand of bureaucracy.

What are the characteristics of a work environment which provide quality to work life. They are, as Ted Mills puts it:
— cooperative rather than authoritative
— evolutionary and changing, not fixed
— open not rigid
— informal rather than rule based
— interpersonal, not mechanistic

Most of you are familiar with the different kinds of experiments and programs that enlightened managements have used to encourage these conditions. At the individual level we have seen systems of job rotation, the most successful ones being those in which the workers or clericals themselves figured out how to organize their work—not by management fiat—not by management telling people "we're doing this to make you happy!" Job enlargement is a familiar concept in which the number of elements to a job are expanded to provide variety and to relieve boredom.

We've heard of job enrichment. I first coined the term when the late Charles Walker and I wrote the book, "The Man on the Assembly Line" back in 1952. Essentially it means (Fred Herzberg not withstanding) not just a rearrangement of the tasks to provide variety, but also giving people a true sense of involvement in the design process, giving them a chance to grow on the job. Recently I observed, for example, what has been happening in two insurance companies. The results are striking. Not only have the employees expressed interest and excitement with the job enrichment efforts but absenteeism and turnover have been reduced and the error rate in processing insurance policies has been reduced by more than 20 percent in some areas.

Then, too, there have been hundreds of examples and experiments where entire work groups have been given latitude to self-regulate themselves and to figure out both the most interesting and productive ways to perform their work. They are known as "autonomous work groups" among which Volvo's Kalmar plant or Saab-Scania's engine assembly are the more dramatic examples. Then there is that Japanese "import" known as Quality Control Circles in which supervision and workers join together in a new kind of worker management relationship to find creative ways of solving quality problems. Many have expanded their focus to take in matters of scheduling, maintenance, the introduction of new technology and a variety of responsibilities which traditionally were responsibilities of staff management and personnel.

Where there are unions we see a burgeoning of joint labor-management committees dealing not with contractual issues, but on matters of mutual interest—joint safety programs, apprenticeship training, alcoholism rehabilitation, pre-retirement education as well as the solution of production problems.

On the compensation side of quality of work life we can predict that the present hourly wage system will change in the future and, as IBM has done, evolve in the direction of weekly, monthly, even annual methods of payments. I predict a new look at the old Scanlon Plans in which workers and management together develop incentive rewards based on cost savings factored from the ratio of standard costs measured against sales.

Technology itself is forcing radical changes in the nature of work. Automation has already eliminated thousands of dull or back-breaking jobs. Many of you have already seen in your own offices what has happened and what will happen because of the revolution of micro electronics. (Intel Corporation has a small general purpose device that can execute 770,000 instructions per second!) In Citibank, to cite one of hundreds of examples, the mini-computer and, more important, the relationship of the operator to the machine has changed with the responsibilities of the person supervising the machine having been enlarged immeasurably—single individuals interacting with clients, customers, vendors, and whatnot all over the country—all over the world. And what is coming down the pike in the mid and late eighties is mind boggling as these changes affect the way work is performed and the quality of work life itself. With enormous cost reductions we can expect the productivity gap which I mentioned earlier to improve substantially.

But the discussion of job enrichment, autonomous work groups, new technology can be deceptive. It is dangerous to embrace programs in a cookbook fashion. Many experiments and programs have gone down the tube—and those of us who have been close to the firing line know why. Too many managements have viewed them as motivational gimmicks to get more work out of people—or to make employees happy. The American business scene is a graveyard of programs, begun with good intentions, but that did not work because the *process* by which they were introduced was superficial and the motives of management were based on the quick payoff.

Fundamentally, what has gone wrong is that many managements have not comprehended the full meaning and impact of the quiet revolution taking place in the minds, the behavior and the social values of the New Breed of employees. Managements can be great risk takers when it comes to promoting a new product or service, making financial and investment decisions, introducing new technologies and systems, but they are often not willing to embrace employee participation in the full meaning of the term I have described. Because of a myriad of pressing distractions among the managers and executives I find them out of touch with what is really going on at the lower ranks of our giant complex enterprises. The concept of greater employee autonomy and flexibility in decision-making process is seen as a threat not a benefit to managerial power and authority. Sharing power is even frightening. Some feel that if you give an inch now the next thing they will demand is to have a say in corporate decisions. American management today is somewhat frightened by what has happened in Germany, Scandinavia and the low countries where by law there must be worker representation on the boards of directors. Nothing in my own studies here and overseas suggests that American workers either as individuals or as members of organized labor want to go the European route. The proposed appointment of Douglas Fraser to the board at Chrysler is a special circumstance. No. The "piece of the act" they seek, and this is not universally true, is limited to the immediate work environment.

In closing, may I underscore, for what it is worth, a few notions—guiding principles, if you will—that I feel are important to any policy-maker or manager who is seriously interested in the Quality of Work Life process. Some were mentioned at the end of the Tarrytown article. They represent my observations and feelings about the *process* of successful organizational change. In enumerating them I am conscious of the fact that a Quality of Work Life effort must be tailored to a particular organization's own history, climate and culture. Here they are:

1. Top management (and top labor officials where there is a collective bargaining agreement) must initially make *explicit commitments* to try innovative QWL activities. The decisions cannot be relegated to a staff function or viewed as a motivational "program" with a finite beginning and ending. They should be accepted as a "way of life" for the entire organization. There must be built-in momentum that is dynamic, on-going and that can continue regardless of personnel and other changes in the organization.
2. Even with agreement at high levels it is essential that middle management down to front line supervisors understand the issues and the challenge. Everyone must not only know what is taking place but also feel that they have a say in the change process. The same can be said about shop stewards where there is a union.
3. For QWL to succeed, management must be not only receptive to new ideas but show managerial competence in running an effective organization as a profit-making business enterprise. Employees, it has been found, are not willing to become involved in participative problem-solving efforts knowing that management lacks the competence to do anything with their ideas.
4. Where there are labor agreements a QWL effort should not be used to circumvent the contract. Management should not give up its right to manage nor the union its right to protect the workers under the contract. Experience has shown, however, than an effective joint QWL program can have substantial spillover effects in reducing labor grievances, bettering communication and in improving relationships.

5. Programs should be initated and carried out on a voluntary basis.
6. A program will not succeed if management's sole purpose in agreeing to it is to increase productivity. Workers quickly see this to be exploitative. But as successful programs show, a healthy QWL effort usually results in cost savings from improved quality performance, lower absenteeism and turnover and in better production methods.
7. Many successful examples do not start off with a master plan. They begin on a limited scale and are allowed to "feed on" success and spread to other segments of the organizaiton. I call this the "healthy infection principle".

One could add many more caveats. Surely to graduates of a prestigious business school it doesn't take one more professor to tell you what you already know. But don't take a professor's word for it. The clarion call has been made by a former top executive and Under-Secretary of Commerce who first initiated, carried out, and sustained one of the most comprehensive Quality of Work Life efforts. Here is what Sidney Harmon said recently:

> "I will flately assert that our problem is not just finding a way to increase technical capacity to improve productivity; we also have to emphasize the role of the individual and at a time when people just aren't interested in their work. I would suggest that the time to do so is now, while progressive thinkers in industry fully recognize that it is good business to build a healthy society. All of society is responsible.

SECTION VI

PRACTICING "WIN-WIN" ADMINISTRATION

INTRODUCTION

In order for organizations to achieve the results they are capable of attaining, in order for organizational members to find satisfaction in their worklife and be healthy productive members of the society, and in order to relieve some of the frustration and anger felt by too many people who have to deal with organizations, the practice of "Win-Win" administration must become a reality. The practice of "Win-Win" administration will become reality as organizational members, non-managers as well as managers, begin to appreciate the potential existing in the concept of "win-win." It will become reality as organizational structure and managerial style change to meet the demands of contemporary society. It is through the practice of "Win-Win" administration that organizations, the people who work in them, and the people served by them will have an opportunity to reach their fullest potential.

Edgar Schein suggests that to effectively practice "Win-Win" administration requires an improvement in interpersonal relations. Managerial problems, he says in his article, can be largely solved by improving face-to-face relationships. He articulates the factors which are involved in building and maintaining effective interpersonal communication, and pays particular attention to the ways in which damaged relationships can be repaired.

Despite the sincerity of managers who wish to practice "Win-Win" administration, it is reality that from time-to-time there will be conflict within even the most well-intentioned organization. When properly handled, says Andrew Hoh in his article, conflicts can stimulate organizational growth and development. He advocates the problem-solving method of reaching consensus as the only technique of conflict resolution allowing for a "win-win" solution because it is a method assuming mutual problems and interdependence.

As a virtual guide toward one method of practicing "Win-Win" administration, the article by Heinz Weihrich and Andre-Jean Rigny presents a specific technique for managers to use. Rensis Likert established what he labeled as "System 4" to represent the participative management style which he advocates, and Weihrich and Rigny have linked their theory to Likert's. In System Four, managers involve non-managers in the organization because they have confidence and trust in them. In order to achieve this System Four style of management, Weihrich and Rigny suggest that Transactional Analysis is a powerful tool to use.

Finally, Hirotaka Takeuchi says that those who wish to practice "Win-Win" administration can learn much from the experience of Japanese organizations. Takeuchi, an expert on Japanese management, has written a scholarly, well-documented article which concludes that employees are any organization's greatest asset. If treated with respect and allowed to be involved, people will contribute to the organization's success. The success of Japanese companies since World War II, Takeuchi has found, is due to strict quality control, grass roots involvement of workers, quality circles, recognition that people are motivated by pride and channels for creativity, and "maternalistic management" in which management demonstrates a sincere interest in every employee.

The articles in this section, in conjunction with the articles in the other sections of this volume, should help to put any manager on the road toward the practice of "Win-Win" administration.

IMPROVING FACE-TO-FACE RELATIONSHIPS

Edgar H. Schein

The challenges of management in the 1980s are enormous, but they are fairly easy to identify. The great difficulties that we face lie not in deciding *what* our goals should be, but in determining *how* to achieve them. Our problems in this area are problems of *implementation: how* can we reach goals that are often perfectly clear but seemingly impossible to attain.

Several explanations of these problems readily come to mind:

— Large systems have become too complex to be understood.
— "Bureaucracy" makes it impossible to get anything done.
— Intergroup hostility paralyzes all constructive effort.
— Power politics undermine and subvert rational action.
— Irrationality and human resistance to change defeat even the wisest programs.

All of these explanations are true, but they are also incomplete. Sometimes they are used only as excuses for failure rather than as constructive analyses of our management problems. On the other hand, we *have* learned something about implementation in the last forty years or so, and what we have leaned takes us back to one fundamental principle: societies, organizations, and families are *human* groups, and the face-to-face relationships among the members of these groups are a basic element of any social action. Whatever else we need in the way of systems, procedures, and mechanisms, the process of social action always starts with face-to-face relationships among people.

Reprinted from "Improving Face-to-Face Relationships" by Edgar Schein, SLOAN MANAGEMENT REVIEW, Vol. 22 (Winter 1981), pp. 43–52, by permission of the publisher. Copyright © 1981 by the Sloan Management Review Association. All rights reserved.

Face-to-face relationships can be thought of as the glue that holds organizations together, and such relationships are the links in the implementation chain. Therefore, we should take a fresh look at these relationships to see if we can articulate some of the skills which can make them more constructive, and thus enable us to move toward solving some of the pressing problems of the 1980s.

THE ELEMENTS OF FACE-TO-FACE RELATIONSHIPS

What does it take to build, maintain, improve, and, if need be, repair face-to-face relationships? I would like to discuss nine different elements, which are all closely interrelated yet distinct in important ways. These elements reflect motives and values, perceptual skills, and behavioral skills:

1. Self-insight and a sense of one's own identity;
2. Cross-cultural sensitivity—the ability to decipher other people's values;
3. Cultural/moral humility—the ability to see one's own values as not necessarily better or worse than another's values;
4. A proactive problem-solving orientation—the conviction that interpersonal and cross-cultural problems can be solved;
5. Personal flexibility—the ability to adopt different responses and approaches as needed by situational contingencies;
6. Negotiation skills—the ability to explore differences creatively, to locate some common ground, and to solve the problem;
7. Interpersonal and cross-cultural tact—the ability to solve problems with people without insulting them, demeaning them, or destroying their "face";
8. Repair strategies and skills—the ability to resurrect, to revitalize, and to rebuild damaged or broken face-to-face relationships;
9. Patience.

I would like to discuss each of these elements in turn, putting most of the attention on those which have been insufficiently attended to in prior analyses and on those which are especially relevant to repair strategies.

SELF-INSIGHT

One can hardly work out common goals with others if one does not know where one's own values and goals lie. Leaders and managers especially must know where they are going, and they must be able to articulate their own goals. Parents and spouses must make a valiant effort to lift to the surface what is often left implicit—their own life goals and targets—so that there can be genuine negotiation among family members in the different life stages.

Self-insight is a *competence*—the ability to see oneself accurately and to evaluate one-self fairly. Through feedback from others and through systematic self-study, we can improve our ability to see ourselves. As we increase in self-insight, we lay the foundations for self-acceptance, which is to some extent, a prerequisite for some of the other skills to be discussed.

CROSS-CULTURAL SENSITIVITY

It goes without saying that we cannot offer leadership if we do not have perspective on ourselves and on others, and we cannot gain such perspective if we continue to be ethnocentric—to notice and appreciate only our own culture and values. Cross-cultural issues are not limited to the dramatic differences which can be identified in how different countries operate. Many of the most harmful cases of cultural misunderstanding occur right under our noses —with our spouses, friends, children, and subordinates—because norms, values, and behavioral codes vary widely within any country. American managers often tell tales of woe of trying to transfer people from the deep South to Manhattan, or from an urban center to a rural plant site.

A costly misunderstanding occurred in the small town where we used to spend our summers. The local wood-turning mill employed both men and women from the community, and the pay scales had developed historically around the status system in the town. A new manager who had experience in a progressive urban mill noticed that some of the skilled women operators were grossly underpaid in relation to their male counterparts. He set about to rationalize the pay structure to reflect actual skill levels. This action led to wives bringing home bigger paychecks, which neither they nor their husbands could accept in terms of the status system in the town. The dissatisfaction and turmoil that resulted from upsetting the social order was completely unanticipated by this manager.

Deciphering values, motives, aspirations, and basic assumptions across *occupational* and *social class lines* is particularly difficult. It is hard for the son of a successful middle-class businessman to understand the values and career aspirations of the son of an immigrant or an unskilled worker. It is hard for the general manager to understand the values and career aspirations of the technically oriented person and vice versa. It is hard for people in the different functional areas of a business to decipher each other's values and aspirations.[1]

Cultural Differences between Countries

When we go to countries where a different language is being spoken and where the culture is obviously different, we do wake up to the need to sharpen our deciphering skills. But even then we have a strong tendency to look for similarities and to rationalize that "people are people" and "business is business" no matter where it is conducted. My own tendency to ignore differences was brought home to me during a visit to Australia, which is superficially and historically similar to the U.S. It took me quite a while to discover that while Australians (like Americans) are achievement oriented, they also have the "tall poppy syndrome": one must not stand out above the crowd; one must accomplish things without seeming to work too hard at them; and one must not take too much personal credit for one's accomplishments. The son of a friend of mine told us how, after waiting all day for the perfect wave, he had finally succeeded in having a brilliant ride on his surfboard. When he hit the beach, he told his watching friends—as he knew he had to—"Boy that was a *lucky* one."

I kept hearing how complacent and security oriented the Australians were even when I was dealing with what seemed to be some pretty tough, aggressive managers. What one's true motives are and what is culturally acceptable as a legitimate explanation of one's motives are, of course, not necessarily the same. In comparing America and Australia, one sees a paradoxical reversal. In Australia, people claim to be mostly security oriented, though companies admitted they had many aggressive, ambitious, power-seeking managers working for them. In the U.S., the popular image is that most people are ambitious and want to climb right to the top of the organization—though I encounter a growing number of allegedly ambitious managers who admit in private that they are not motivated to continue the "rat race," that they would like early retirement, or that they are considering another career altogether. Both public images reflect cultural norms, yet both are to some degree a misrepresentation of the actual state of affairs. The public selves we wear—the way we are supposed to present ourselves to others—is a strongly ingrained set of cultural values in its own right, and tact prevents us from puncturing the illusions which cultures teach us to project.

"Face Work"

Erving Goffman has written articulately about what he calls "face work"—the behavior of people in a social situation which is designed to help everyone maintain the self which they choose to project in that particular situation.[2] Selves are forever constructed, and the audience for any given performance is culturally bound to uphold as much as possible the identities which the actors claim. At the minimum, we nod and say "uh huh" when someone is talking to us, or we try to laugh politely at a joke that is not really funny, or we ignore embarrassing incidents. If our boss tells us through his actions or demeanor that he believes himself to be very competent in handling a given meeting, we rarely challenge this claim even though we may privately believe that he will totally mismanage it. The skill in this situation is our ability to compensate for his incompetence or to repair what damage may have been done. But we do not destroy his face.

The Reciprocity of Relationships

One of the most interesting features of the cultural norms of face-to-face interactions is their symmetric, reciprocal, exchange nature. We sometimes get into difficulty because we do not know how to complete an interaction. When someone in a strange country offers you an object in his house because you have admired it, are you supposed to take it and reciprocate at some future time when the visitor is in your home, or is it appropriate to refuse? The whole question of when and how to say yes or no is fraught with difficulty if we are talking across cultures or subcultures. And, as many businessmen have found out, how to interpret a yes or a no is even more difficult.

The ability to detect the subtleties of how others perceive situations and of what the values of others are requires both formal training and practical experience. Learning a new language would seem to be a prerequisite since so much of every culture is encoded into the language. Many people pride themselves on their extensive travel, even making lists of how many countries they have been in, without ever encountering or deciphering any of the cultures of those countries; they do not learn the languages and therefore miss the important nuances of what is going on. On the other hand, I have heard repeatedly from multinational companies that one of the best prescriptions for success in an overseas assignment is to take time to learn the local language.

CULTURAL/MORAL HUMILITY

Beyond self-insight and the ability to understand others, we need something which we might call cultural/moral *humility*. Can we not only sense the values of other people but, more importantly, positively appreciate them? Can we see our own culture and values only as *different*, not necessarily as *better*? Our tendency to think of things as "funny" or "odd" is a good diagnostic here. I have often been shown or told about funny things people do in other countries. An American visitor to the mainland of China found it very amusing that some Chinese farmers were so proud of owning tractors which were, in fact, useless; the tractors could not turn on the tight terraces and they did not have attachable plows to pull. The fact that a Chinese farmer did not even know the function of the pin to which the plow attaches struck this American as very funny and weird. It never occurred to him that his own utilitarian, pragmatic values might not be the only relevant ones in this situation.

A few years ago, a group of American students teased one of their German peers about his heel-clicking, head-nodding, hand-shaking formality. After some months of being teased, he stopped them one day with the statement: "When I go to work in the morning, I go to my boss's office, click my heels, bow my head, shake his hand, and then tell him the truth." The teasing stopped.

Many American managers lack cultural humility. We are more pragmatic than other people, and if we encounter people less pragmatic, we view *them* as odd rather then wonder about the oddity of our being so pragmatic. We don't consider our own culture as funny, odd, and in need of explanation, yet *it is our culture which is probably in a statistical sense the most different from all other cultures.* Let me give a couple of examples:

1. Our mercantile attitude—embodied in our marketing skills and our efforts to sell anything to anybody—strikes people in other parts of the world as being rather crass and superficial. I have encountered managers in other countries who have real reservations about making products which they consider to have no intrinsic value, and who have even greater reservations about using advertising skills to create markets for such products.
2. Our attitude toward efficiency—attempting to reduce all costs for the sake of higher profit margins, even if those costs are people's jobs—is clearly out of line with the value systems in some other countries. Yet we take the importance of efficiency for granted. We do not think of people as capital investments and we find it hard to comprehend systems of guaranteed lifetime employment.

My point is not to dissect the value system of the U.S. but rather to identify a strong tendency I have seen in managers all over the world (Americans and non-Americans alike) to be ethnocentric—to assume that one's own values are the best, and that one is excused for having to know what others think and value, or at least from having to take very seriously what others think and value. Such an absence of cultural humility can be a dangerous weakness when we are attempting face-to-face negotiations or problem solving. This point is important whenever we deal with people whose values are different from our own, whether these people are within our society or are from other countries.

PROACTIVE PROBLEM-SOLVING ORIENTATION

Solving face-to-face problems, especially where difficult cross-cultural under-standing and humility are required, presupposes a faith that problems *can* be solved if one works at them and an assumption that active problem solving will produce positive results. Communication and understanding are difficult to achieve, but if one does not even try, then there is no possibility for achieve-ment.

A proactive orientation is itself to some degree a cultural characteristic. When Americans take the "can do" attitude, how do we determine when we are coming on too strongly, or when we are actually intruding in private lifespace in our eagerness to establish constructive face-to-face relationships in order to solve problems. The anthropologist Edward Hall has given us many excellent examples of how conducting business in different cultural contexts must be delicately handled, lest we invade people's territory and unwittingly destroy the possibility of better relationships.[3]

What I mean by a "proactive orientation" is a *motivation* to work on problems, not necessarily a high level of overt *activity.* We must base our actual course of action on genuine cultural understanding and not simply on a desire to act. As in the case of international diplomacy, we should always be ready to negotiate. No matter how bad the situation is between management and employees in a company or industry, each party should always be ready to sit down and try again to talk face-to-face.

PERSONAL FLEXIBILITY

It does us little good to sense situations accurately if we cannot take advantage of what we perceive. I know people who can tell you exactly what is going on but who cannot alter their own behavior to adjust to what they know to be the realities. One of the reasons why experiential learning methods—such as sensitivity training or transactional analysis workshops—have been so successful is that they allow experimentation on the part of participants, thus permitting the participants to enlarge their repretory of face-to-face behavior. Role playing is perhaps the prototype of such behavioral training and is clearly a necessary component of face-to-face skill development.[4]

NEGOTIATION SKILLS

Much has been written about the process of negotiation and the skills needed to be an effective negotiator. To a considerable degree, what has been said reflects the same themes that I am focusing on here. Negotiation requires great sensitivity, humility, self-insight, motivation to solve the problem, and behavioral flexibility. Part of the sensitivity required is the ability to decipher others' values. Another part is the ability to elicit information from others and to judge the validity of that information. Face-to-face relationships are not always benign, not always comfortable, not always safe, and not always open, yet they are always crucial to problem solving. Especially in situations where there initially is conflict, we need the ability to maintain relationships so that negotiations can continue, to decipher messages when deliberate concealment is attempted, to convince and to persuade, to bluff when necessary, and to figure out what the other will do in response to our own moves.

As we know, negotiations can become so dangerous and threatening to one's face that we have to resort to neutral third parties as catalysts, go-betweens, message carriers, and the like. Often what is most needed is to explain the values and goals of each principal to the other. Principals often lack the skills to reveal themselves to each other without making themselves seem either too vulnerable or too threatening.[5]

One of my Australian manager friends speculated that a lack of verbal articulation skills seriously hampers negotiation in his country. He notices that in many labor-management confrontations in Australia each side would blurt out bluntly, and with some pride at their own ability to be so open, exactly what their *final* demands were. When these demands proved to be incompatible, an impasse occurred. The situation then deteriorated to name calling and to seeing the other side as being stubborn and exploitative. This manager speculated that the educational system was partly responsible for this situation in that written English is heavily emphasized in school while spoken English is hardly attended to at all. He thought of Australians as being quite inarticulate, on the average, and therefore at a real disadvantage in face-to-face negotiations.

The important point is to recognize that openness is not an absolute value in face-to-face relationships. For some purposes, it is better not to reveal exactly where one stands. One of the ways that relationships become more intimate is through successive minimal self-revelations which consitute interpersonal tests of acceptance: if you accept this much of me, then perhaps I can run the risk of revealing a bit more of myself. Total openness may be safe and charming when total acceptance is guaranteed, but it can become highly dangerous when goals are not compatible, and acceptance is therefore not guaranteed at all.[6]

INTERPERSONAL AND CROSS-CULTURAL TACT

Negotiation requires great tact. The tactfulness I refer to here is the *behavioral* manifestation of the cultural humility discussed above. If we don't feel humble in the face of others' values, we will certainly offend them. On the other hand, if we feel that there is genuinely room for different values in this world, then we have the basis for showing in our speech and behavior an adequate level of respect for others.

REPAIR STRATEGIES AND SKILLS

The repair strategies and repair skills needed to fix broken or spoiled relationships, careers, lives, negotiations, and other interpersonal or intergroup situations are probably the most important yet least understood of face-to-face skills. As the world becomes more complex and more intercultural, there will be more communication breakdowns, diplomatic disasters, losses of confidence and trust, hurt feelings between individuals and groups, hostilities, wars, and other forms of social pathology and disorder. It will not help us to resign ourselves to such situations, to lament our cruel fate, or to merely explain why something happened; what *will* be helpful is our attempting to repair these situations.

The concept of "repair strategies" was brought to my attention by Jacqueline Goodnow, a cognitive social psychologist who now teaches in Australia. She has been struck by the Australian tendency to "knock" things rather than to solve problems. I often heard the phrase in Australia that "we are a nation of knockers," which means that when things go wrong there is a tendency to blame government, unions, management, multinationals, OPEC, or any other handy group rather than to figure out how to repair the situation.

The Perception of New Elements

Repair strategies presume and require not only constructive motivation but also *the ability to see new elements in the situation which one may not have noticed before.* The new elements may be in *oneself*; one may discover that one has been unfair or selfish, or lacking insight concerning the consequences of one's own behavior or concerning one's true motives. In this instance repair may begin with apology.

One may also discover new things in the *other people* in the situation; *they may have changed in significant ways.* One of the most damaging things we do in our face-to-face relationships is to freeze our assumptions about ourselves and others. Our stereotype of the other person can become a straight jacket of a self-fulfilling prophecy. McGregor gave us the best example of this years ago in noting that if we assume people are lazy we will begin to treat them as if they *are* lazy, which will eventually train them to *be* lazy.[7] The energy and creativity which they might have applied to thier jobs then gets channeled either into other situations or into angry attempts to defeat the organization.

We want and need predictability in our relationships, but that very need often prevents us from repairing damaged relationships. It may be psychologically easier to see the worker as lazy and hostile because we can then predict his or her behavior and can know exactly how to respond. To renegotiate the relationship, to permit some participation, or to admit that we may have been wrong in our assessment is to make ourselves psychologically vulnerable. We then enter a period in the relationship that may be less predictable.

As in the case of negotiation, we may need the help of third parties—counselors, therapists, consultants, or other helpers—to get through the period of vulnerability and instability. Often the motivation to repair is there but the skill is not—in the sense that neither party has self-insight, the capacity to hear the values or goals of the other, the articulateness to negotiate without further destruction of face, or the emotional strength of self-confidence to make concessions to reach at least a common ground of understanding.

Taking the Other's Perspective

Sociologists taught us long ago that in childhood the very process of becoming social is a process of learning to take the role of the other. We could not really understand each other at all—even though we live in the same culture and speak the same language—without the ability to put ourselves in the other person's shoes. We could not develop judgements, standards, and morals without the ability to see our own behavior from the standpoint of others, which gradually becomes abstracted into what sociologists call the "generalized other," or what we sometimes label as our "reference group." Guilt and shame, the products of one's internalized conscience, can be thought of as the accumulated empathy of a decade of growing up. As adults we have the capacity to see ourselves from others' perspectives and this capacity should help us to develop repair strategies. Why is it, then, that so often we end up in complete disagreement, convinced that the only thing the other party really wants is to gain a selfish advantage at our expense?

One factor certainly is our need to maintain our position and our pride. Having suffered an affront, a loss of face, or a loss of advantage sometime in the past, we feel the only safe thing to do is to protect ourselves from any repetition of such an unpleasant event. We may, in addition, recognize that our own interest and that of the other party are genuinely in conflict. If we are in a zero-sum game, we may not be able to afford too much sympathy for our opponent. In such an instance, a repair strategy would call for the ability to locate some superordinate goals, where goal conflict is not intrinsic, and to build a new set of interactions around such superordinate goals. Skillful diplomats, negotiators, and statesmen build their entire careers around the development of such repair strategies. They create one repair strategy after another as the people they deal with destroy one relationship after another.

Ordinary day-to-day relations with families, between managers and subordinates, and between groups in organizations are forever in danger of breaking down. We must be prepared to diagnose the situation when breakdown occurs and to have the skills to repair it, if repair is needed. Let me give two examples of what is involved.

REPAIR STRATEGIES IN MIDLIFE

Much of the research on midlife is beginning to point to the presence of two very broad phases, each lasting a decade or more.[8] In the first phase, which lasts roughly from age twenty-five to age forty, the family in a sense colludes with the primary career occupant to build a successful career. The primary career occupant, his or her spouse or partner, and the children all learn that our occupational structure requires that one go to school and then put in an intensive decade or so building up one's career (and one's organizational membership if the career is pursued within an organization). The support by the family may be silent and stoic. The children are kept out of the career builder's hair while he or she is busy. The spouse or partner—gladly or resentfully—makes sacrifices and actively develops a viable ancillary support role as homemaker and as mother and father combined.

But something else is going on during these years. The homemaker is in a terminal career and knows it; at some point the children will be off to school, the house will have had all the attention it needs, and being the ancillary spouse may not be a full enough life. The spouse builds up expectations that at some point "it will be my turn; I have helped you to build your career and now I want something in return—something for myself." As these feelings grow and are articulated, as teenage children begin to say "Why are you working so hard? What's it all about anyway?", and as the career occupant begins to reexamine his or her career, a new phase begins. In this phase, there may be a need for repair strategies, renegotiation of the family contract, and reassessment of who wants what and how it is best achieved. People discover either that their relationships are already damaged and need to be repaired or that they *will* be damaged if no preventive maintenance is undertaken.

Cross-Cultural Sensitivity within the Family

It should be noted that each family member has, in a sense, been living in a different subculture and that cross-cultural understanding and humility will therefore become very important. The career occupant will have to understand and respect the serious requirements of the spouse and the young adult children. The spouse and children will have to understand and respect the serious requirements of the world of work and organizations with which the career occupant grapples. This will tax each member's self-insight, commitment to the family, sensitivity, and perspective.

The moral humility issue is central here because the cause of a damaged relationship is often a devaluing of each other's goals and aspirations. The career occupant looks down on what may be regarded as the trivial or threatening values of the next generation; he or she cannot really appreciate why the homemaker spouse should have an issue about self-identity, the need to feel important and worthwhile in a society in which worth is defined almost exclusively by paid work and career involvement. The spouse (and most likely the children) find it easy to devalue organizational goals, to identify organizational careers with exploitation of the poor, marginal product quality, questionable business ethics, overworked people who are eventually cast off by cruel employers, and so on. If midlife family relationships are damaged by such feelings, then how can they be repaired?

The Interplay of Face-to Face Skills

Each party in the relationship must first achieve some self-insight, some sense of one's own commitments so that defensiveness and denial can be reduced. We cannot hear others if we cannot accept ourselves. Next we need the kind of cross-cultural sensitivity I have been talking about, the relaxed, open ability to hear others' values with empathy and perspective. Once we can hear each other, we can begin to seek the common ground, the goals or aspirations around which some common activities can be designed; we can begin to renegotiate the relationships to make it possible for the desirable activities to happen. If, in hearing each other, we find a genuine lack of common ground, we can negotiate a reduced level of intimacy in the relationship yet maintain a high degree of mutual acceptance of what each cares about; this can lead to nondestructive separations, more limited interactions with children, or both.

LABOR-MANAGEMENT RELATIONS

My second example has to do with face-to-face skills and repair strategies in labor-management situations. I am struck by the degree to which these situations seem to turn into intergroup struggles—struggles among unions, managements, and government bodies or political parties. Once the conflicts have escalated to the intergroup level, it is easy to give up one's proactive problem-solving orientation and to resign oneself to the idea that the problem is essentially unsolvable. Yet when one looks at successful enterprises—those which have managed to maintain harmony between management and employees—one realizes that the key to this harmony is a high degree of mutual trust, active listening, appropriate levels of participation, and consistently constructive face-to-face communications.

An example will highlight what I mean. A plant manager told me that he had spent many years developing a constructive relationship with his employees, in spite of the fact that they belong to a strong national union which periodically calls for national strikes. One year his employees refused to strike. They were told by the national union that it would get all the suppliers of the plant to refuse to deliver, thus effectively shutting the plant down. Under these conditions, the manager and the employees should go out on strike, but everyone knew that it was not over local issues. The manager did not hold it against his subordinates that they had gone out on strike.

Intergroup trust, reinforced by open face-to-face communications on relevant issues, was strong enough to keep this plant functioning well even in a larger context that made periodic strikes inevitable. What we can learn from this is that constructive face-to-face relationships are necessary even though they may not be sufficient. Solving a problem at the national level will probably be useless if there continue to be destructive low-trust relationships within the enterprise.

DISENGAGING THE CRITICAL MIND

Achieving trust in a labor-management situation that has developed into a hostile intergroup conflict over a period of decades seems like a tall order. One prerequisite to working out the problem at the group level will be, as I have argued, the reestablishment of constructive face-to-face relationships. This will only be possible if both managers and workers find a way to see each other in less stereotypic ways. There is a need here to introduce in the interpersonal arena what Zen, gestalt training, encounter groups, and other training programs have emphasized—relaxing the active critical mind enough to let our eyes and ears see and hear what is really out there rather than what we *expect* to see and hear. Just as the person who is learning to draw must suspend what he or she knows intellectually about what things should look like, and, instead, must learn to see what is really out there, so the person concerned about repairing human relationships must first see not what he or she expects or knows should be there, but what is actually there.[9]

I don't think it is accidental that Americans are so preoccupied with sensitivity training, Zen meditation, inner tennis, and, most recently, right-side brain functions.[10] What all of these programs and approaches have in common is a focus on learning how to perceive oneself, others, and the environment realistically, which apparently requires a certain relaxation of our active critical functions and a deliberate disengaging of our analytical selves. We cannot improve face-to-face relationships if we cannot perceive accurately. And accurate seeing and hearing is for many of us a lost skill that we must somehow regain. The place to begin practicing this skill is in our families and in our immediate superior-subrodinate and peer relations.

If we cannot see ourselves and others in this relaxed, uncritical way, then we cannot develop perspective, humility, or tact, and we run the danger of acting on incorrect data. On the other hand, if we can really learn to see each other, and if we can combine more accurate perception with the ninth element in my list—patience—then we have some chance of improving and repairing face-to-face relationships.

> "Even though you try to put people under some control, it is impossible. You cannot do it. The best way to control people is to encourage them to be mischievous. Then they will be in control in its wider sense. To give your sheep or cow a large, spacious meadow is the way to control him. So it is with people: first let them do what they want, and watch them. This is the best policy. To ignore them is not good; that is the worst policy. The second worst is trying to control them. The best one is to watch them, just to watch them, without trying to control them. The same way works for yourself as well." S. Suzuki, Zen Mind, Beginner's Mind.[11]

REFERENCES

1. See P.R. Lawrence and J.W. Lorsch, *Organization and Environment* (Boston: Division of Research, Harvard Business School, 1967).
2. See E. Goffman, *Interaction Ritual* (Chicago: Aldine, 1967).
3. See E. Hall, *Beyond Culture* (Garden City, NY: Anchor, 1977).

4. See: E.H. Schein, *Organizational Psychology,* 3rd ed. (Englewood Cliffs, NJ: Prentice-Hall, 1980), chs. 9 and 13; T.A. Harris, *I'm OK—You're OK* (New York: Avon, 1967); E. Polster and M. Polster, *Gestalt Therapy Integrated* (New York: Bruner/Mazel, 1973).

5. See R.E. Walton, *Interpersonal Peacemaking: Confrontations and Third-Party Consultation* (Reading, MA: Addison-Wesley, 1969).

6. See W. Bennis, J. Van Maanen, E.H. Schein, and F.I. Steele, *Essays in Interpersonal Dynamics* (Homewood, IL: Dorsey, 1979).

7. See D. McGregor, *The Human Side of Enterprise* (New York: McGraw-Hill, 1960).

8. See F. Bartolomé and P.A.L. Evans, *Must Success Cost So Much?* (London: Grant McIntyre, 1980); E.H. Schein, *Career Dynamics* (Reading, MA: Addison-Wesley, 1978); C.B. Derr, ed., *Work, Family, and the Career* (New York: Praeger, 1980).

9. See B. Edwards, *Drawing on the Right Side of the Brain* (Los Angeles: J.P. Tarcher, 1979); F. Frank, *The Zen of Seeing* (New York: Vintage, 1973).

10. See R.E. Ornstein, *The Psychology of Consciousness* (San Francisco: W.H. Freeman, 1972).

11. See S. Suzuki, *Zen Mind, Beginner's Mind* (New York: Weatherhill, 1977), p. 32.

CONSENSUS-BUILDING: A CREATIVE APPROACH TO RESOLVING CONFLICTS

Andrew K. Hoh

Conflict, especially in today's complex business environment, is a fact of organizational life. Neither inherently good nor evil, disagreements and disputes may foster creative insights and closer relationships among employees or they may generate lasting resentment and hostility.

Whether conflicts are constructive or destructive depends on how they are handled. To suppress conflict in an attempt to avoid trouble and minimize open discord is often extremely destructive. Top executives should accept the inevitability of conflicts and learn how to manage them in a way that will mitigate their harmful aspects and capitalize on their potential for good.

HOW TO RESOLVE CONFLICTS

Basically, there are four ways in which conflicts can be resolved:

Forcing. This method relies on overcoming the opponent through the use of authority, violence, threats, majority rule, and coalitions. The conflict is solved, but not resolved because there is always a loser. The loser may withdraw cooperation and commitment from the resolution and start looking for ways to retaliate.

Compromising. This consists of an attempt to find a middle ground that both parties find acceptable. A compromise, by definition, can result only in partial fulfillment of the needs of each party. By recalling King Solomon's classic compromise, it is easy to see that compromise does not always work: half a baby is worse than none.

Reprinted by permission of the publisher from MANAGEMENT REVIEW, March 1981, © 1981 by AMACOM, a division of American Management Associations. All rights reserved.

Mediating. This involves an appeal to a neutral third party for resolution on conflicts. Mediation depends on both parties' acceptance of the mediator as a fair, knowledgeable, and wise person. Even so, the loser will probably attribute his loss to the mediator's poor judgment.

Problem solving. This is the only technique that seeks a solution that is fundamentally acceptable to both parties. Through direct, open communication, a third alternative is worked out that both integrates and is superior to the two original positions. It is the most successful method for resolving conflicts, but it is also the most difficult. Considerable interpersonal skills and an adequate investment in time are required.

WIN-LOSE VS. WIN-WIN

Forcing, compromising, and mediating share several characteristics that may turn all three methods into zero-sum games—what each side gains is at the expense of the other. First, there is a clear we-they distinction between the parties, rather than a we-versus-the-problem orientation. This means that energies are directed toward the other party in an atmosphere of total victory or total defeat. Second, the emphasis is on attaining a solution, rather than on seeking mutually defined goals or values. Therefore, each party sees the issue strictly from his own point of view, without regard for mutual needs. Also, the conflict is reduced to a battle between personalities, while the emphasis on issues and facts is lost. Finally, communication is defensive: Each party tries to obtain as much information about the other's preferences while disclosing as little as possible about his own point of view. Exchanges are judgmental and critical, rather than descriptive and empathetic.

In contrast to the win-lose and lose-lose strategies of forcing, mediating, and compromise, the problem-solving method focuses on shared goals. The negotiating process is rooted in the following questions: What is our common goal? Why do we have conflicts? What are the obstacles that prevent us from reaching our goals? What are alternative solutions? Which alternative is most acceptable to all of us?

A problem-solving approach helps the opposing parties focus on defeating the problem rather than each other. It guarantees, at the least, that all participants receive an equal chance to express their points of view. Because the approach assumes a mutual problem and interdependence, it may foster assertive rather than aggressive behavior. Differences and similarities in opinions can be expressed in a noncompetitive climate.

TOWARD A CONSENSUS

Reaching a consensus is an effective problem-solving approach to resolving conflicts. Consensus is commonly defined as a collective opinion arrived at by a group of people working together under conditions that allow everyone a fair chance to influence the decision. Consensus is not necessarily unanimity—an ideal that is often impossible to achieve.

Chances are that a group working together toward a consensus will arrive at a better solution than that offered by any single individual. Further, the participants will understand the solution they settle on and therefore will accept the final decision with more enthusiasm and commitment. Since all members have had a chance to air their views, even those who still disagree or have doubts will say they are willing to give the solution a chance.

Within the synergistic framework that a consensus approach creates, differences of opinion provide an opportunity for gathering information, clarifying issues, and forcing the group to seek better alternatives that will integrate the valuable assets of each position.

HELPFUL GUIDELINES

Here are some rules to follow when using the consensus-building approach:

- Avoid blindly arguing for your own individual judgments. Present your position as clearly and logically as possible, but listen to the reactions of other members and consider them carefully before you press your point.
- Avoid changing your mind just to reach agreement and avoid conflict. Support only the solutions that you at least partially agree with. Yield only to positions that have objective and logical foundations.
- Avoid conflict-reducing procedures such as using majority votes, tossing a coin, averaging, ridiculing, or bargaining to reach decisions.
- Do not assume that someone must win and someone must lose when the discussion reaches a stalemate. Instead, look for the most acceptable alternative for all members.
- Encourage the participation of all members. Avoid a prolonged two-way exchange between two participants. Introduce deliberate pauses for reflection.
- Clarify differences in positions and integrate similarities in opinions. Periodic summarizing is useful for this purpose. It also gets the discussion back on course, checks understanding of opinions expressed, improves communication within the group, and indicates and measures progress toward an agreement.
- Make occasional use of the role-reversal technique to ensure that each participant understands both the position and the frame of reference of his opponent.

Encourage active listening during the discussion. Practice the use of "I hear you say. . . ." in which each person summarizes the statements made by the previous speaker before presenting his own opinions. Avoid the "yes, but" discussion in which party A gets party B to stop talking with the "yes" and then counters with the "but" and a full report on the errors in B's thinking.

When a tentative decision is reached, test the consensus by playing the devil's advocate, by introducing outside experts, and by calling second-chance, follow-up meetings.

When an agreement is reached, point out the role that conflict has played and specify what each participant has agreed to do to implement the solution.

All the parties involved in a conflict should feel like winners who can satisfactorily achieve their individual needs. "The group that fights together stays together" can be the motto of an organization where problem solving is used to resolve conflict.

TOWARD SYSTEM FOUR THROUGH TRANSACTIONAL ANALYSIS

Heinz Weihrich and Andre-Jean Rigny

The effectiveness of an organization depends largely on its people. In the past, managing the human component was primarily based on the often imprecise subjective judgments of managers. Now, however, considerable research is available on the measurement of variables that are critical in the effective management of human resources.

One such approach has been developed by Rensis Likert and his associates.[1,2] Their model, consisting of four systems of managing, facilitates the accessment of the existing organizational environment. An important benefit of this model is that it can also be used for moving the enterprise from an ineffective managerial system toward the more effective participative group, which Likert calls "System 4." To achieve this, several tools have been employed, including dissemination of information, feedback, training in leadership, participation in decision making, team building, and job enrichment. However, the new tool of Transactional Analysis (TA) has been overlooked in moving organizations toward System 4. The purpose of this article is to fill that gap.

First, the four systems of management are outlined in this article and the application of this theory in organizational development is shown. Then, TA is introduced. Specifically, the focus is on the ego states that comprise the personality, the analysis of transactions between people, and the importance of life positions for determining behavior. Finally, the application of TA is recommended as a tool for moving the organization from the ineffective System 1 (exploitative-authoritative) toward the effective System 4 (participative group).

Reprinted by permission of the authors and the Association for System Management from *Journal of Systems Management*, Volume 31 (July 1980).

FOUR MANAGERIAL SYSTEMS

Likert identified several managerial styles and related organizational factors. These are measured through a questionnaire and the responses to the questions are then grouped into four management systems: the exploitative-authoritative, the benevolent-authoritative, the consultative, and the participative group.

System 1: Exploitative-Authoritative—In System 1, leadership is rather autocratic. Motivation is primarily through fear, threats, punishment, and occasional rewards. The usual direction of communication is downward. Decisions are made mostly at the top of the organization. Goals are set through orders. Control and review are concentrated at the top.

System 2: Benevolent-Authoritative—System 2 is characterized by a condescending attitude of managers. The motivation is through the use of rewards and some punishment. Communication is mostly downward. Policy decisions are made at the top, but there is some delegation. Although goals are ordered, some comments by subordinates are invited. Control is still concentrated rather high in the organization.

System 3: Consultative—In System 3, there is a substantial amount of confidence in subordinates. Motivation is through rewards, occasional punishment, and some involvement. The communication flow is downward and upward. Furthermore, subordinates are generally consulted on decisions related to their work. Goals are set by orders after discussion. Control is exercised through moderate delegation to lower levels.

System 4: Participative Group—In System 4, superiors have a great deal of confidence and trust in their subordinates. Motivation is achieved through involvement and rewards based on group actions. Communication is downward, upward, and sideways. Well-integrated decisions are made at all levels of the organization. Goals are set by the group, except in a crisis situation. Control is widely shared by members of the organization.

APPLICATION OF THE FOUR SYSTEMS

Several studies have indicated that when organizations moved toward System 4, they became more effective in the long-run. One successful experiment was conducted in the General Motors Lakewood Plant.[3]

Their Organizational Development (OD) was based on Likert's theory consisting of three sets of variables: casual, intervening, and end-result. The change effort focused on the casual variables, such as organizational climate and leadership. First, a survey was conducted which showed that the Lakewood plant operated approximately as System 2. Training sessions were held to promote and improve trust, teamwork, communication, and goal setting. Emphasis was on frequent feedback, availability of information, and participation. The long-term result was improvement of plant efficiency, greater savings, and improved quality.

The tools applied to achieve these results emphasized rational decision making, improvement of personal competence, and an enhancement of a feeling of personal worth. At the time of the General Motors OD efforts (1969–1972), TA was little known in management circles. It is only recently that TA has been linked to the managerial process.[4,5] The aim here is to introduce basic TA concepts and indicate their application for moving organizations to System 4.

WHAT IS TRANSACTIONAL ANALYSIS?

Originally, TA was primarily a method of psychotherapy.[6] Later, the general value of TA in improving interpersonal relationships and communication was also recognized. TA is a rational approach to the understanding of behavior. It is logical, then, to go one step further and apply TA to managerial leadership and processes.

TA considers both the emotional and intellectual aspects of behavior, but the emphasis is on the rational and analytical side. Furthermore, the focus is on observable behavior—not on the inner psyche. Managers can hardly deal with the latter, but they can learn to observe, interpret, and change their behavior and that of others. TA is concerned with transactions between people. Although it consists of various aspects, the most pertinent ones for our discussion are: (1) the concept of ego states with the focus on the personality of the individual, (2) the analysis of transactions between people, and (3) the basic life positions in respect to whether people are OK or not OK.

THE EGO STATES

According to TA theory, every person has three ego states: The Parent, the Adult, and the Child. Each ego state is a distinct source of particular behavior. However, one does not stay in only one ego state; instead, a person switches occasionally from one to another, as can be noted through observing behavior and listening to *what* is said and *how* it is said.

The *Parent* ego state includes the experiences and related behavior patterns influenced by the external environment, especially during early life. The parent ego state may be indicated by words and phrases such as: always, don't, do as I say and do not ask why.

The *Adult* ego state is the rational aspect of the personality. It includes information gathering, problem solving, and rational decision making. Words and phrases generally indicating the Adult are: who, what, when, where, how, why, which is the best alternative course of action based on the facts, and so on.

The *Child* ego state is the source of fear, rebellion, anger, hurt, happiness, laughter, and creativity. Words and phrases indicative of this ego state are: I can't, help me, I want what I want now, wow! great!

No one ego state is necessarily better than the other. Problems usually occur when an ego state that is not appropriate for a situation becomes a source of behavior. Generally, however, the Adult state is the one that is underutilized in most organizations.

TRANSACTIONS

Individuals do not operate in isolation; they interact and talk with other people. This is called a *transaction.* There are different kinds of transactions between the ego states of individuals. This article will concentrate on complementary transactions, also called parallel transactions, between superior and subordinate.

In a *complementary* transaction, the transactional stimulus is followed by the predicted response. For example, the superior may say, "John, clean the engine plugs, change the distributor points; never mind why—just do it." (Parent injunction.) The subordinate, John, may answer, "Yes, sir, I'll do as you say." This transaction, as shown in Figure 1, illustrates Likert's System 1.

If John is a good "order taker" this transaction may not cause a communication breakdown; but, if this kind of interaction continues, it does not provide sufficient growth opportunities for the subordinate. Today's work force is generally better educated and may not accept orders blindly. Furthermore, in many organizations, professional subordinates may have more detailed knowledge about their area of competence than their boss. In short, the Parent-Child interaction has considerable limitations.

Parent-Child Transactions

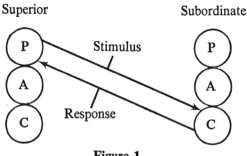

Superior   Subordinate

Figure 1

An alternative approach would have been the superior saying, "John, this engine does not run right. Can you check it?" The subordinate might have answered, "I will find out what the problem is. If the spark plugs and distributor points are the problem, I will do the necessary work. The car will then be ready by four o'clock." This transaction, as shown in Figure 2, is based on a rational analysis of the problem and the actions required to solve it. As will be seen later, this kind of interaction is characteristic of System 4.

Adult-Adult Transactions

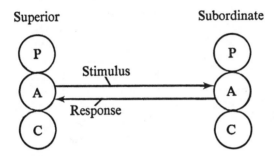

Figure 2

LIFE POSITIONS

In TA, four life positions are identified. The first is, *I'm not OK—You're OK,* a rather depressing position. Such people have little confidence in themselves, take little initiative, and often follow the orders of others they consider OK. The second life position, *I'm not OK—You're not OK,* is futile. Little gets done and the organization operates in disarray. The third position, *I'm OK—You're not OK,* can be observed in enterprises when managers do not trust subordinates and consider them not OK. The result is lack of delegation and the feeling on the bosses' part that nothing gets done unless *they* take over the task. Such superiors may behave rather arrogantly in their relationships with subordinates. In contrast, persons with the fourth position, *I'm OK—You're OK,* recognize their own worth and that of others; they have good relationships with superiors, subordinates, and peers. It is position that is very conducive to System 4 management.

TOWARD PARTICIPATIVE MANAGEMENT WITH TA

Likert and his associates found the System 1 or System 2 organizations were associated with poor performance. As organizations moved toward the participative approach of System 4, long-run performance generally improved. Since the effectiveness of an enterprise depends to a great extent upon its people, it is necessary not only to measure organizational variables, but also to develop tools that help improve the human organization.

Transactional Analysis is such a tool. It is simple and easy to learn, yet it can be used to understand relatively complex interactions. It also gives insights into one's own behavior—a first step toward change—and facilitates the analysis and improvement of communications. Finally, TA may be used to move the organization toward System 4.

In this article, System 1 will be contrasted with System 4 and the relationship to TA will be shown. System 1 tends to emphasize Parent-Child relationships between superior and subordinate which may be workable at times, but are generally not the most effective means for utilizing people's potential. Furthermore, in System 1 the superior frequently assumes the position of *I'm OK—You're not OK,* which has serious implications for managing.

In contrast, System 4 is flexible; members of the organization use the ego state that is appropriate for the specific situation. Clearly, the often underutilized Adult ego is emphasized, and transactions between superior and subordinates tend to be—although not exclusively—on the Adult-Adult level. Furthermore, people are confident and secure, operating from the *I'm OK— You're OK* life position. Table 1 contrasts System 1 with System 4 and shows the corresponding concepts in Transactional Analysis.

SYSTEM 1 AND TA

In System 1, superiors operate primarily from their Parent ego state and the life position in which subordinates are considered not OK. This has serious implications for leadership, motivation, communication, decision making, goal setting, and control.

Leadership. In System 1, the superior has no trust in subordinates who then feel that their ideas are not sought. The superior operates from his Parent ego state, often criticizing subordinates. Consequently, subordinates do not feel free to talk to their superior, and respond from their Child ego state. Suggestions from subordinates are hardly ever considered seriously. The boss often assumes that he is OK and his subordinates are not. There is little delegation of real authority, and subordinates are expected to follow instructions. It is no surprise, therefore, that they do not develop a healthy self-concept nor do they feel a sense of real accomplishment.

Motivation. The superior, operating from his Parent state, primarily uses fear, threats, punishment, and occasionally rewards. The boss wants dependent subordinates who behave in their Child ego state; that is what he gets. There is no participation, no involvement, and there is low satisfaction. Furthermore, subordinates do not feel responsible for taking the initiative to achieve organizational goals. To make matters worse, the superior reminds

Table 1. The Analyses of Trasactions in Managerial Systems

	System 1: Exploitative-Authoritative	System 4: Participative Group
1. Leadership	Superior has no trust in subordinates; their ideas are not sought. Superior operates from his P[a], often the Critical P. Subordinates do not feel free to talk to boss. Subordinates are expected to respond from their C[c]. Their suggestions are seldom taken seriously. Boss often assumes that he is OK—but not subordinates. Little delegation. Subordinates follow instructions; they develop no healthy self-concept.	Superior has great deal of trust in subordinates. Their ideas are sought and they feel free to talk to their boss. Transactions are on the A-A[b] basis: subordinates are expected to develop their own ideas. Boss and subordinates feel OK about each other. Superior is a member of a team with emphasis on competence, not authority. There is a great deal of delegation. Subordinates feel accountable for their actions and they feel OK about their accomplishments.
2. Motivation	Superior operating from P uses especially fear, threat, and punishment, and occasionally rewards. The boss wants dependent subordinates in their C. This is what he gets. No participation, no involvement, low satisfaction. Subordinates do not feel responsible for achieving organizational goals. Superior reminds them that they are not OK. Not conducive for teamwork.	Great emphasis on involvement based on group actions and teamwork. Interactions based on A. Responsibility is shared, with a great deal of individual commitment to organizational results. Great deal of cooperation by members who are OK and also consider others OK.
3. Communication	The boss, from his P, gives orders, which are viewed with suspicion by subordinates. They also do not dare to level with their boss, who considers himself OK but not the employees. Consequently, upward communication is inaccurate and the boss is not aware of what is going on in the enterprise.	Free communication flow in all directions. Since communication is primarily in the A mode, it is very accurate. This means superiors are well informed about problems facing subordinates. The focus is on objective problem solving, not on finding scapegoats for difficulties. Superior and subordinates consider each other OK—a prerequisite for genuine communication.

Table 1.   (Continued)

	System 1: Exploitative-Authoritative	System 4: Participative Group
4. Decision Making	Decisions are made by the top managers who view others are not OK. Subordinates are hardly ever involved in decisions related to their work. They operate in their C, follow orders, but are not motivated to contribute.	Decisions are made at all levels of the organization. Decisions are made objectively, based on the A ego state. Problems and their causes are identified and alternative courses is selected after objective analysis. Subordinates are involved in this process which reinforces their OK life position.
5. Goals	Organizational goals are established at the top in an autocratic manner in the superior's P ego state. Although subordinates may appear to follow the directions there is a great deal of resistance to the aims. In fact, the Rebellious C ego state of subordinates often determines behavior behind the boss's back.	Organizational and personal development goals are set at all levels primarily through group actions. Subordinates, based on their A ego state, set the goals primarily through group actions. Subordinates, based on their A ego state, set the goals primarily by themselves and discuss them with the superior. There is a great deal of participation, and individuals set high performance goals. The sense of direction makes superiors and subordinates feel OK and enhances their self-image.
6. Control	External, rigid controls are concentrated at the top. The boss, driven by his P, tries to control everything. Since subordinates are considered not OK, they cannot exercise self-control. Subordinates, in their C ego state, try to meet control standards—even if inappropriate—instead of speaking openly to the superior. There is considerable hidden resistance to control.	Review and control is shared by members of the organization. Subordinates, based on their A, exercise self-control and self-guidance. Controls are used for feedback; not to pin blame on individuals. Analysis of deviations from plans is objective. Emphasis is on forward-looking controls to prevent deviations. Measurement of performance is in a positive environment in which superior and subordinates adopt an OK position.

^aP = Parent ego state
^bA = Adult ego state
^cC = Child ego state

subordinates that they are not OK. Clearly, this is not conducive to teamwork that achieves results.

Communication.   The boss issues orders from his Parent ego state. These directives are viewed with great suspicion by subordinates. Yet, they are afraid to level with the superior who considers himself OK but not the subordinates. In this organizational climate, upward communication is inaccurate. Consequently, the boss does not really know what is going on in the enterprise.

Decisions.   Top management, viewing others as being not OK, makes decisions with insufficient information input from people at lower levels of the organization. Subordinates are hardly ever involved in decisions related to their job. Their behavior is often based on their Child ego state—they follow orders, but they are not motivated to contribute.

Goals.   In System 1, organizational goals are set in an autocratic manner at the top. Superiors, operating from their Parent ego state, issue directives and communicate them down the organization. There is no subordinate participation in the goal-setting process. Subordinates may follow directions, but there is a great deal of hidden resistance to the organizational aims. In fact, subordinates are often rebellious behind the boss's back with their behavior derived from their Child ego state. They feel not OK and avoid confronting their boss with the real issues. In this organizational climate, therefore, there is no commitment to objectives by the subordinates.

Control.   System 1 is characterized by rigid external controls concentrated at the top of the organization. The boss, influenced by his Parent ego state, wants to control everything. Since subordinates are considered "not OK," they are not permitted to exercise self-control. In this environment, the subordinate's behavior is determined by his Child ego state. Subordinates may even work toward the achievement of obsolete or inappropriate standards because they do not feel free to discuss the relevance of these standards. Also, there may be hidden resistance to control. The problem is that subordinates have little opportunity to develop a healthy self-concept and a sense of competence.

SYSTEM 4 AND TA

Obviously, System 1 has serious limitations. In contrast, research has shown that organizations that moved toward System 4 became more effective in the long-run. It is suggested that System 4 is basically congruent with behavior derived from the Adult ego state and the *I'm OK—You're OK* life position.

Leadership.   In this organizational environment, the superior has a great deal of trust in subordinates. Their ideas are sought and they feel free to talk to their bosses. Transactions are primarily on the Adult-Adult level, and subordinates are encouraged to develop their own ideas. The boss and subordinates feel OK about each other. The superior, as a member of the team, derives his power largely from his competence and deemphasizes formal authority. There is a great deal of delegation of authority, and subordinates, in turn, feel accountable for their actions. They also feel OK about their accomplishments which are acknowledged by their superior.

Motivation. In System 4 a great deal of emphasis is placed on involvement in group actions and teamwork. Most interactions are on the Adult ego state level. Responsibility is shared by the group, yet there also is great individual commitment to organizational results. People not only feel motivated and OK about themselves but create an environment in which others feel OK as well.

Communication. Communication flows freely in all directions. Since it is primarily in the adult mode, with emphasis on factual analysis and clarity, it is very accurate. Consequently, superiors are well informed about the problems faced by subordinates; the focus is on rational problem solving, not on finding scapegoats for organizational difficulties. The superior and subordinate consider each other OK, an important prerequisite for genuine communication.

Decisions. Decisions, made at all levels of the organization, are made on a rational basis derived from the Adult ego state. Problems and their causes are identified, and alternative courses of action are evaluated. Based on this analysis, the best course is selected. Subordinates become active participants in this process which, in turn, reinforces their OK life position.

Goals. In System 4, organizational and personal development goals are set at all levels of the enterprise through group action. Subordinates, in their Adult ego state, set objectives for themselves and discuss them with their boss and others. The aims are challenging, yet attainable. Agreement on goals is accomplished through participative interaction, not by decree of the boss. Clear objectives give a sense of direction which makes superiors and subordinates feel OK about themselves and the organization.

Control. Review and control are shaped by members of the organization. Subordinates, operating from their Adult ego state, exercise self-control and self-guidance. Analysis of deviations from plans is objective. Controls are used for feedback, not to pin blame on individuals. Moreover, emphasis is on forward-looking controls, with the aim of preventing deviations from occurring in the future. In all, the measurement of performance is conducted in a positive environment; the focus is on improvement by building on personal strengths of individuals.

WHAT TO DO

The practicing manager and the organizational development (OD) consultant are, naturally, interested in the application of TA in making the organization effective. The different methods may include action planning, confrontation meetings, team building, or intergroup development, just to mention a few. The appropriateness of each is, of course, contingent upon the particular situation.

The OD model recommended in this article not only utilizes TA, but it is also research-based. Specifically, it involves the following steps: first, the organization is diagnosed through data collection on important managerial and organizational variables. Likert's questionnaire may be used to develop an organizational profile which indicates the position of the enterprise between System 1 and System 4.[7]. These findings then are discussed by members of the organization. At that time, the concepts of Likert's four systems are further explained. In addition, Transactional Analysis is taught and applied as an important tool to move the organization toward System 4.

Transactional Analysis can be used in several ways. People learn to recognize their predominant *ego states* and their effect on managing. Although the Parent ego state of the superior may be appropriate at times—such as in an emergency—if used exclusively, it may inhibit the development of subordinates. Similarly, the Child ego state may facilitate the development of new and creative ways to accomplish the task, but it would be inappropriate as a dominant mode of behavior for most organizations. The Adult ego state, unfortunately, is often underutilized. Consequently, subordinates have only limited growth opportunities. Yet, through the Adult state, superiors and employees would recognize alternative ways of behaving, thus building a flexible organization that can respond to the ever-changing environmental demands.

The *analysis of transactions* may benefit both the superior and the subordinates. Both can use TA as a tool to identify their predominant interactions and consciously decide to improve them. Although parallel transactions from the Parent state of the superior to the Child state of the subordinate may not cause a breakdown in communication, if they become the prevailing modes of interaction, the result is usually not the most effective use of human potential. Furthermore, through TA, both superior and subordinate may recognize the psychological game they play—that is, a set of transactions with a gimmick —and hidden meanings underlying their communication patterns. This insight is the first step in stopping the game and, instead, using the psychological energy to move the organization toward greater effectiveness.

The recognition of one's *life position* can also aid in moving the organization toward System 4. For example, a boss who thinks that only he is OK, and others are not, may realize that he overlooked certain talents in his subordinates. Promoting their growth will not only encourage their professional behavior, but will also help the superior to carry out his job. Moreover, rewarding productive behavior through positive reinforcement will result in repetition of this behavior and the development of a better self-image by organizational members. The aim is to build on the strengths of people, help them to overcome their weaknesses, and create an *I'm OK—You're OK* environment.

SUMMARY

The organizational effectiveness depends on its people. Likert's approach facilitates the scientific measurement of the human organization. Research has shown that System 1, the exploitative-authoritative approach, is ineffective. As the organization moves toward the participative approach of System 4, long-term effectiveness increases.

Although in the past a number of approaches have been used to move organizations toward System 4, the new and potentially powerful tool of Transactional Analysis has not been utilized. This article has shown that the ineffective System 1 is characterized by Parent-Child transactions between superior and subordinates. In addition, the *not*—OK position of employees is often institutionalized through negative reinforcement and punishment. In contrast, System 4 is congruent with Adult-Adult leadership and personal growth. Thus, managerial behavior is based on a potentially healthy psychological life position of *I'm OK—You're OK*.

In conclusion, it is suggested that TA can be a powerful, yet easy to learn, tool for organizational development. It can help individuals to identify their predominant ego state and evaluate its appropriateness for the specific situation; this is the first step to personal growth and effectiveness. TA also facilitates the analysis of transactions between superior and subordinates. The traditional Parent-Child transaction can be supplemented—if not largely replaced—by Adult-Adult interactions that provide greater opportunities for utilizing employees' potentials. Finally, an environment which promotes the development of OK life positions by all organizational members is not only satisfying to individuals but also congruent with System 4, the managerial approach which may result in greater organizational effectiveness.

REFERENCES

1. Rensis Likert, *The Human Organization.* New York: McGraw-Hill Book Company, 1967.
2. Rensis Likert and Jane Gibson Likert, *New Ways of Managing Conflict.* New York: McGraw-Hill Book Company, 1976.
3. William F. Dowling, "At General Motors, System 4 Builds Performance and Profits." *Organizational Dynamics,* Vol. 3, No. 3 (Winter, 1975), pp. 23–38.
4. H. M. F. Rush and Phyllis S. McGrath, "Transactional Analysis Moves into Corporate Training." *The Conference Board Record,* (July, 1973), pp. 38–44.

5. Heinz Weihrich, "MBO: Appraisal with Transactional Analysis." *Personnel Journal,* Vol. 55, No. 4 (April, 1976), pp. 173–175, 183.
6. Eric Berne, *Games People Play.* New York: Grove Press, Inc. 1964.
7. Rensis Likert and Jane Gibson Likert, *op. cit.,* p. 75.

PRODUCTIVITY: LEARNING FROM THE JAPANESE

Hirotaka Takeuchi

Everyone seems to agree that lagging productivity is a serious problem in the U.S. Everyone seems to agree that something ought to be done about it soon. After three decades of diminishing growth rate, productivity of the private economy actually declined in the first three quarters of 1979. But no one seems to agree on what is causing the slowdown or who should be taking responsibility. The bulk of the blame has been placed, rightly or wrongly, on the following:

- the government, for increasing the number of federal, state, and local regulations, for enacting equal opportunity rules, for maintaining large military spendings, and for not providing tax incentives to boost investment;
- unions, for being responsible for featherbedding and for spiraling wage costs;
- OPEC, for creating a sharp rise in energy costs;
- environmentalists, for demanding stringent pollution control measures;
- the worker, for taking days off from work, for being inexperienced and undereducated, and for being "more interested in the 'me' in his life than in keeping his nose to the grindstone";[1]
- corporate managers, for making workers feel alienated and for not investing more in long-term research and development.[2]

Given the long list of possible "suspects," productivity experts have been struggling to determine from where to start the investigation. These experts, who are mostly comprised of economists, have tended to concentrate their investigative efforts at the macro-economic level. As a consequence, relatively

© 1981 by the Regents of the University of California. Reprinted from CALIFORNIA MANAGEMENT REVIEW, Volume XXIII, no. 4, pp. 5 to 19 by permission of the Regents.

little has been said thus far on what corporate managers or workers could do to improve the productivity problem.

The prevailing view among corporate managers has been to treat productivity as "someone else's problem." Those who hold such a view would point out that any of the causes of the productivity slowdown cited by experts are beyond their own control. Some managers would go a step further to argue that they have been the victims of actions taken by the government, unions, and others.

There may be other reasons why corporate managers have opted to take a noncommittal attitude towards the productivity problem. For one thing, corporate managers are sensitive to the tradition in the U.S. of dismissing concern for productivity as "right-wing patter." They fear that a call for steps to improve productivity would be linked to work speed-ups and layoffs. Yet another reason may be rooted in the fact that the U.S. is still ahead of other countries in terms of the absolute level of productivity. In 1977, the output per employee hour of Japan, which recorded the fastest productivity growth rate in recent years, stood at about 62 percent of the U.S.'s.[3] A plausible response to the U.S. decline could be: "Don't panic—we're still the most productive nation."

In recent years, more and more corporate managers in the U.S. are beginning to realize the direct impact of declining productivity on their business. Productivity, these managers argue, is very much "their problem." These managers see productivity as playing some part in the loss of U.S. companies' share in the domestic and world markets to foreign competition. Others are alarmed by a report published by the New York Stock Exchange suggesting that a small productivity decline may have a large "multiplier" effect on inflation.[4] Still others are concerned with empirical results that show productivity as a significant determinant of profits.[5] To the extent that these concerns —loss of market share, inflation, and profits—are of pivotal importance to everyday business, it seems logical that corporate managers are beginning to show much more than a casual interest in productivity.

Some U.S. companies—Westinghouse, General Motors, IBM, General Electric, Honeywell, TRW, and Nashua Corporation, to name a few—have put their productivity concerns into action by adopting various productivity improvement programs. Westinghouse has recently started a multimillion-dollar project to study how robots, computer-aided systems, office and paperwork systems, energy conservation, value engineering, quality control teams, and reorganization can improve productivity in the plant and office. The companies named above have been enthusiastic about the results of such programs—namely, an improved rate of productivity growth for the company and improved morale among the workers.

One of the characteristics common to all these U.S. companies has been their willingness to learn from how Japanese companies manage productivity.

Many Japanese companies have been testing and implementing productivity improvement programs for almost three decades. These long years of experimental efforts have now produced a unique way of thinking about and managing productivity, which I call the "Japanese productivity system" in this article.

This article addresses three questions regarding the Japanese productivity system:

- What is unique about the Japanese productivity system?
- Can a management technique developed within the context of Japanese companies be transferred to U.S. companies?
- What can U.S. managers interested in initiating successful productivity programs learn from past experiences?

I believe that corporate managers can do something about the productivity problem perplexing the U.S. I invite managers to evaluate, for themselves, whether the Japanese productivity system can deliver to them the kinds of benefits currently enjoyed by a small number of U.S. companies and their workers.

WORDS OF CAUTION

A casual observer may note that Japanese companies must be doing something right to post a rate of productivity growth more than three times faster than their own in the past decade. According to the Bureau of Labor Statistics, output per hour of manufacturing worker rose 9.9 percent annually in Japan between 1967 and 1977, compared to 2.7 percent in the U.S. for the same period.[6]

A casual observer may also note that the Japanese have been able to record a higher level of productivity in some key industries. According to the latest census data, an average Japanese auto worker produces 50 cars per year, compared to 25 cars for an average U.S. worker. An average Japanese steelworker turns out 420 tons of output per year, compared to 250 tons in the U.S.

Some words of caution are in order. First of all, an unwary use of readily available raw data may render comparisons meaningless. Taking the auto industry comparison, an informed observer may respond: "How can you call that a legitimate comparison when you know that differences in the size of the car produced, the length of the work days, the level of automation, the degree of participation by outside suppliers, the attitude and skills of the workers, and a host of other factors distort the understanding of what's really happening in the two countries?" An informed observer may also explain that the difference in the annual growth rates may be largely due to the differences in the stages of industrial development in the two countries.

Second, there is a danger of obscuring the focus of the Japanese productivity system if corporate managers in the U.S. become too preoccupied with numbers. The focus should be more on the process by which productivity programs are implemented and less on the results of having implemented them. To the extent that productivity programs are implemented by people, managers should be concerned primarily about people and secondarily about numbers. There is already some criticism that U.S. managers have become too preoccupied with short-term performance results (such as returns on sales and investments, earnings per share, and equity ratios) at the risk of becoming myopic in their thinking. Translated within our context, a myopic manager may possibly run the risk of going to the extreme in thinking, "What we need to do is to get those 'automatons' to crank out more products, even at the expense of increased defective rates."

The digression was needed to strike a sense of balance. We should be cautious of unqualified claims made by overly eager advocates of the Japanese productivity system. We should also be cautious of becoming too preoccupied with playing the numbers game. On the other hand, we should guard ourselves against becoming overly critical of the advocates' claims because differences between the two countries have not been accounted for entirely, and against shunning all comparative numbers that show differences between the two countries. An appropriate frame of mind to maintain is to recognize that differences do exist and to see if something can be learned from them.

JAPANESE PRODUCTIVITY SYSTEM

Some U.S. managers seem to feel that Japanese companies must have developed secret formulas for dealing with the productivity problem. There is nothing secret or magical about the productivity improvement programs (such as the suggestion box or quality control program), or the measures of productivity that they employ. In fact, most of the programs and measures were developed in the U.S. and subsequently borrowed by the Japanese (more on this topic later).

There are also no major gaps in the resources employed in the two countries. As the manager of a Japanese consumer electronics company aptly observed, "Our workers are no smarter [than U.S. workers]; our technology is no more advanced; our materials are no different; and our energy is less abundant."

What is unique about the Japanese productivity system is not the ingredients or pieces that go into the system, but how the pieces are put together. Productivity is like a jigsaw puzzle—all the pieces must be fitted together before the entire picture can be seen. Japanese companies seem to have mastered the art of putting together a workable productivity system.

The following describes five major idiosyncrasies of the Japanese productivity system. These idiosyncrasies are the key factors for success. Each is indispensable because without one the entire picture cannot be appreciated.

Product Quality Control. Productivity improvement came about among Japanese companies as a by-product of the emphasis placed on product quality control. The most urgent problem that most export-minded Japanese companies faced in the 1950s was the "cheap and shoddy" image associated with made-in-Japan products. In order to compete in the world market, these companies placed their top priority in improving the quality of their products.

One of the first steps taken was to invite American experts to lecture on statistical quality control techniques. Visits by W. Edwards Deming, a statistician, in 1950 and J.M. Juran, a consultant, in 1954, helped to spread the use of the methodology and practice needed in carrying out quality control programs. Every new technique subsequently developed in the U.S.—such as Zero Defects or Value Engineering—has been studied and adopted by Japanese manufacturers. By the 1970s, quality control had almost become a religion.

This religious dedication towards quality control seems to have paid off for the Japanese. Taking the television industry as an example, J.M. Juran observes:

- Between 1.5 to 1.8 defects per television set were discovered at the Motorola TV factory before Matsushita Electric took over in 1974. In 1978, under new management but virtually the same employees, the new Quasar brand had a defective rate of 0.03 to 0.04 per set. In the Japanese parent company, the defective rate at the factory averages 0.005 per set.
- Once on the market, Japanese televisions have from one-half to one-fourth the failure rates as compared to U.S. and European sets.[7]

Of the computer industry, a representative from Hewlett-Packard recently reported the test results conducted on three hundred thousand 16K RAMs (random access memory microcomponents) supplied by three Japanese vendors and three U.S. vendors. The incoming inspection failure rates of the 16K RAMs supplied by the three Japanese vendors were all 0.00 percent to 0.19 percent for the three U.S. vendors. Similarly, the field failure rates of the 16K RAMs supplied by the three Japanese vendors ranged from 0.010 percent to 0.019 percent, compared to a range between 0.090 percent to 0.267 percent for the three U.S. vendors.[8] Although considerable caution must be taken in interpreting these results and in generalizing these findings to other industries, the fact still remains that made-in-Japan products no longer suffer from the stigma that was attached to them up to a decade ago.

What does quality control have to do with productivity? Quality control affects both output and input. On the output side, Louis P. Bucklin notes, "If the television sets that move off the assembly line fail to function, then there is no real output, even though the physical presence of something that would otherwise be described as a television undeniably exists."[9] From a marketing perspective, lower defective rates in the factory and on the market are likely to be translated into higher trial rates and repeat purchase rates—higher sales, in other words. On the input side, a large number of rejected items means: more human resources required to repair them; duplicated use of materials; and more energy consumed per unit produced.

Grassroots Involvement. With such dedication to quality, it was natural for technical experts to assume a leadership role in promoting productivity in Japan. But the major driving force behind its productivity movement came from millions of rank-and-file workers who have taken the initiative to suggest changes to their superiors. This "bottom-up" process constitutes the backbone of the Japanese productivity system.

The number of suggestions reported by some companies is astonishingly high:

- In the past few years, both Toyota Motor Company and Mitsubishi Motors have been averaging close to twenty suggestions per worker a year at their factories.
- In the ten months ending October 1976, Matsushita Electric averaged fifty suggestions for each of the fifteen hundred production workers in its Ibaragi television factory.[10] The company as a whole has been averaging over ten suggestions per worker (factory and office workers combined) per year in the last few years. These numbers should be treated with discretion because they include all suggestions for change. But a Matsushita manager points out, "All these suggestions somehow relate to making the product better, the job easier, or the worker happier. Wouldn't that lead to better productivity?"

Once the suggestions are submitted in writing, using preprinted forms in most cases, a suggestion committee evaluates the ideas, and, if necessary, hands over the acceptable set to technical experts for further evaluation. At Matsushita, the acceptance rate has been averaging about 10 percent.

One interesting feature of the suggestion program is its rapid increase since the mid-1960s. Toyota averaged only one suggestion per worker in 1965 and Matsushita averaged 1.1 suggestion per worker in 1966. The rapid increase in worker involvement since the mid-1960s corresponds directly with the rise of small-group activities discussed next in the same time period.

Another interesting feature of the suggestion system is the heavy promotional effort directed towards the newcomers to the company. Slogans such as "Make Every Worker a Manager" and "Make Every Worker an Engineer" are emphasized to encourage initiative taking on the part of even the lowest ranked workers. Some companies put the program into practice by offering newcomers small incentives (such as a meal ticket) in exchange for suggestions, whether used or not. If accepted, the name of the contributor is publicized through a company newspaper or a bulletin board. In such a way, workers are conditioned early in their career to thinking that there is room for creativity even within the routine operations of the factory, and to thinking that "giving is rewarding."

A personnel manager at Toshiba Electric asked a twenty-one-year-old factory worker what prompted her to make seventy technical suggestions a year, half of which were accepted. "Her answer was simply, 'It makes me feel good,'" said the manager. "Our strength lies in the fact that we can mix the scientific management approach and the behavioral approach (self-actualization, job enrichment) together and come up with rank-and-file workers with a very constructive frame of mind."

Quality Control Circles. Quality control circles are a natural outgrowth of the suggestion program. As in the suggestions program, workers offer solutions towards job-related problems, but the problems addressed by QC Circles are often more complex and less obvious to uncover. Also, the solutions no longer consist of untested ideas, which may or may not work. Members of QC Circles devote a considerable amount of their time toward testing their recommendations and putting them into practice. QC Circles thus serve to further enhance worker involvement.

Although the QC Circle is well-known in Japan, the concept as it is understood in Japan is still relatively unknown in the U.S. A quality control circle is a voluntary study group dedicated to solving job-related problems. Two commonly held misconceptions need to be dispelled. First, the study group does not consist of quality control specialists with extensive prior technical training. QC Circle members are mostly rank-and-file workers and foremen who receive virtually all of their technical training once they join the study group. Some see the inclusion and training of foremen, who usually serve as circle leaders, as the most innovative characteristic of the Japanese approach to quality control.[11] Second, problem solving is not restricted to the area of product quality control. According to a 1979 survey, the kinds of projects being conducted by over five hundred of the QC Circles in Japan include (in order of importance) cost reduction, product quality control, improvement of workshop facilities, safety precautions, employee morale improvement, pollution control, and continued employee education.[12] Directly or indirectly, these projects become instrumental in improving productivity and quality of work life.

QC Circles have grown explosively in Japan since their establishment in 1962. In 1965, fewer than 5,000 QC Circles were registered with the Japan Union of Scientists and Engineers (JUSE), a nonprofit association serving as the QC Circle coordinator. By the end of 1979, there were over 100,000 circles. Membership of these registered circles totalled 980,000 in 1979, with an average of nine members per QC Circle. A high-ranking JUSE official estimates the number of unregistered and quasi-QC Circles in Japan to reach as high as eight times the number of registered circles. Assuming the same number of members per group, as many as one out of five employees in the entire Japanese labor force (thirty-seven million) could be taking part in some form of job-related group activities today.

This rapid diffusion of QC Circles in Japan is credited largely to JUSE's pioneering efforts. Among other activities, JUSE has been responsible for:

- Holding training sessions for managers and foremen. In 1979, more than thirty such sessions, usually lasting from two to six days, were held in its Tokyo headquarters and its eight regional offices. In addition, close to thirty-five hundred foremen took two training courses conducted via radio and TV.
- Publishing a monthly trade journal called FQC (Quality Control for the Foreman), whose subscription reached over one hundred thousand in 1979. In addition, it publishes numerous textbooks and training manuals.
- Sponsoring a series of conferences and visitor programs. In 1979, a total of 107 conferences, in which some two thousand successful case stories were presented by QC Circle members, were held throughout Japan. Exchange visits among different Japanese companies active in QC Circles (initiated in 1963) and exchange visits with foreign countries (initiated in 1968) are increasing every year.

JUSE's activities are financed through nominal fees charged for these training programs, publications, and conferences. It does not, however, charge membership fees. "It's a voluntary movement," said a JUSE official. "This movement will grow as long as we can continue to deliver the hoped-for benefits to member companies and their workers."

According to the 1979 survey cited earlier, the QC movement delivered different benefits to company managers and circle members. The intangible benefits cited most often by the two groups are shown in Table 1. The survey also tried to ascertain the extent of tangible monetary benefits enjoyed by both groups. About 80 percent of the managers reported that the company gained annual monetary benefits ranging from $12,000 to $1.2 million per business unit.[13] Taking the mode, the ratio of these benefits to incremental, out-of-pocket costs was ten to one per business unit.[14] On a company-wide basis, one large Japanese elecronics company with forty-six thousand employees interviewed by the author estimated its benefits at $13.3 million a year and its incremental costs at $2.7 million in 1978 (a benefit-cost ratio of five to one). Monetary benefits to QC Circle members, on the other hand, appear to be relatively insignificant. As in indication, only 2.7 percent of over five hundred QC Circle leaders surveyed mentioned higher pay as one of the benefits of participating in QC Circles (more on this topic later).

Table 1.

Managers	Circle Leaders
1. Improved worker morale	1. Provided good opportunity for learning
2. Improved safety	2. Improved communication with superior
3. Strengthened teamwork	3. Heightened problem awareness
4. Improved product quality	4. Heightened consciousness to improve
5. Led to better human relations	status quo
	5. Improved working environment

Of course, companies will not be able to amass such large benefits by simply providing moral encouragement. Active company support is a necessary condition for the successful operation of QC Circles. First, workers are encouraged to use company facilities to test out their ideas or to develop prototypes. Second, workers are encouraged to conduct QC Circle meetings during working hours—two-thirds of the circles surveyed did so in 1979. On the average, QC Circles met twice a month for more than an hour per session. Third, even if meetings are held outside of regular working hours, most companies (69 percent in 1979) offer some financial support. For the most part, such support consists of nominal overtime pay. Fourth, almost all the companies bear the costs associated with putting together intercompany QC Circles contests. These intercompany contests, usually held two or three times a year regionally and once a year nationally, can turn into fiercely competitive events. QC Circle members spend long hours rehearsing their case study presentation, oftentimes on stage. The presentations are often accompanied by skits or music to make the potentially dry technical content as appealing as possible. "Sometimes these contests turn into talent shows," said one manager. "It can also become as thrilling and exciting as an Academy Award when the time for selecting the winner is reached. I've seen many winners in tears."

The case study method has been used very effectively within QC Circles. In the early stage of the case study, much of the effort of the study group is directed towards identifying crucial problems that may have a far-reaching impact if resolved. This search process tests the creativity of QC Circle members and heightens their sense of mission. In the analytical stage, QC Circle members make extensive use of basic statistical and graphical techniques that they've learned in the training program. The major objective of the analysis is to derive meaningful relationships and inferences from the raw data that have been collected. The most frequently utilized analytical tools include histograms, Pareto analysis (similar to "80–20" analysis), cause-and-effect diagrams, and flow charts. This analytical process conditions QC Circle members to argue with facts rather than with intuitions. In the recommendation stage of the case study, QC Circle members try to convince their superiors that the solution makes a positive contribution to the company. The number of case studies that reach this stage is low (an average of 2.4 per QC Circle in 1979), but the rewards are high for the workers.

Nonfinancial Rewards. The reward that seems to work best within the Japanese productivity system is the pat on the back. The success of many Japanese companies in applying positive reinforcement, such as praise and recognition, suggests that rewards do not necessarily have to take the form of a fat check.

Some Japanese companies, to be sure, are offering cash rewards to individual workers and QC Circles, but payments appear to be nominal. A worker at Matsushita Electric's TV factory suggested a device to stop solder from dripping down the endplates of television sets and causing short circuits.[15] His suggestion, which was designated as a fifth-grade award under Matsushita's eight-grade system, earned him thirteen dollars. Another worker received a total of one hundred dollars for sixty suggestions that were accepted in a year. The cash reward came out to sixty cents per suggestion. At Mitsubishi Electric, ten members of a QC Circle jointly received a cash reward of two hundred dollars for suggesting the best cost-reduction idea of the year. According to Robert E. Cole, "Symbolic payments are common, with rewards for even the best suggestion, leading to say a patent, seldom exceeding $600."[16]

Most companies prefer to rely on some form of nonfinancial reward. At a Honda Motor Company plant small rectangular cards are hung from the ceiling directly above some of its workers. These cards are the most visible rewards that Honda's workers receive for contributing to the suggestion program. Under the system, workers can receive up to a hundred points per suggestion, depending on the value of the suggestion made. Cumulative record is kept of the points earned by each worker and a gold-colored card is awarded once he or she reaches fifty points.

Extensive use is also made of trophies, plaques, medals, diplomas, and other commemorative items to honor the contributors. According to the 1979 survey of QC Circles, 93 percent of the companies handed out some variations of the above awards in their intercompany contests. For some QC Circles fortunate enough to be selected to attend the national contest, positive reinforcement may result from something less tangible that a trophy or a medal. The opportunity to visit the corporate headquarters, to present their case studies to top management, and for a presidential handshake have been mentioned by QC Circle members as morale boosters.

Another positive reinforcement tool, within a broader context, is the posting of performance results—such as defective rate, output per employee hour, number of suggestions, attendance rate, and repair rate—on the factory bulletin board. The results are charted and updated on a regular basis. Performance results of other factories or the norm for the entire company are frequently charted to provide a basis for comparison. Workers are praised for internal improvements and for superior performance over others

Are cards hanging from the ceiling, trophies, presidential handshakes, and performance charts too sophomoric as mechanisms for reward? Call it whatever you please, but the Skinnerian principle of offering positive rewards in the form of praise and recognition has become an integral part of the Japanese productivity system.

Maternalistic Management. The missing link in understanding the Japanese productivity system is the role the company plays in making the worker become closely involved with productivity. The answer lies in the "maternalistic" way in which the company relates to the worker on a day-to-day basis. Maternalistic management is characterized by the close, caring, nurturing type of relationship that companies build in trying to motivate, guide, and develop their workers.

Many readers may be puzzled at this point with the seemingly perverse use of the word *maternalistic* to describe a management style traditionally called *paternalistic*. As M.Y. Yoshino observes, "The [Japanese] company was regarded as one vast family, with management playing the benevolent 'father' role and the workers accepting the submissive role of 'children'."[17] To be sure, Japanese companies still adhere to a paternalistic style of management in building enduring employer-employee relationships. A paternalistic system—which connotes security, solidarity, loyalty, and authority—is reflected in their personnel practices, such as the "guarantee against dismissal, regularized wage increases to meet the rising needs of a growing family, and fringe benefits."[18]

But many Japanese companies switch over to a more maternalistic style when managing the short-run execution of specific programs. Within the context of productivity improvement programs, this style is reflected in the following practices:

- Presence of top managers: frequent visits of top managers to the factory and their participation in training programs or in companywide events (such as sports competition or QC Circle contests) help to convey the message that "top managers care." Taking QC Circle contests as an example, 89 percent of the five hundred or so companies interviewed in 1979 responded that their presidents regularly attended these contests.
- Guidance and support provided by middle managers: 98 percent of QC Circle leaders interviewed acknowledged receiving some form of guidance and support from their immediate supervisors (mostly section or department managers).
- Daily contacts with productivity "facilitators": all the companies interviewed assigned one of more full-time administrative staff members to serve as facilitators between the company and QC Circle members. Workers are on "equal" terms with these facilitators, unlike the "submissive" role suggested within paternalistic system.

- Support of QC activities: as seen earlier, the company supports QC activities by providing materials and equipment necessary for workers to conduct experiments, arranging QC Circle meetings on company premises and during working hours, sponsoring contests, organizing visits to other companies, and sending its managers and foremen to training sessions conducted by JUSE. Company expenditure for these activities averaged thirty dollars per QC Circle member annually, according to the 1979 JUSE survey.

Attempts to motivate and nurture the workers start as soon as the workers join the company. As cited earlier, the seeds for an active suggestion program are planted during the first few days of training when the workers are encouraged to stretch their creative thinking. The seeds for teamwork are also planted during the initial training program in which the new employees are organized into study groups. Some companies go as far as sending their new recruits to Zen temples, farms, camps, or even the Self-Defence Force. "By eating together, sleeping together, and organizing daytime activities around groups, we want the trainees to have a first-hand experience in what teamwork means and what it can accomplish," said the personnel manager of a company which recently incorporated climbing Mt. Fuji into the training program.

The company enables workers to feel like "part of the system" by providing a constant flow of information from different sources. Mention was made earlier of the use of charts to disseminate information regarding worker performance. In addition, general information on the financial status of the company, industry and competitive trends, long-run corporate strategy, and other areas is shared with everyone in the organization via formal channels (such as company newspapers or routine morning gatherings) and informal channels (social gatherings, company clubs).[19] Information about QC Circle activities is also disseminated in some companies. According to the 1979 survey, 40 percent of the companies published intercompany QC Circle newsletters; 60 percent of these companies published such newsletters over six times a year.

The bottom-up nature of the Japanese productivity system does not come about simply as a result of positive-thinking workers becoming personally "turned on" with solving problems. Considerable effort is expended by the company in laying out the necessary network of people and communication to support the workers. The maternalistic nature in which the day-to-day programs are executed, combined with a paternalistic framework, helps to foster the belief among the workers that "the best interests of company are also my own best interests."

Regarding the key factors of the Japanese productivity system just discussed, U.S. managers may legitimately raise the question, "So, what's new?" Suggestion boxes, for example, have been around for a long time in many companies. Statistical quality control, work groups, positive reinforcements, and human relations (a broader concept encompassing maternalistic management) are not unheard of either. In fact, many of the original ideas date back to the experiments conducted at Western Electric Company's Hawthorne plant in the late 1920s.

Again, the distinguishing feature of the Japanese program lies in how the pieces are put together. In planning and organizing productivity improvement programs, Japanese companies rely on almost a fanatic dedication to details. In implementing and controlling the programs, they resort to tender loving care. In orchestrating the entire effort, they mobilize managers from different levels and staff members from different departments. And at all times, they keep sight of why productivity is being pursued—to benefit the workers, the company, and the product simultaneously.

IS IT TRANSFERABLE?

The discussion thus far has centered on the successful implementation of a productivity system in a country several thousand miles away that shares little, culturally, with the U.S. Before discussing what lessons can be drawn from the Japanese experience one must ask whether its success is endemic to Japan or whether it could be transferred across cultural boundaries.

Managers who hold a negative view (it will never work in the U.S.) would argue that the differences in the business culture between the two countries are too many for any meaningful transfer to take place. They would call the idiosyncrasies of the Japanese business culture—close government-business ties, company-based unions (which play a less adversary role than in the U.S.), commitment to a lifetime employment, and innate group orientation—barriers to entry. Their arguments could run as follows:[20]

- Under the cozy government-business partnership known as "Japan, Inc.," the government gives companies direct and indirect support for productivity improvement. For companies in selected growth industries, the government provides direct support in the form of tax breaks, technology transfer, and preferential financing. The government also provides indirect support to all companies by funding the Japan Productivity Center (JPC), which it established in 1955 as a means of involving management and labor unions in a national movement towards achieving higher productivity. In the U.S., a nonprofit organization similar to the JPC (last known as the National Center for Productivity and Quality of Working Life) was established by the U.S. Government in 1970, but was closed in 1978.
- Although the percentage of the work force participating in labor unions is somewhat higher in Japan, the locus of union power does not reside at the industry level, but resides within the company. Unlike local trade unions in the U.S., which are "outside" unions, the so-called enterprise unions in Japan (sometimes referred to as home unions) are based "inside" the company. Most Japanese companies consider their unions as friends, not as adversaries. Company managers involve union leaders in key decisions, so-

cialize with them, and regard "bringing up good union leaders" as part of their responsibility. Such practices are unheard of, if not illegal, in the U.S.
• The lifetime employment practice of Japanese companies has dual benefits for productivity. Knowing that the employees will be around until they retire at age fifty-five or sixty, companies can make substantial investment in training programs and efforts directed at human resources development. Knowing that their personal well-being hinges on how well the company performs, workers are induced to making as much contribution to the company as possible. In the U.S., several companies—IBM, Hewlett-Packard, and Eli Lilly, among others—are committed to job security (a no-layoff policy). These companies, however, are the exceptions rather than the rule.
• Japanese workers are prone to working in groups and teams, given the emphasis placed on traditional values of cooperation, harmony, and group consensus within the culture. Companies foster this group spirit by having their own uniforms, badges, mottos, and songs, and by organizing training programs, sports competition, and social events around groups. In the U.S., work teams are still a novelty. Although experiments with work teams have been conducted in General Foods' Topeka, Kansas plant, in Procter and Gamble's Lima, Ohio plant, in four Donnelly Mirrors plants in Holland, Michigan, and more recently in Sherwin-Williams' Richmond, Kentucky plant, they are still the exceptions rather than the rule.[21]

Although these arguments may support Kipling's contention that "East is East, and West is West, and never the twain shall meet," recent developments indicate that the twain are beginning to meet. We now turn to two groups of companies—U.S. subsidiaries of Japanese companies and U.S. companies that have established QC Circles—to present the view that the ideas basic to the Japanese productivity system can be transferred to the U.S.

JAPANESE COMPANIES IN THE U.S.

Japanese companies that have established subsidiaries in the U.S. are finding that American workers are responding very positively towards concerns for product quality and human resources development. Mention was made earlier of how Matsushita was able to improve the factory defective rate of its TV sets by a factor of almost fifty to one in the four years since it took over the Motorola factory in Chicago. Other examples abound.

Sanyo Electric Company took over a unionized Forrest City, Arkansas television factory of Whirlpool-controlled Warwick Electronics in December 1976, and in less than a year reduced the retail failure rate of its TV sets from 10 percent to less than 2 percent. In the computer industry, Fujitsu America reduced the factory defective rate of its subassemblies by a factor of ten to one in the past two years. Its president describes the process as follows:

I conducted a meeting once every week and had the American managers discuss their work openly. I encouraged everyone to think through problems together, to an eventual solution. Working together, we found these problems: carelessness, poor handling of delicate parts, inaccurate testing of equipment, improper placement of parts to be tested and, most important, failure of managers to act on the foregoing.[22]

Japanese companies in the U.S. are as commited to people building and team building as they are to product quality. Concern for the workers is best reflected in the words of the Fujitsu America president: "We Japanese managers consider our employees to be our greatest asset. We treat them as treasures, and they respond with loyalty and hard work."[23] This commitment is put into practice by the chairman of Hitachi Magnetics Corporation in Edmore, Michigan, who organizes and personally attends softball games and weekend picnics; by the president of NTN Bearing in Des Plaines, Illinois, who works as a manual laborer in the warehouse during the semiannual physical inventory count; and by the plant managers of Sony Corporation of America's San Diego plant, who hold monthly meetings with all its workers (over twelve hundred) to keep them abreast of relevant information related to marketing, production, and personnel matters.

These efforts seem to be paying off, as many companies are reporting superior performance records in absenteeism, employee turnover, and productivity. Sony's San Diego plant's absenteeism and turnover rates were 25 percent to 50 percent below those of other electronics companies in that area. Output per unit of labor was 22 percent higher than that of a U.S. counterpart.[24]

To be sure, Japanese companies are not free of problems in their U.S. subsidiaries.

- A dispute over wages led to a strike by the United Auto Workers at the Ann Arbor, Michigan plant of Nippon Seiko, a bearing manufacturer. In general, Japanese companies are discovering that a pat on the back and trophies alone do not provide adequate incentives for American workers.
- Charges of discrimination over promotion, wages, and fringe benefits has led three American workers to file a law suit against C. Itoh and Company, a large trading company. Charges of sexism and racism led women employees of Sumitomo Bank to demonstrate in front of its San Francisco office. Japanese companies are discovering the penchant for American workers to put their complaints into immediate action.
- Japanese companies in the service areas see the high turnover among middle managers as a major problem. They are discovering the difficulty of preventing American workers from job hopping.

- When the Forrest City, Arkansas plant of Sanyo constructed a softball field for employee and community use, one employee's reaction was the following: "When I leave here, my interest is on my things, not Sanyo's. I am a Christian, and I put my non-company time into serving the Lord."[25] Japanese companies are discovering a clear-cut distinction of company time from personal time.

Japanese companies are generally confident that these problems can be worked out in the long run. According to the manager of a Japanese bank in New York, "It is going to take time for us to learn about how American workers think and behave. It is also going to take some time for American workers to understand how we operate. If both sides are willing to adapt, the learning curve will be steep."

U.S. COMPANIES WITH QC CIRCLES

Japanese quality control circles, or work groups modelled after them, are beginning to spread among U.S. companies. QC Circles were first "imported" to the U.S. in 1974 by Lockheed Missiles and Space Company, which had sent its manufacturing manager to Japan to visit JUSE and eight companies actively involved in QC Circles. Lockeed adopted training programs developed by JUSE and followed suggestions from Japanese companies on how to organize and implement QC Circles. After two years, the company had some fifteen QC Circles and had accumulated savings of almost $3 million from problems solved by circle members. In one operation, the manufacturing defective rate declined from twenty-five to thirty per thousand hours of work to less than six per thousand hours.[26]

Other aerospace companies soon followed Lockeed's steps in installing QC Circles (or whatever names the companies decided to call them). These companies provided an ideal setting for QC Circle activities to expand since their work environment is characterized by acute sensitivity towards product quality, non-routine jobs that often require group involvement, and a cooperative relationship between management and workers. Similar characteristics also helped the diffusion of QC Circle activities among such electronics companies as Tektronix, Hewlett-Packard, and IBM. These companies were also better prepared than others to install QC Circles due to their prior commitments to people-building and quality-improvement programs.

Companies in other industries have also incorporated QC Circles. General Motors' Buick Division spearheaded the introduction of QC Circles in the automobile industry in late 1977. QC Circles soon spread to a number of other divisions within General Motors and to other automobile manufacturers as well. The enthusiasm of these companies can be seen in the fact that circle activities are continuing to expand despite sales declines and worker layoffs.

Automobile companies join several diversified manufacturers that have actively pursued QC Circle activities—Westinghouse, General Electric, the 3M Company—in emphasizing that a QC Circle program should be looked upon primarily as a people-building tool and secondarily as a means to realize savings and quality improvements.

Application of QC Circles is not limited to the production lines alone. QC Circles can now be found in the offices as well. Lincoln National Life Insurance Company of Fort Wayne, Indiana has found that circles have been able to make improvements in job structure, work flow, paper flow, and service quality to customers. Experiments are also underway to establish QC Circles in retail stores and in other service-oriented workplaces.

Assistance in setting up a QC Circle program appears to be readily available in the U.S. Companies can turn to nonprofit organizations, such as the American Productivity Center, the American Society for Quality Control, and the International Association of Quality Circles, to gain a better understanding of the QC Circle concept. They can also turn to a number of consultants in California who specialize in organizing training sessions and conducting pilot programs within the company.

Several U.S. companies have modified the Japanese version of the QC Circle program to fit their own needs. One company incorporated a hefty financial incentive program into the QC Circle program, offering one-sixth of the savings (up to twenty-five hundred dollars) as cash reward. Another company paid overtime wage rates for the extra time that workers put in after work on QC Circle activities. Another created QC Circles that operated on a revolving basis; a QC Circle worked on solving job-related problems, but once its recommendations were presented to management (usually between six to eight months after its inception), the circle was dissolved automatically. Another company made participation in QC Circle meetings mandatory because they were being held during working hours. The same company assigned first-line managers as QC Circle leaders, rather than allowing circle members to elect their leaders, as is the case in Japan. Yet another company significantly curtailed the training period to thirty minutes because "the workers preferred solving problems rather than sitting down for twenty hours of lecture." Although some are concerned that too liberal a deviation from the Japanese model may cause the basic philosophy behind QC Circles to be misconstrued, most believe that adaptations have to be made to suit the American work environment. As one manager put it, "After all, didn't the Japanese adapt ideas that originated in the U.S. to develop what is today called QC Circles?"

Some observers are starting to voice other concerns over the development of QC Circle activities in the U.S. Are QC Circles being sold as an instant panacea? As one U.S. manager aptly remarked, "It takes extreme patience and painstaking regularity to make QC Circles work. It's one thing to come up with buzz words, but it's another thing to make QC Circles a 'way of life.' " Why is the attrition rate of QC Circles in some companies so high? In one company, for example, 20 percent of the circles ceased to function in the last two years. The common thread among companies facing these situations is the lack of commitment and support from both middle and top management. Are cost savings resulting from QC Circle activities being overemphasized? Excerpts from recent articles include the following:

- An assembly line circle at the solar-turbines division of International Harvester found a way to simplify the production of a compression disc for a turbine. As a result, several production steps were eliminated and $8,700 a year was saved.[27]
- The circle at a GM plant in Michigan decided it should do something about the large number of automobiles leaving the assembly line with flat tires. Their analysis eventually traced the problem to a defective tire stem. The part was replaced and the company's annual savings turned out to be $225,-000.[28]
- A purchasing department circle [of Westinghouse] noted that when supplies were ordered, many vendors routinely sent more than requested. The company either paid the bill or shipped the parts back at its own expense. The solution was to inform suppliers that the company would either keep the extra material or charge for returning it. The saving: $636,000 a year.[29]

Fortunately, the articles quoted above give a balanced view, as does the following quotation of a factor worker: "It's the best thing that's happened in a long time around here. It gives you a feeling of accomplishment when a solution your circle thought up is enacted by management."[30] The concern is on whether overemphasizing cost savings may lead U.S. managers to become further preoccupied with end results rather than the process.

Whatever concerns observers may have, QC Circles are generally receiving high marks from companies that are actually implementing the program. The number of U.S. companies that have already implemented QC Circles has reached over two hundred as of this writing. Some of these companies—General Motors, General Electric, Hewlett-Packard, IBM, TRW, and Eaton Corporation—have also been active in pursuing quality of work life programs. The basic concerns of such programs—humanization of work, job enrichment, and participative management—are integral parts of QC Circle activities as well.[31] QC Circles are also receiving high marks from the workers. "I feel like I've put in my two cents worth," said one worker. "I'm discovering that I can solve lots of problems if several of us get together," said another. The unions have generally been supportive of QC Circle activities. Some companies have invited union representatives to participate during pilot programs; others have assigned union representatives as QC Circle leaders or trainers.

Enough evidence has been accumulated to suggest that the underlying principles of the Japanese productivity system have taken root in the U.S. The East and West have met in a number of U.S. subsidiaries of leading Japanese companies and in a number of U.S. companies described above. The question to be addressed now is whether the current momentum behind productivity improvement programs can be sustained in the U.S. Will the productivity improvement program become a way of life or will it whither away as just another fad?

CONCLUSION

The fate of productivity improvement programs in the U.S. rests on the shoulders of managers. Growth will be sustained if managers can provide the leadership required to tap the reservoir of productivity improvement potential within the company. To begin with managers need a proper frame of mind. The Japanese productivity system has taught us that productivity should not be looked upon as someone else's problem or as right-wing patter, but as something that managers can have control over and something that can benefit the company, workers, and products.

The Japanese productivity system has also taught us where to tap the reservoir of productivity improvement potential and how to tap it. The first and most obvious place for managers to look is at themselves, because without top management commitment and support, productivity improvement programs are doomed to failure. In some U.S. companies, top managers have demonstrated their commitment and support by establishing productivity seed-money funds, visiting Japan as members of the productivity task force, participating in productivity training seminars, attending QC Circle meetings, or presenting awards in productivity contests. In implementing productivity improvement programs, they should not expect an overnight success nor a panacea. After all, it has taken almost three decades of trial and error for the Japanese productivity system to reach where it is now. A Japanese saying best describes how managers should view the process: "When dust accumulates, it makes a mountain."

Second, managers should solicit assistance from a wide variety of departments within the company to facilitate productivity improvement programs. To "make every worker an engineer" managers should rely on the support of departments such as production, research and development, quality control, and others. To "make every worker a manager" they should turn to departments such as employee relations and personnel for education and training, and to data processing, finance, accounting, and marketing for relevant managerial information. At the same time, managers should solicit support from appropriate outside constituents, especially labor unions. The Japanese experience has shown that a broad-based internal support system and an early involvement of outside constituents are indispensable to the success of productivity improvement programs.

Third, managers should draw substantially more from their own workers, who are probably one of the most untapped and undervalued resources available. Managers should start with the premise that workers know best when it comes to identifying problems that exist in their workplace. The Japanese experience has shown that managers should go a step further in challenging workers to actually solve those problems. In trying to crack the problems, workers should be encouraged to resort to practices followed by many management consulting firms—working in teams, analyzing issues in depth, searching for creative solutions, and presenting the analyses and solutions in graphical form. Workers should also be asked to implement the solutions, which allows them to see what they have been able to accomplish and "feel mighty good" about it. One U.S. manager warned that "you should not try to 'nickel and dime' on savings or try to set minimum ROI requirements because, you have to remember, the primary focus throughout the exercise is on people building." Shouldn't human resources deserve as much attention and care from managers as financial resources?

Fourth, managers should utilize product quality control as a catalyst toward improving productivity. One of the most innovative characteristics of the Japanese productivity system has been the infusion of quality control consciousness into the blood of everyone in the organization, including the president, foremen, and rank-and-file workers. Quality control became a grassroots activity, rather than "a little room adjacent to the factory floor, whose occupants make a nuisance of themselves to everyone else."[32] Through the formation of QC Circles, quality control has been pursued within a cooperative environment. This dedication to quality control has been instrumental in bringing about greater acceptance of made-in-Japan products in the world market. At the same time, improved product quality and improved market performance has instilled a sense of craftsmanlike pride among Japanese rank-and-file workers.

Managers in the U.S. should realize that the Japanese originally learned about advanced quality control techniques from the U.S. They first invited leading American authorities in the field to Japan and later sent study teams to leading companies in the U.S. that were practicing new quality control programs (such as Zero Defects and Value Engineering). In general, sending study teams to the U.S. appears to be a prevalent mode of learning for the Japanese, as exemplified by the fact that the Japan Productivity Center had commissioned about a thousand productivity study teams to this country in the last twenty-five years. The Japan Union of Scientists and Engineers also initiated a similar program in 1968. Based on the belief that "there is so much to be learned in the U.S.," numerous Japanese companies have been sending study teams to this country. Several companies in the U.S. have reciprocated in recent years by sending task forces to study the quality control circle movement in Japan. These companies are finding that "seeing is believing."

Ten years ago, Peter Drucker warned that it would be folly for managers in the U.S. to attempt to imitate the Japanese management system.[33] The same could be said today about the Japanese productivity system. But, it would be folly not to attempt to learn from other people's successes, especially when lagging productivity is one of the most pressing problems facing the U.S. today. Success should be contagious.

REFERENCES

1. *The New York Times* (26 January 1979), p. 28.
2. For more detailed description of what is causing productivity to slow down, see Campbell R. McConnell, "Why is U.S. Productivity Slowing Down?" *Harvard Business Review* (March–April 1979), pp. 36–60.
3. U.S. National Center for Productivity and Quality of Working Life, *Productivity in the Changing World of the 1980s* (U.S. Government Printing Office, September 1978), p. 24.
4. The New York Stock Exchange, *Reaching a Higher Standard of Living* (The New York Stock Exchange, January 1979).
5. Hirotaka Takeuchi, *Productivity Analysis as a Resource Management Tool in the Retail Trade,* unpublished dissertation (Berkeley, California: University of California, Berkeley, 1977).
6. *Monthly Labor Review* (November 1978), p. 15.
7. J. M. Juran, "Japanese and Western Quality: A Contrast in Methods and Results," *Management Review* (November 1978), pp. 27–45.
8. *The Rosen Electronic Letter* (31 March 1980), p. 4.
9. Louis P. Bucklin, *Productivity in Marketing* (Chicago: American Marketing Association, 1978), p. 20.
10. *International Management* (February 1977), pp. 36–39.
11. See Robert E. Cole, *Work, Mobility, and Participation: A Comparative Study of American and Japanese Industry* (Berkeley, California: University of California Press, 1979).
12. Japan Union of Scientists and Engineers (JUSE), *Current Status of QC Circle Activities* (Tokyo: JUSE, 1979), in Japanese.
13. These benefits took the forms of savings in labor hours, capital expenditures, energy, or materials, as well as quantifiable improvements in product quality or output rate.
14. This benefit-cost ratio is inflated to the extent that wages and overtime pay of the workers and expenses for materials and energy utilized in carrying out the projects are not included.
15. Example taken from *International Management,* op. cit.
16. Cole, op. cit., p. 140.
17. M. Y. Yoshimo, *Japan's Managerial System* (Cambridge, Massachusetts: The MIT Press, 1978), p. 78.
18. Ibid.

19. Employee-initiated clubs are strongly supported by most Japanese co mpanies. One of the divisions of Matsushita Electric, for example, has over twenty sports, cultural, and other company clubs. According to a Matsushita manager, "These clubs serve to counterbalance the intensity and pressure the work place may create. Our intent is to develop a 'total' person."

20. For more details on these idiosyncrasies, see M. Y. Yoshino, op. cit.; and Ezra F. Vogel, *Japan as No. 1: Lessons for America* (Cambridge, Massachusetts: Harvard University Press, 1979).

21. See Richard E. Walton, "How to Counter Alienation in the Plant," *Harvard Business Review* (November–December 1972); Louis E. Davis and Albert B. Cherns (eds.), *The Quality of Working Life, Volume II* (New York: The Free Press, 1975); Edward M. Glaser, *Productivity Gains Through Worklife Improvement* (New York: Harcourt Brace Jovanovich, 1975); Ernesto J. Poza and M. Lynn Marjus, "Success Story: The Team Approach to Work Structuring," *Organizational Dynamics* (Winter 1980), pp. 3–25.

22. *The New York Times* (30 March 1980) p. 16F.

23. Ibid.

24. Richard T. Johnson and William G. Ouchi, "Made in America (Under Japanese Management)," *Harvard Business Review* (September–October 1974), p. 63, and "Are Japanese Managers Really Better?" *International Management* (July 1976), p. 35.

25. *Industry Week* (19 February 1979), p. 74.

26. Ed Yager, "Examining the Quality Control Circle," *Personnel Journal* (October 1979), p. 684.

27. *Wall Street Journal* (21 February 1980), p. 48.

28. Ibid.

29. "The Workers Know Best," *Time* (28 January 1980), p. 65.

30. *Wall Street Journal,* op. cit.

31. For further readings on quality of work life programs, see Robert H. Guest, "Quality of Work-Life-Learning from Tarrytown." *Harvard Business Review* (July–August 1979); and Richard E. Walton, "Work Innovations in the United States," *Harvard Business Review* (July–August 1979).

32. *The New York Times,* op. cit.

33. Peter F. Drucker, "What We Can Learn from Japanese Management," *Harvard Business Review* (March–April 1971).

EPILOGUE

The articles presented in this book provide, I feel, persuasive evidence of the organizational benefits accruing from the adoption of a "win-win" philosophy. It is clear that in a number of instances organizational structures and attitudes are changing. Managerial style and behavior, and the values upon which they are based, are likewise going through change which renders that change dramatically different from past patterns. The articles in this book can serve as a positive example leading open-minded readers to move ahead with an optimistic attitude toward the future of organizational life. We have seen that many organizations have taken on new postures and new ground rules by which they play. For the players in these organizations there are only winners.

I am aware of the existence of cynics and skeptics who may refer to these arguments for humanizng the workplace as simply attempts to "make people feel good." Although one might argue that making people feel good is a viable goal itself, we must remember that the majority of the foregoing articles stress increased productivity as the ultimate result of these new humanistic structures and managerial styles. Indeed, productivity and what is represented by "quality of worklife" are inextricably related.

The concern of enlightened managers, though, transcends their serious interest in productivity. They care about results, about organizational effectiveness and efficiency. But they also care about much more. They care about all the people who spend so much of their lives in work organizations. This concern for organizational members does not deter managers from reaching high levels of productivity; there is no conflict between satisfying individual needs and the accomplishment of organizational goals. In fact, the articles in this book are further evidence of the mandate to be sensitively responsive to the needs of people throughout the organization if one is genuinely concerned about maximizing productivity.

The focus of these "win-win" articles seems to be the increasing demand of people for more interesting and self-satisfying work, and for participation in the decision-making process which governs that work. Rapidly increasing numbers of people want to feel a genuine sense of belonging within their organization. The people who must carry out the work in an organization want to be involved in decisions relating to that work. More and more people are also indicating that it is important to them to be rewarded in proportion to the individual contribution they make to their organization. People want to feel that they are a part of a humane organization; people being served by organizations want to be served by humane ones. It is the enlightened manager who has become aware of these emerging realities.

The challenge to those blessed with the responsibility of organizational leadership is to build and maintain open communication, cooperation, and trust within their organizations. They will do this because they will recognize that it is right to operate this way, and they will do it because it's the only way to accomplish their organization's goals on a sustaining basis. These enlightened managers will operate this way because they desire to be involved in the practice of "win-win" administration. These managers, like the non-managers throughout their organization and the people served by their organization, want to be involved with an organization in which the "win-win" philosophy is prevalent. Is there a manager amongst us who cannot support and enthusiastically endorse the goal of managing their organization so that everybody wins?

The techniques, structures, and styles discussed in the foregoing articles are important. They are important because they open the door to allowing organizations to be managed in such a way that everybody wins. How do we obtain "win-win" administration? It is achieved by internalizing the values promoted in these articles and by applying the various techniques discussed in the articles. Enlightened managers know that the depth of their responsibility is awesome. They realize that their role requires the establishment of a "win-win" organization as the only viable means of producing on-going organizational results. As important as organizational efficiency is, they recognize that any technical competency which takes no account of the individual humanness of every person involved stands self-condemned.

Essentially, the contributing authors in this book are all seeking the same result. We want to see a humanization of the workplace. We want to make life at work more meaningful. We want people to have opportunities at work to become more self-fulfilled, to grow, to be productive in the best sense of the word. Organizational benefits, and benefit to the society, will simultaneously accrue. Not the least of the societal benefit will be the more positive feelings held toward organizations by the people served by the organizations. Enlightened managers will remember always that there is a relationship between the way they manage the people in their organizations and the way those people then in-turn relate to the people they serve.

It is my fervent hope that more and more organizations will strive to become humane; will seek to humanize themselves; will adopt an enriching spirit of "win-win" administration. I trust that the preceding articles have served to inspire managers, present and future, to take steps to achieve this "win-win" result.

BIBLIOGRAPHY OF "WIN-WIN" ARTICLES

Bennis, Warren G. "Changing Organizations." *Journal of Applied Behavioral Science,* 2 (July–September, 1966), 247–63.

Blumberg, Stephen K. "Notes on the Art of Administration." *Midwest Review of Public Administration,* 14 (September, 1980), 191–99.

Briscoe, Dennis R. "Organizational Design: Dealing with the Human Constraint." *California Management Review,* XXIII (Fall 1980), 71–80.

Bruno, Jim and Lippin, Paula. "New Trend: Nice Guys Finish First." *Administrative Management,* June, 1979, pp. 30–31ff.

Cleveland, Harlan. "The Public Executive: A Sense of Responsibility for the Whole." *Public Management,* 62 (December, 1980), 2–7.

Gibson, James L. "Organization Theory and the Nature of Man." *Academy of Management Journal,* 9 (September, 1966), 233–44.

Glaser, Edward M. "Productivity Gains Through Worklife Improvement." *Personnel,* 57 (January–February, 1980), 71–77.

Guest, Robert H. "Quality of Work Life—Prospects for the 80s." *Vital Speeches of the Day,* 1 March 1980, pp. 310–13.

Hoh, Andrew K. "Consensus-Building: A Creative Approach to Resolving Conflicts." *Management Review,* March, 1981, pp. 52–54.

McConkey, Dale D. "Participative Management: What It Really Means in Practice." *Business Horizons,* 23 (October, 1980), 66–73.

Pascarella, Perry. "Humanagement." *Industry Week,* 204 (7 January 1980), 85–90.

Pogrebin, Letty Cottin. "The Working Woman." *Ladies Home Journal,* April, 1978, pp. 60ff.

Rosenbaum, Bernard L. "Understanding and Using Motivation." *Supervisory Management,* 24 (January, 1979), 9–13.

Schein, Edgar. "Improving Face-to-Face Relationships." *Sloan Management Review,* 22 (Winter 1981), 43–52.

Silverman, Robert Stephen and Heming, D. A. "Exit The Organization Man: Enter The Professional Person." *Personnel Journal,* March, 1975, pp. 146–48.

Sinetar, Marsha. "Management in the New Age: An Exploration of Changing Work Values." *Personnel Journal,* September, 1980, pp. 749–55.

Swart, J. Carroll. "The Worth of Humanistic Management." *Business Horizons,* 16 (June, 1973), 41–50.

Takeuchi, Hirotaka. "Productivity: Learning from the Japanese." *California Management Review,* XXIII (Summer 1981), 5–19.

Tannenbaum, Robert and Davis, Sheldon A. "Values, Man, and Organizations." *Industrial Management Review,* 10 (Winter 1969), 67–84.

Webb, Ronald J. "Supportiveness: A Recurring Theme in Organizational Effectiveness." *University of Michigan Business Review,* 28 (July, 1976), 16–21.

Weihrich, Heinz and Rigny, Andre-Jean. "Toward System Four Through Transactional Analysis." *Journal of Systems Management,* 31 (July, 1980), 30–36.

White, Harold C. "Perceptions of Leadership By Managers In A Federal Agency." *Personnel Administration/Public Personnel Review,* 1 (July–August, 1972), 51–56.

CONTRIBUTING AUTHORS

WARREN G. BENNIS, Professor of Research, School of Business, University of Southern California

STEPHEN K. BLUMBERG, Associate Professor and Assistant Director, Center for Public Policy and Administration, California State University, Long Beach

DENNIS R. BRISCOE, Associate Professor of Management and Personnel, School of Business, University of San Diego

JIM BRUNO, Managing Editor, *Administrative Management* (at time of article publication)

HARLAN CLEVELAND, Director, Hubert H. Humphrey Institute of Public Affairs, University of Minnesota

SHELDON A. DAVIS, Vice President, Personnel, Digital Equipment Corporation, Maynard, Massachusetts

JAMES L. GIBSON, Professor, Department of Business Administration, University of Kentucky

EDWARD M. GLASER, President, Human Interaction Research Institute, Los Angeles and managing associate of Edward Glaser & Associates

ROBERT H. GUEST, Professor of Organizational Behavior, Emeritus, The Amos Tuck School of Business Administration, Dartmouth College

D. A. HEMING, Head of the Drug Quality Assessment Unit, Health Protection Branch, Health & Welfare Canada, Toronto, Canada

ANDREW K. HOH, Assistant Professor of Management, College of Business Administration, Creighton University

PAULA LIPPIN, Features Editor, *Administrative Management* (at time of article publication)

DALE D. McCONKEY, Professor of Management, University of Wisconsin in Madison

PERRY PASCARELLA, Executive Editor, *Industry Week*

LETTY COTTIN POGREBIN, Writer/Editor; Author of *Getting Yours: How to Make the System Work for the Working Woman* and *Growing Up Free: Raising Your Child in the 80s*

ANDRE-JEAN RIGNY, Teaching experience at the University of Sherbrooke, the Administrative Institute at the University of Grenoble, and the European Institute of Business Administration in Fontainebleau, France

BERNARD L. ROSENBAUM, President, MOHR Development, Inc., Stamford, Connecticut

EDGAR SCHEIN, Sloan Fellows Professor of Management, Sloan School of Management, Massachusetts Institute of Technology

BUDDY ROBERT S. SILVERMAN, Program Manager, Merit Pay Development Division, U.S. Office of Personnel Management, Washington, D.C.

MARSHA SINETAR, Organizational Psychologist and President, Sinetar and Associates, El Segundo, California

J. CARROLL SWART, Professor of Management Science, College of Business, Ball State University

HIROTAKA TAKEUCHI, Assistant Professor, Graduate School of Business Administration, Harvard University

ROBERT TANNENBAUM, Professor of the Development of Human Systems (Faculty Early Retirement Program), Graduate School of Management, University of California, Los Angeles

RONALD J. WEBB, Chairman and Associate Professor of Business, Department of Business and Management, Messiah College, Grantham, Pennsylvania

HEINZ WEIHRICH, Professor of Management, McLaren College of Business Administration, University of San Francisco

HAROLD C. WHITE, Professor of Management, Arizona State University, Tempe, Arizona